D0710347

ENVIRONMENTAL SITE ASSESSMENT
PHASE I: A BASIC GUIDE

Kathleen Hess, MS, CIH

LEWIS PUBLISHERS

Boca Raton   Ann Arbor   London   Tokyo

Library of Congress Cataloging-in-Publication Data

Hess, Kathleen.
   Environmental site assessment, phase I : a basic guide / Kathleen
Hess.
      p.   cm.
   Includes bibliographical references and index.
   ISBN 0-87371-798-8
   1. Hazardous wastes--Risk assessment.   2. Hazardous waste sites.
 I. Title.
   TD1050.R57H47   1993
   363.7--dc20   93-12470
                                                                   CIP

COPYRIGHT© 1993 by LEWIS PUBLISHERS
ALL RIGHTS RESERVED

This book represents information obtained from authentic and highly regarded sources. Reprinted material is quoted with permission, and sources are indicated. A wide variety of references are listed. Every reasonable effort has been made to give reliable data and information, but the author and the publisher cannot assume responsibility for the validity of all materials or for the consequences of their use.

Neither this book nor any part may be reproduced or transmitted in any form or by any means, electronic or mechanical, including photocopying, microfilming, and recording, or by any information storage and retrieval system, without permission in writing from the publisher.

Direct all inquiries to CRC Press, Inc., 2000 Corporate Blvd., N.W., Boca Raton, Florida 33431.

PRINTED IN THE UNITED STATES OF AMERICA
2 3 4 5 6 7 8 9 0

Printed on acid-free paper

PREFACE

In recent years, the United States has identified hazardous materials in the soil, surface water, groundwater, and building structures. Most of these contaminants are the result of the evolution of technology without the benefit of chemical regulatory controls. The cost for cleanup is projected to exceed a trillion dollars, the burden of which is to be borne by the taxpayer and responsible parties. The term "responsible party" is broad and in the final analysis involves the property owner. The purpose of an environmental site assessment is to project the possibilities of hazardous substance contamination on and/or around a property.

The purpose of this book is to address these issues in a clear, concise method so as to allow the reader to: 1) better understand the rationale and process necessary to protect those associated with the property, 2) become familiar with methods used by leaders in the industry, and 3) develop an easy-to-follow investigative strategy to performing an in-house assessment.

The intended audience includes, but is not limited to: 1) environmental consultants, 2) industrial hygienists, 3) geologists, 4) structural engineers, and 5) commercial real estate loan officers. Others who may find the topic of interest are: 1) building inspectors, 2) business owners who invest routinely in property, 3) real estate agents, 4) environmental lawyers, and 5) land developers. The book is written such that it is informative for those who are new to the subject, and it is a quick reference guide for those already knowledgeable in the field.

The performance of environmental site assessments is an ever-evolving process, and there are as many different approaches as there are consultants. Some consultants perform a minimal service, while others dig into all possible realms. An attempt has been made in this book to discuss most of the investigative tools which are presently being used by many of the environmental consultants.

The legal concerns involved with the purchase of property are discussed. An historic overview provides the reader with a sense of evolution, and the rest of the book provides guidance. It is up to the reader to use the tools in developing methodology.

Methods currently used by most professionals are discussed, as are procedures of major lending institutions. Many of the methods are similar, but they do vary from one institution to the next. Many are summarized in the appendices.

Many of those who read this book may never perform an assessment. They will, however, be informed and able to make better decisions on property purchases.

Should the reader decide to proceed with the aid of this guide, the first assessment will be more easily managed. Without this guide, however, the reader could be as a climber preparing to scale Mount Everest without the proper equipment. This book is intended to save the reader from re-inventing the wheel.

With this guide, the reader approaches a challenge not unlike some taken on in a Sherlock Holmes mystery. The reader becomes the mastermind. The investigative tools are unlimited. The manipulation of these tools is left up to the resourcefulness of the investigator.

Kathleen Hess, MS, CIH
Georgetown, Texas

Acknowledgments

I wish to thank my publisher, Jon Lewis, for his patience and willingness to work with me through the challenges of preparing this book. Special thanks to Shirley Ness, Claren Kotrla, Paul Heidgerd, and Mark and Lisa Baker for spending their vacation time and evenings assisting me. Last, but not least, I would like to acknowledge Mary Hess, Hamlet, Nicki, and John for their support.

About the Author

Kathleen Hess is an industrial hygiene/environmental consultant with Omega Southwest Consulting in Austin, Texas. She was introduced to environmental site assessments in the early 1980s while working for a major insurance firm, evaluating hazardous substance exposures to workers in industrial environments ranging from sawmills to foundries in both large and small operations. She has also assessed exposures to office occupants regarding such subjects as indoor air pollution and asbestos.

Since then, field experience and additional study expanded her areas of expertise into the environmental field and hazardous waste cleanup/management. She holds a Master of Science degree in industrial hygiene from Texas A&M University and is certified by the American Board of Industrial Hygiene.

Contents

Chapter 1

Liability Associated with Environmental Pollution[1,2,3]

INTRODUCTION

A recent cost estimate for site cleanup of environmental pollution identified on U.S. properties is between $484 billion and $1.177 trillion.[4] This figure does not include cleanup costs for hazardous substance spills, waste oil contamination, leaking underground storage tanks, other uncontrolled releases into the environment, or hazardous waste sites which have yet to be identified. Nor does it consider the costs for removal of hazardous materials from buildings and the escalating costs for legal services. The actual expense could well exceed the above estimate.

Whatever the expense, however, all costs will be incurred by the American public—in government dollars and private money. As government dollars are limited, most of the costs will be deferred to responsible private parties. The term responsible is loosely interpreted and is discussed later in this chapter.

Private parties includes corporations, small businesses, individual investors, and groups of investors. They may be past or present owners or lessors, and they may not be associated with the property other than having dumped waste on the premises. The cleanup cost to responsible private parties may be as low as five hundred dollars or as high as several million. Reduction of these risks is sought.

An environmental site assessment will reduce the possibilities for liability claims and cleanup costs as well as provide a means by which a buyer may assess real value prior to a property purchase. As liability is established by law, acceptable practices are dictated by the interpretation of legal statutes and precedent.

It is vital that the reader become familiar with the legal terms and the role played by each participant. The reader should also be aware that each state has its own laws which may either amplify or further define these

1

terms. The environmental laws applicable to the state in which the property is located will require additional research by the reader.

SIGNIFICANT LEGAL TERMS

Under the Comprehensive Environmental Response, Compensation, and Liability Act of 1980 (CERCLA), an "environmental pollutant," or contaminant, is:

> "Any element, substance, compound, or mixture, including disease-causing agents, which after release into the environment and upon exposure, ingestion, inhalation, or assimilation into any organism, either directly from the environment or indirectly by ingestion through food chains, will or may reasonably be anticipated to cause death, disease, behavioral abnormalities, cancer, genetic mutation, physiological malfunctions (including malfunctions in reproduction) or physical deformations in such organisms or their offspring; except that the term...shall not include petroleum...[or] natural gas, liquefied natural gas, or synthetic gas of pipeline quality..."[5]

As amended by the Superfund Amendments and Reauthorization-Act of 1986, CERCLA is also referred to as the "Superfund law." It contains the regulatory mandates which identify and classify hazardous waste sites, defines the limits of liability, and establishes a trust fund for the management of site cleanups.

Under CERCLA there are five classes of parties who may be responsible for cleanup costs. A "potentially responsible party" (PRP) may be any of the following:

- Current owners and operators
- Previous owners or operators who were present at the time the hazardous substance contamination occurred
- Intervening owners who actually had knowledge of the presence of hazardous waste and failed to disclose this information to the prospective buyer
- Hazardous waste generators who arranged for the disposal of hazardous substances to the property
- Persons who accepted hazardous substances for transport to facilities which resulted in a subsequent release

Public policy has been that cleanup costs must be borne by all those presently and previously connected with a property and those engaged in activities resulting in contamination of property.

Under the law, liability for a site cleanup is strict, joint/several, and retroactive. "Strict" means the liable party may be without fault, i.e., ignorance of a preexisting or ongoing occurrence is not a defense. This applies to the seller, buyer, lender, lessor, and other associated parties. Any or all of these parties may be charged with damages.

"Joint and several" means that the liability may be shared by one or several parties, including owners, operators, transporters, and waste management companies. Any or all persons involved, both directly or indirectly, may find themselves sharing a piece of the pie, irrespective of their relative degree of contribution.

"Retroactive" means that any party who owned or conducted business on the property at the time the contaminants were disposed of may be held liable for cleanup costs. The same holds true for an intervening landowner. If the landowner obtained knowledge of the contaminant and did not disclose it upon selling the property, he may be held liable for cleanup costs along with all others found to be responsible.

In 1986, the Superfund Act as amended by SARA, the "innocent landowner defense" was created to provide a buyer who is reasonably inquisitive about environmental issues with a means of protection—provided certain conditions were met. At this point, the law becomes vague.

If the purchaser can show "due diligence" in the performance of a property investigation prior to purchase, their liability may be reduced—as long as they did not contribute to the contamination. Under the Law, due diligence is an appropriate inquiry into previous ownership and uses of the property, consistent with good commercial or customary practice.

"Good commercial or customary practice" is generally determined by precedent which is set by state-of-the-art practices commonly accepted in the industry. Environmental site assessments have become customary, but the methodology for performing a site assessment is controversial. The courts have yet to clarify an acceptable methodology, and state-of-the-art practices remain subject to interpretation. For this reason, many institutions set their own standards.

Lending institutions and insurance companies began to express concern for their liability and protecting the value of their property investments in the early to mid 1980s. Environmental claims were making a significant dent on these industries, and they sought to protect their investments. Many of the larger banks and government agencies (e.g., Fannie

Mae) have developed very precise methodologies. Smaller lending institutions generally know they need to have an assessment performed but don't dictate the "scope of the work." The Small Business Administration requires assessments for small business commercial loans, and they provide minimal direction as to what they require. The Resolution Trust Corporation is managing repossessed properties for the government and has developed very precise procedures which must be followed by the environmental consultants for investigating their property. Professional journals are a good source for "state-of-the-art" procedures, and some states have provided their own guidelines. There have been a few attempts by the federal government, in 1989 and 1991, to legislate the duties to be undertaken to comply with good commercial and customary practice. A summary of some of these various requirements is found in the appendices.

In early 1990, various segments of the real estate community joined under the auspices of the American Standards and Testing Materials (ASTM) to form a subcommittee on Environmental Assessments in Commercial Real Estate Transactions to clarify good commercial practices for performing Phase I environmental site assessments that satisfy the due diligence clause. As ASTM standards are recognized by legislatures, courts, and regulatory bodies, it is felt that compliance with these practices will provide a means of defense for the innocent landowner. This standard should, thus, be used as the "minimal" approach. The guidelines are to be published in 1993. Copies may be purchased from:

ASTM
1916 Race Street
Philadelphia, PA 19103-1187

As some states (e.g., Illinois) have their own guidelines, the reader should become familiar with the state laws as well. Where there are state laws, the "state guidelines" may be more stringent than that of the ASTM.

SELLER

Where contamination predated the acquisition of property, a seller may wish to make a disclosure in order to preserve his own intervening landowner status. "Intervening landowners" have federal Superfund liability *only if they fail to disclose known or unknown conditions when selling* the property.

When hazardous waste contamination is known and the seller is the responsible party, the seller has an obligation to disclose this information to the prospective buyer. Yet, the potential liability under the Superfund law, in some cases, may exceed the value of a property. When this happens, property value becomes a deficit.

Even where the cleanup costs are manageable and the seller is willing to pay for remediation, cleanup may take years. Desired property transfers may be delayed and interest in the property diminishes. There is another alternative.

In some cases, the buyer may be willing to close the transaction while the property has yet to be remediated. The seller's concern in such an agreement will leave the seller exposed to the Superfund liability and allow the buyer to continue as planned. Yet, the buyer must be concerned that the seller will not manage the remediation properly and run up the costs.

In some instances, the buyer has agreed to assume the risk of environmental problems. According to federal law, the transference of liability is not binding. The seller remains the primary responsible party (PRP) in the eyes of the government.

To further complicate matters, third party claims from personal injuries or property damages caused by the hazardous substance(s) may arise. Should the buyer agree to indemnify the seller against environmental claims, he can indemnify the seller only if he has good credit.

Where there is no known existing hazardous waste contamination, a future discovery will revert once again to the seller. Numerous cases are on record of cost recovery claims against former owners who remain liable, even when the sale was made prior to the Superfund law.

Although a prior owner has no liability for contamination which occurred after the property was sold, it may not be clear when contamination actually did occur. The buyer may be the responsible party, but without a site assessment, the seller has no proof of his having not contributed to or been the exclusive responsible party. If the seller has no documentation of the condition of the property prior to the sale, he may find himself floating down a fast moving river without a means for escape.

BUYER

The buyer who purchases contaminated real estate could face strict Superfund liability and possibly cleanup costs for contamination which existed prior to the purchase, particularly if it is unclear that the seller contributed to or caused the pollution. If the buyer had performed an environmental site assessment prior to acquisition of the property and found no contamination, the innocent landowner defense is his. Yet, the government may argue that the assessment was inadequate. This brings us back to good commercial or customary practice. A token gesture as an assessment will not provide a viable defense. As it is neither feasible to test every inch of soil nor to predict certain incidents (e.g., illegal dumping), even the best site assessment does have its limits, but good customary procedures are covered under "due diligence." Thus, state-of-the-art guidelines for the time the survey was performed is a viable defense.

When assessing the possibility of an undisclosed or unknown environmental problem, the buyer should appreciate that the risk is greater for some kinds of properties than others, and no property is immune. Properties at risk are in order of increasing threat as follows:

- Raw land
- Agricultural property
- Residential property
- Commercial property
- Industrial property

The buyer must be alerted to the potential for even property which appears to be raw land to have been previously used for industrial activities or waste disposal. The probability for raw land to have preexisting hazardous waste is diminished but should not be discounted.

Even where preexisting contamination is discovered on the property after the sale, the buyer, having had an assessment performed, may have a legal recourse in deferring to the previous owners or seller. Yet, if the responsible party(ies) don't have money, a suit may be like drawing blood from a tree stump. There may be no recourse for action. Even if there is recourse, fixing liability on another party may be a drain on time and energy, cost for legal expenses, negative publicity, and forestall land use/development plans.

LENDER

If environmental liabilities issue a devastating blow to the buyer, the ultimate result may be a loan default and bankruptcy. A default will result in the lending institution accepting the liability. Lenders are wary of this possibility. As they have the benefit of experience, most lending institutions require environmental site assessments as part of their prerequisites for lending commercial money.

Land as collateral is also subject to the same scenario. Where the lenders are offered mortgages or deeds of trust with real estate as security, there must be sufficient value to cover a default, and the value of the property may be subject to undiscovered property contamination. This may reduce the value of the collateral or deplete it entirely.

Another concern for the lender is the possible restrictions which may apply to property for which they intend to lend money. A developer may intend to use the land for a specific project and then discover, after the purchase, restrictions. Such a disclosure may threaten the project as well as the prospects for repayment of the loan.

LESSOR AND LESSEES

Lessors have no exemption from liability merely because the property is leased to a lessee who is actively contaminating the land. The lessors are exposed to strict liability for environmental contamination as a result of activities of their lessees. Even though the lessor has a right to claim contributory actions against the lessee who caused the contamination, the lessor will spend time and legal fees. Also, if the lessee is financially unable to shoulder the costs for cleanup, the problem reverts to the lessor.

Lessor be forewarned—lessees of previously contaminated property whose lease has expired or was terminated before cost recovery action was commenced would not be considered under CERCLA a primary responsible party, regardless of any disclosures. Otherwise, the lessee has strict liability as the current operator of contaminated property.

BROKERS

Brokers do not have liability under CERCLA or state Superfund laws if acting solely in the capacity of a broker. However, brokers have a professional duty to inspect and disclose. Under this premise, they may be held liable where environmental matters have not been handled properly during a real estate transaction.

Real estate brokers must obtain extensive disclosures from the seller regarding the seller's knowledge of the condition of the property as to both environmental and other matters. The broker also has a duty to inform the parties to a transaction of the existence of environmental laws and concerns, to recommend steps be taken to assess the risk through qualified environmental consultants, and to counsel as is appropriate to the circumstances. The broker is obligated to inform the buyer of any potential problems found during an inspection. Thus, it is a smart practice for brokers to document and discharge in writing their professional duty in regard to the environmental arena.

CORPORATE OFFICERS, DIRECTORS, SHAREHOLDERS, AND SUCCESSORS

The corporate structure has traditionally been used as a means for limiting the liability of shareholders. The shareholders risk loss of their stock investments, but have no personal liability if the assets of the corporation are insufficient to satisfy obligations.

However, the corporate structure does not provide protection against direct liability for one's own breach of civil or criminal law. Unlawful conduct by an individual shareholder is not shielded by the corporate veil.

The system may be breached if the "corporate veil is pierced." Operators of contaminated real estate sometimes circumvent the corporate shield. Strict liability for cleanup of hazardous substance releases is imposed on operators of contaminated property and on others who did operate the property at the time of disposal. "Operators" may include corporate officers, employees, and shareholders who manage or operate the property. Generators (those who arranged for treatment, transportation, and disposal) may also be included.

SUMMARY

The impact of environmental pollutants/hazardous substances on the value of property and its associated liability can be far-reaching, encompassing both those who are innocent and those who were not the direct cause of the existing situation. Ignorance is not a defense, and the best protection for all parties concerned is the completion of a "state-of-the-art" environmental site assessment. The ASTM guides, to be published in 1993, should be used as a "minimal" approach, and some states define their own requirements for property investigations. The latter should be researched by the reader on a state-by-state basis.

This book provides not only a guide for accomplishing the minimum practices, but much more. Some assessments may require additional investigation, and many of these methods are provided herein.

Keep in mind, there are no absolutes. Yet, the possibilities for incurring liability for a site cleanup can be reduced significantly with an environmental site assessment.

REFERENCES

1. Wilson, Albert R.: *Environmental Risk: Identification and Management.* Lewis Publishers, Chelsea, Michigan, 1991.
2. Ashton, Donald, et. al.: *Environmental Evaluations for Real Estate Transactions: A Technical and Business Guide.* Ed. Frank D. Goss. 2nd Printing, Government Institutes, Inc., Rockville, Maryland, 1989.
3. Nanney, Donald C.: *Environmental Risks in Real Estate Transactions: A Practical Guide.* McGraw-Hill, Inc., 2nd ed., Executive Enterprises Publications Co., Inc., New York, New York, 1993.
4. Ibid. p. 6.
5. 42 U.S.C. 9601 § 101(33).

Chapter 2

An Historic Overview

INTRODUCTION

The history of environmental contamination by hazardous substances is involved and complex. Although some of these substances abound naturally in the environment, many are the result of technology and man's manipulation of the earth's resources.

An abbreviated definition for hazardous substance is "any solid, liquid, or gas which is toxic, flammable, caustic, reactive/explosive, and/or radioactive." Today's technological products may be any one or a combination of these, and over 80% of all industrial chemicals can be classified as hazardous.

Past reports have given press to "aquatic graveyards," resulting in a usage ban for those who would avail themselves of the water for fishing, drinking, or recreation. Rivers, lakes, and streams have been contaminated with industrial waste. Fish populations have been destroyed or rendered inedible, and communities have reported noxious odors emanating from local surface waters. Many of these sites are in the process of being remediated or have already been cleaned.

Groundwater has shown signs of hazardous chemical migration through the soils, both horizontally and vertically. Many of these occurrences are the result contaminates in the soil for over twenty years. Soil and surface water contamination, past and present, is an ever-present threat to potable drinking water.

Hazardous materials have been quietly discharged through industrial effluent, dumping into sanitary sewers, industrial/automotive air emissions, and ground/soil contamination through mismanagement of hazardous wastes. Many of the discharges can and have been corrected. Yet, some previously contaminated soils and water remain undiscovered, and more recent contamination is being generated by carelessness and criminal activities.

11

The U.S. government response has been to identify locations for remediation and prevent further incidents from occurring. Identification of these "locations" requires investigation (e.g., environmental site assessments), and prevention comes in the form of regulatory controls. Examples of many of these unrestricted practices of the past are contained herein. Many of the older incidents which resulted in discovery many years after discharge were legal, accepted practices at the time of the environmental contamination. Regulations are having an impact on present day contamination, but the impact of past practices has yet to be fully realized.

Past occurrences pose the greatest concern, and discovery of these events may be traced through media disclosures. These press releases impact public opinion and ultimately the creation of new laws/regulations. Within the next section, trends in the news and regulatory issues are presented in a chronological order.

EVOLUTION OF THE TOXIC SCARE

Toxic substances have prevailed on earth since the "big bang." Volcanic eruptions expel clouds of metal fumes and deadly hydrogen sulfide gas into the atmosphere. Silica, lead, and heavy metals are ubiquitous in the ground. Ground cavities trap petroleum and flammable gases. Rock formations contain deposits of asbestos and radioactive ores. It wasn't until man learned to mine, manipulate, and process the earth's rich bounty that he began to experience the consequences of the intrusion.

The earliest recorded information acknowledging toxic materials was the Ebers papyrus about 1500 B.C. The papyrus is a recipe book for "poisons," pointing out that lead, copper, and antimony are deadly metals when consumed. By 400 B.C., Hippocrates, the father of medicine, recorded an illness in the mining industries.[5] It is postulated that arsenic was the poison with which Agrippina killed Claudius to make Nero the emperor of Rome.[6] Five hundred years later, Pliny the Elder, a Roman scholar, made reference to the dangers inherent in working with lead, zinc, and mercury.[7] In the 16th century, Paracelsus introduced and advocated the use of mercury for treatment of syphilis. This treatment was used for the next 300 years until a more suitable substitute was discovered. It was known at the time that mercury was toxic, but Paracelsus presented an irrefutable argument, "Only the dose determines that a [chemical] is [a] poison."[8] This was the first acknowledgment that toxic effects are dose related.

During the Renaissance, illness associated with mining was attributed to "malevolent demons" emanating from the caverns of the earth. The Industrial Revolution saw the extraction and use of metals and ores to create machines of unprecedented size and complexity. In the early 1700s, physicians began to relate certain ailments with various industrial activities. Scrotal cancer was associated with soot and chimney sweeps.

Air pollution saw its origin around the rise of the Roman Empire. A Roman philosopher, Seneca, observed that "as soon as I had gotten out of the heavy air of Rome and from the stink of the smoky chimneys thereof, which being stirred poured forth whatever pestilential vapors and soot they had enclosed in them, I felt an alteration of my disposition." In the mid 1100s, Edward I of Great Britain announced, "Be it known to all within the sound of my voice, whosoever shall be found guilty of burning coal shall suffer the loss of his head." Later, Edward II had a man hanged outside St. Bartholomew's Hospital for burning coal and filling the air with the "pestilential odor."[9] In 1977, a news headline proclaimed "Premature Deaths Linked to Coal and Oil Burning." The article speculated that by the year 2010, as many as 35 thousand premature deaths could be expected annually.[10] An American doctor in 1900 announced that the horseless carriage, by replacing horses, would also drive the flies off the streets. "Thus, a serious channel of infection will be done away with and many lives spared. The horseless carriage will reduce the death in cities."[11]

In 1854, a cholera epidemic in England sparked an investigation which revealed that untreated sewage was being dumped into the Thames River, upstream of a public drinking water source. Raw sewage was the culprit. In the late 1800s and early 1900s, water treatment processes were developed which dramatically decreased the incidence of sewage borne typhoid fever.[12] By 1924, the news media disclosed various incidents involving raw sewage and industrial waste discharge into the nation's streams. In the mid to late 1970s, the media unveiled events involving contamination of the nation's surface and groundwaters.[13]

World War I saw the advancement of industry and chemical processing. World War II saw the advancement of the nuclear bomb and an arsenal of nerve gases. Technology boomed. Plastics and synthetics were formulated, and pesticides were improved. Computer chip production required exotic, toxic substances (e.g., gallium arsenide and arsine).

In the 1960s, environmental concerns were for disease-carrying vermin and pests, smog, pesticides, detergent contamination of water, and oil spills. News articles read as follows:[14]

- Waterborne communicable disease...is still a problem in the U.S.
- Smog disintegrates nylon stockings in Chicago and Los Angeles, eats away historic stone structures.
- Modern chemical technology that invented the detergents that produce cleaner clothes (has) led to the pollution of waterways.
- The country's ranchers, loggers, and farmers, who form the agriculture pollution sector, continue to be the "worst polluters in the entire nation."
- (Global oil) spills have reached the point where the entire world ocean is affected.
- A beach on Barbados Island in the Antilles is fouled with tar and oil, although ships rarely pass.

Rachel Carson's *Silent Spring* was published in 1962, a controversial exposé which stirred up the public internationally.[15] It contained a treatise on our environment and its deadly contamination by industry and the advances in technology. Private interest groups and communities rallied, and the Clean Air Act of 1963 was created to regulate air pollution and set forth emission standards. Some claim that the public response to Carson's book was also the impetuous for the eventual creation of the Environmental Protection Agency.

The Occupational Safety and Health Act (OSHA) and National Environmental Policy Act (NEPA) were voted into law in 1970, and under the NEPA, the Environmental Protection Agency (EPA) was formed. OSHA is concerned with worker exposures, and the EPA is concerned with environmental hazards.

In the mid 1970s, Dr. Samuel Epstein, a professor of medicine at the University of Illinois Medical Center in Chicago, and his journalistic counterparts, most notably Ralph Nader, began to speculate on the subject of environmental issues. The media spread "doom and gloom." A membership solicitation letter from Ralph Nader's Public Citizen organization began with—"Earlier generations lived in fear of polio and smallpox. Nowadays, the most deadly epidemics are man-made." The public demanded government intervention.[16]

In the late 1970s, stories about chemicals "oozing from the ground" got front page news coverage. Groundwater/surface water was being contaminated, and environmental interest groups were more vocal. Government intervention became necessary, and regulations escalated as media coverage of environmental issues increased.

The Toxic Wastelands: Media Coverage

Although often inflammatory, media coverage of environmental events is of historic value. Disclosures give times of discovery and trends in public opinion. Regulatory controls of hazardous substance and environmental pollution followed.

Although hazardous waste has been a sleeping giant for many years, evidence was not apparent until the 1970s. Contaminated groundwater is the end result, the evidence of toxins gone awry. Newspaper and magazine articles read as follows:[17]

- Organic contamination forced the closing of nearly one hundred drinking wells in New Jersey. (Jackson Township, New Jersey; 1972)
- A shallow aquifer outside Denver was contaminated when chemical wastes infiltrated the groundwater from unlined holding ponds.
- Sixteen wells closed because of contamination from a number of chemicals from a nearby facility which processed waste oil. (Gray, Maine; 1977)
- Four wells supplying 80 percent of the town's drinking water were found to be contaminated with trichloroethylene and dioxane. (Bedford, Massachusetts)
- Groundwater in San Joaquin Valley was contaminated with a pesticide. Approximately 35 percent of the valley has been affected.
- Fourteen city wells and 80 private wells were closed due to the presence of vinyl chloride, trichloroethylene, and benzene. (Battle Creek, Michigan)
- Eleven of 13 people who drank from a well fell ill from arsenic poisoning. The arsenic-containing pesticide had been buried in the 1930s. (Perham, Minnesota; 1972)
- Residents in a small Indiana town were alarmed to find their private well water coated with an oily substance. The EPA found volatile organic compounds, believed to be from a leak in a gasoline tank years earlier. The groundwater flow presumably brought the chemicals to the water supply of the affected neighborhood. (Elkhart County, Indiana; 1978)

Surface water contamination had its own symptoms. Newspaper and magazine articles read as follows:[17]

- The blood of local residents in a town on a tributary of the Tennessee River was found to have five times the national average level of PCBs and ten times the average level of DDT. (1979)
- The Mississippi River, a source of drinking water for New Orleans, contains measurable amounts of 66 chemical compounds. (1974)
- Twenty miles of Colorado streams are void of all aquatic life. Blame is placed on acid drainage from an area mine. (1978)

Industrial dumping of mercury in Japan's Minamata Bay and Agano River occurred in the 1950s and early 1960s. The fish became contaminated, and an epidemic of "Minamata's disease" surfaced. Thousands complained of symptoms including loss of motor control; loss of hearing; and, in some cases, blindness, coma, and death. Infants born to exposed mothers had mental retardation and cerebral palsy with convulsions. This event received considerable international attention.[19]

In 1977, the Clean Water Act was passed to protect the U.S. rivers and streams. However, preexisting conditions prevail. Ground contamination may not have impacted the waterways as yet. Already contaminated waterways may have not been identified and illegal dumping in the rivers is alleged.

In 1975, a combination of oil and industrial wastes contaminated with dioxin were sprayed on a horse arena near Times Beach, Missouri. Soon after the spraying, numerous birds, rodents, and horses died in the vicinity of the arena. Two children were hospitalized after playing in the area. Later, unpaved roads in and around the Times Beach area were sprayed with the same material for dust control. In December 1982, severe rains and flooding spread the dioxin-contaminated waste throughout the entire town. The Center for Disease Control recommended evacuation. EPA bought the homes for $30 million.[20]

Industrial dumping has occurred at sea. Ocean dumping was legal until 1970, and there were no controls on that which was dumped. A fisherman was hired to haul toxic and radioactive waste 20 miles from Boston into the Massachusetts Bay, in an area now referred to as the "Foul Area." From 1947 until 1970, fisherman hauled tens of thousands of barrels of hazardous, nonradioactive waste to the general vicinity of the area and shot holes in the drums so they could sink. EPA estimated that just over 4,000 barrels of radioactive material was also dumped into the Foul Area since 1952. There were no prior records. During this time, there were three other ocean dumping sites as well. One was the Farallon Islands site, 40 miles west of San Francisco, in water depths greater than 3,000 feet. Two others were 120 and 200 miles off the coast of Delaware and Maryland, at 9,300 and 13,000 feet depths, respectively. The Boston site was not only closer to land in relatively shallow water, but also it was a fish-spawning ground. According to EPA, there is no apparent danger to the environment or the public from the dumping yet. As of this writing, there has been no coverage to indicate any monitoring being conducted for hazardous materials in the "Foul Area."[21]

In the late 1970s, midnight dumpers and gypsy haulers became prominent in the news. Articles read as follows:[22]

- A transformer company paid $75,000 to a hauler to dispose of 31,000 gallons of transformer fluid, containing highly toxic PCBs. Instead, the hauler dumped the chemicals along the side of 270 miles of North Carolina roads.
- Small firms throughout Kentucky hired a hauler to dump their hazardous waste. What they did not know was that the hauler was dumping the barrels of waste on a 17-acre field 20 miles south of Louisville.
- It is becoming commonplace for investigators to find drums of chemicals of unknown ancestry hidden in abandoned warehouses, stored on small lots in rundown sections of cities, stashed under elevated roadways or in open fields, poured onto the ground on vacant lots or rented farms, or simply dumped into municipal sewers and private wells.
- About 75 percent of hazardous wastes were disposed of on the property of the companies that generate them. Only 10 percent were disposed of in a manner consistent with regulations.
- A major chemical processing plant contracted with a disposal firm to carry away 4,500 drums of hazardous waste. The hauler abandoned the 55-gallon drums on a former chicken farm near a river. When the owners discovered the barrels, Union Carbide was charged with part of the cleanup. EPA paid the rest.
- A research and development laboratory has been dumping chemical wastes, principally arsenic, onto a seven-acre site since 1953. The arsenic is now leaching into the nearby river.
- A plant producing fungicides and mercury compounds has operated for years under several owners. EPA estimates that as much as two kilograms of mercury per day was slopped onto the floor and washed into a nearby swamp. The concentration of mercury in the ground has exceeded generally accepted limits 750-fold.

In the late 1970s and early 1980s, headlines touted environmental disasters with greater frequency. Some of the articles follow:[23,24]

- Approximately 6,000 pounds of plastic and other wastes were buried in an Arkansas landfill between 1972 and 1979. In late 1979, the dump ignited and burned out of control for 12 days, producing a cloud of toxic hydrogen chloride. (Gassville, Arkansas; 1979)
- Over 1,000 cubic yards of resins, left over from a redistilling process have been ordered removed from a dumpsite which was located within 10 feet of the owner's house. Previously, assorted toxic wastes, which had been leaking from over 15,000 drums and 43 tanks within 100 yards of homes, were removed. (Rehoboth, Massachusetts; 1979)
- A small working-class community north of Boston fears a chemical disaster in the making. Radioactive wastes, arsenic, chromium and other deadly chemicals have produced foul-tasting water and concentrations of explosive swamp gas within the town's boundaries. The property had been previously owned by a chemical company. (1980)
- Officials are cleaning up oil and chemicals from a river in Pennsylvania. The origin is an old, abandoned mine where the chemicals were poured into open shafts. (1981)
- A 17-acre "Valley of the Drums" still contains 100,000 barrels of highly toxic chemicals. All EPA could do is stop the chemicals inside the rotting, rusting drums from leaking into a nearby stream. (Bullitt County, Kentucky; 1981)
- A chemical corporation has dumped 300,000 drums of pesticide-production waste in unlined trenches on a 242-acre site near town. The water table has become contaminated and the residents are suing the corporation. (Toone, Tennessee; 1980)
- A fire broke out at a dump that had been used by the Chemical Control Corporation. A major incident was averted when winds blew toxic clouds away from populated areas.

In response to all the stories of "doom and gloom," the U.S. Congress enacted the Resource Conservation and Recovery Act (RCRA) and Toxic Substances Control Act (TSCA) in 1976. The RCRA was enacted to regulate hazardous substances. Subtitle C of Title II regulates treatments, storage, disposal, generation, and transportation of hazardous wastes. Subtitle I regulates the management and reporting of underground storage tanks, and Subtitle J regulates medical waste. The TSCA was enacted to regulate the manufacture and distribution of hazardous chemical substances within the U.S. Then, in 1980, the Comprehensive Environmental Response, Compensation, and Liability Act (CERCLA) was enacted to identify hazardous waste sites, establish a trust fund for cleanup (i.e., "Superfund"), and require notification of uncontrolled releases.

Between 1980 and 1985, the U.S. EPA recorded 6,928 accidents involving toxic chemicals and radioactive materials. This is an average of five per day. A congressional research team concluded that nearly half of the 1,246 hazardous waste dumps it surveyed showed signs of polluting nearby groundwater, and the Office of Technology Assessment estimated that at least 10,000 hazardous waste sites in the U.S. pose a serious threat to public health and need to be cleaned up.[33]

In 1986, the environmental problems were noted to be more extensive than they had originally been. Thus, the Superfund Amendments and Reauthorization Act (SARA) was enacted to amend CERCLA, increasing the trust fund for hazardous waste site cleanups, and disclosing the Emergency Planning and Community Right-to-Know Act. The latter, mostly in response to the Bhopal incident, requires business to prepare inventory reports, listing hazardous chemicals in their possession, to assist in the development of local emergency response plans, to prepare annual reports of hazardous substance releases, and to report immediately certain ultrahazardous releases.

The impact of environmental pollution was still being discovered, even after many of the environmental laws had been enacted. Groundwater ills were being diagnosed in the late 1980s and early 1990s. Articles read as follows:[25]

- The federal government estimates that one to two percent of the nation's groundwater is at least moderately polluted by "point sources" alone, such as leaking landfills or hazardous waste dumps.
- One-fifth of California's large drinking water wells fed by groundwater exceed the state's pollution limits.
- Pesticides and other synthetic chemicals have been detected in half of Iowa's city wells.
- More than 1,000 wells have been shut down as drinking water sources because they are contaminated with the nematocide ethylene dibromide, a suspected human carcinogen. The levels exceed the state limit 60-fold.
- Florida state authorities in 1979 tallied 6,000 lagoons and ponds filled with toxic waste.

In the early 1980s, the EPA began to notice contamination of groundwater by leaking underground storage tanks. Due to the large numbers of underground storage tanks and the potential for leaks, greater controls were indicated.

In 1984, the U.S. Congress directed the U.S. EPA, under Subtitle I of RCRA, to respond to the leaking underground storage tank problems. This regulation was promulgated in 1988. It covered requirements for new tank systems, leak detection, recordkeeping, reporting, closure techniques, corrective action, and financial responsibility.

It has been speculated that the ground abounds with hazardous substances which have yet to reach the ground and surface waters. The presence of some hazardous materials in the ground went undetected until it created a problem (e.g., a high incidence of illness in a small community), and there were reports of illegal dumping (e.g., dumping in storm sewers). A couple of press releases follow:

- Louisville's sewers exploded in 1981, collapsing some streets and sidewalks when a 150-gallon load of untreated hexane-contaminated wastes entered from an animal food plant.[26]
- Abandoned mines have a variety of wastes which have been poured in their unboarded-up holes in Texas. (1990)[27]

The cost for waste disposal and cleanup began to escalate. Consequently, industry looked for alternate means of disposal. Some U.S. firms have been accused of turning Mexican border towns into a backyard dump. As labor costs in Mexico attract these firms, the lack of adequate waste disposal controls becomes a big plus for the industrial corporations. Accusations follow:[28]

- A Matamoros company signed a contract to dispose of several hundred barrels of paint sludge. The barrels never arrived at the prescribed hazardous waste site. They were dumped in the desert. (1988)
- Even though a 1987 agreement between the two countries requires U.S. companies in Mexico to return their waste products to the U.S., the companies have poured chemical wastes down drains, dumped them in irrigation ditches, left them in the desert, burned them in city dumps, and turned them over to Mexican recycling firms not qualified to handle toxic waste. (1988)
- Of 634 U.S. toxic waste-generating companies surveyed in Mexico, only 20 had notified the U.S. EPA that they were returning waste to the country. (1986)
- Poor Mexican residents in nearby areas collect their drinking water in 55-gallon drums still labeled with their previous contents, e.g.,

copper cyanide, zinc chromate epoxy, caustic sodium hydroxide. Many drums still have residues of solvents and other harmful substances. The poor say they "know it's dangerous, but [they] don't have a choice. It is [their] only means for storing the water" which they buy off trucks. (1988)

- The New River, a 75-mile waterway along the border of California and Mexico has been found to have 28 strains of infectious diseases—including typhoid, cholera, hepatitis, and polio—and at least a hundred types of toxic chemicals. The chemicals have been traced back to U.S. companies in Mexico. (1988)

- A growing number of Southern California businesses are clandestinely trucking their hazardous wastes to Mexico to dodge increasingly stringent and costly environmental laws in the U.S. (1990)[29]

Some firms remaining in the U.S. have found other loosely regulated places to dispose of their hazardous waste—Indian reservations. The attraction is the isolation and relative freedom from state and federal regulations or political pressures. The reservations are sovereign. Stories follow:[30]

- Indian tribes across America are grappling with some of the worst uranium tailings, chemical lagoons, and illegal dumps. (1990)

- Mohawks have fought a long battle with several manufacturers who have fouled the river which they once relied on for food and income. The perch and pike can no longer be eaten, and fluoride poisoning has decimated herds of cattle. (1990)

- California's Campo Indians have contracted for a 600-acre landfill. (1990)

- Arizona's Kalbab-Palutes are accepting a huge hazardous waste incinerator. (1990)

Industries responsible for the greatest quantity of hazardous waste discharges in the past have been the aluminum plants, petroleum refineries, and drilling, and the largest concentration of petrochemical plants are in Texas and Louisiana.[31] The following press release is dated 1989:

- Louisiana's Mississippi River is so polluted that it has become known as "cancer alley." The 85-mile stretch of river, between Baton Rouge and New Orleans, is lined with 136 petrochemical plants and seven oil refineries.[32]

In 1980, the EPA assigned 1,245 hazardous waste sites a high priority and placed them on the National Priority List. As of October 1992, only 105 sites had been remediated.[35]

Love Canal[36]

In 1978, the sleepy residential community of Love Canal in Niagara Falls, New York, was declared a toxic disaster, and residents were to be evacuated with financial assistance from the Federal Disaster Assistance Administration. Between 1942 and 1952, Hooker Chemical had disposed of more than 21,000 tons of chemical wastes at the site, at a depth of 20 to 25 feet. At this time, waste disposal was a simple process. A waste hauler simply acquired a permit affirming that the site would not endanger public health by attracting flies and vermin.

At the time, the site seemed ideal for their purposes. The ground was an impermeable clay, and the site was located in a scarcely populated area. In December 1952, Hooker Chemical sold 16 acres, inclusive of the site which was landfilled, to the school board of Niagara Falls with the understanding that it would be used for school buildings or for recreation purposes. In their warranty deed, Hooker Chemical included a disclaimer, stating that:

> "The grantee herein has been advised by the grantor that the premises...have been filled, in whole or in part, to the present grade level thereof with waste products resulting from the manufacturing of chemicals by the grantor at its plant...and the grantee assumes all risk and liability incident to the use thereof...as a part of the consideration...thereof, no claim, suit, action or demand...shall ever be made...against [Hooker]...for injury to a person or persons, including death resulting therefrom, or loss of or damage to property caused by, or in connection with or by reason of the presence of said industrial wastes."

In 1957, Hooker's attorney warned the school board that damage to water/sewer lines, building foundations, and danger to human health could result from improper use of the property. The school attracted a burgeoning community of modest two and three bedroom homes to the boundaries of the property. Occupants began to notice noxious odors emanating from the area at times of high humidity.

By the mid 1970s, the land began to show signs of settling as the disposal containers deteriorated. Residents noticed exposed waste drums. Exposures to the soil caused itchy, burning skin and blisters to barefoot children playing and workers digging in the area. Between 1976 and 1978, several investigations were made on the area—initially brought about by an effort to trace the source of contaminants found in the Great Lakes. Local citizens began paying greater attention to the warning signs. Community groups were formed, and residents became aware that the problem was not singular.

The Love Canal community asked for assistance. The media brought attention to the area, and Love Canal became a "hot" topic for television special reporting. President Carter declared the area a national emergency. The U.S. government sued Hooker for $125 million in cleanup costs, and the local citizens sued Hooker for $3 billion in damages. This incident was the spark which ignited the creation of the "Superfund" regulation.

Ironically, the cost of the property had been a gift to the school for $1 back in 1952. Hooker officials claimed it was a charitable donation.

The Bhopal Incident

In 1984, there was a methyl isocyanate gas leak in Bhopal, India. Over 2,000 people were killed and thousands more injured. At the time, this was labeled the "worst civilian technological disaster in history." A year later, as the U.S. was speculating as to whether a Bhopal disaster could occur in the U.S., a release occurred at a Union Carbide plant in Institute, West Virginia. There were 135 injuries and no deaths. Although the civilian population was not affected, heightened public awareness caused the big wheels of government to legislate the Community Right-to-Know Law, a community awareness and emergency response program.

HAZARDOUS SUBSTANCES WHICH RECEIVED SPECIAL ATTENTION

Some hazardous substances have received more publicity and created concerns which go beyond the general concerns of hazardous wastes. These include asbestos, lead, polychlorinated biphenyls, and some pesticides. The historic events and regulations are discussed in this section, while details and specific information relevant to performing a site assessment are discussed in a later chapter.

Asbestos

Asbestos, a thread-like, fibrous rock which can cause lung disease, is ubiquitous in the earth's crust. Major deposits have been found in North America, Canada, South Africa, and the former Soviet Union.

It was used by the Greeks over 2,500 years ago to weave "stone flax." The product was used for eternal wicks, handkerchiefs, and napkins, each of which was not washed but placed in a fire to burn off the stains—magic! Yet, many of the craftsmen suffered from a "sickness of the lungs."[37]

In the late 1800s, the industrial revolution was met head on with problems. Roofs were ignitable and dangerous. Steam engine gaskets were deteriorating as fast as they were put on, and tenders were not shielded from the sparks and heat extremes created by the steam boilers. Boiler pipes were being wrapped in old carpet and mortar. A corpulent inventor and roof manufacturer, Henry W. Johns, read about an Italian fireproof paper and linen. This sparked his imagination, and the would-be roofing magnate and asbestos zealot proceeded to develop a fireproof roofing material. Later, he expanded the use of this miracle fiber to durable gaskets, heat shields, and pipe insulation. In 1898, Mr. Johns died of a dust "phthisis pneumonitis." It appears as though his death was the result of exposures to the "miracle fiber." In 1902, C.B. Manville bought out the Johns estate, changed the Johns to John, and created the John-Manville Corporation.[38]

By 1936, asbestos had been promoted to the single most common construction material in the U.S. Some of the uses included ceiling tiles, floor tiles, insulation on electrical wires, circuit boxes, caulking, spackling, and thermal/acoustical surfacing material. It was also used for automobile convertibles, boat and auto insulation, Christmas tree flock, papier-maché mixes, baby blankets, mattress stuffing, and curtains. The list goes on.[39]

Throughout the 1920s, British medical journals published accounts of patients suffering a peculiar lung disease, and by 1930 a report was published, indicating an association between the lung disease and asbestos exposures. By 1935, the U.S. legal profession had acknowledged the association, and the relationship became widely published information.[40] Over the next 40 years, evidence mounted, and asbestos exposures were positively linked with lung cancer, mesothelioma, and "asbestosis"—a progressive, deadly, lung disease. Public interest and concern set off a chain reaction.

In 1972, the Occupational Safety and Health Administration (OSHA) set a limit to the acceptable levels that workers could be exposed to and establish proper handling procedures in 1972. The standard was modified in 1976, and OSHA published regulations to cover asbestos removal work practices in 1986.

In 1973, the Environmental Protection Agency (EPA) issued regulations (National Emission Standards for Hazardous Air Pollutants, NESHAPS) which set forth procedures requiring asbestos removal in buildings prior to demolition and banned the manufacture/use of asbestos-containing, sprayed-on surfacing insulation in buildings. This regulation was later revised.

The 1975 and 1978 NESHAPS Amendment banned the manufacture and use of "all" types of *insulating* asbestos-containing materials (ACM) in new buildings and special controls/work practices for removing friable ACM from areas under renovation. In abbreviated terms, the special controls call for wet removal and no visible emissions during removal, transportation, or disposal.

In 1982, EPA promulgated guidelines for controlling "friable" ACM in school buildings (Friable Asbestos-Containing Materials in Schools: Identification and Notification Rule). They applied a 1983 deadline for compliance.

In 1986, EPA promulgated guidelines for identifying and controlling "non-friable," as well as friable, ACM in school buildings and the development of ACM operations and management plans. This law is the Asbestos Hazard Emergency Response Act (AHERA) and is directed toward the public/private schools up through the 12th grade. Some feel that a similar law will be passed for all public buildings, and lawyers advise present day adherence to the AHERA protocol when inspecting any building for asbestos.

In November 1990, a clarifying rule (amended 40 CFR 61) to the NESHAPS asbestos regulations limits the 1973 requirement for removal of all ACM prior to demolition. This is discussed in greater detail in the section on Asbestos in Chapter 9.

In July 1989, the EPA promulgated a rule providing for a seven year phase-out plan for all asbestos-containing material. This ban was later vacated and remanded by the Fifth Circuit Court of Appeals. Although the Court clarified that the decision still held for products that were not being manufactured, imported, or processed on July 1989. In 40 CFR 763, the EPA identifies those products they "believe" remain subject to the ban. As of March 1993, an attempt is being made to clarify the restrictions.

Asbestos manufacturers are being sued for damages associated with the "deadly substance." Schools and public buildings are scurrying to remove the liability, often at considerable expense. Building occupants have sued for associated emotional trauma from occupying asbestos-containing buildings. Commercial real estate investors are expressing concern for the devaluation of their property due to preexisting asbestos. The laws regulating asbestos are abundant, sometimes confusing, and the cost for removal escalates.

Lead[40]

Current levels of lead in an average body are estimated to be 1,000 times higher than that of the caveman. Lead exposures, particularly to children, have become problematic over the years as a child may suffer irreversible effects (e.g., learning impairment). A study performed by the Second National Health and Nutrition Examination Survey, conducted between 1976 and 1980, demonstrated blood lead levels in children, under the age of six, to be 16 to 20 micrograms of lead per deciliter of blood (µg/dl). The acceptable level is 10 µg/dl.

Subsequently, the Center for Disease Control recommended that a child with a blood lead level in excess of 25 µg/dl be given a full-day test to determine whether hospitalization was needed. A recent case involved a child with a blood lead level of 144 µg/dl. The child died from massive brain damage.

As much as half of the total exposures have previously been attributed to airborne lead from automotive exhausts when tetraethyl lead was used as a gasoline additive. Lead-containing gasoline, today, has less than half a percent of that which it had prior to public awareness. All lead-containing gasoline is being phased out and will be banned completely by 1996.

Another source of lead exposures is drinking water which has passed over lead-soldered joints in copper pipes or lead-containing, galvanized pipes, and more recent exposures, particularly to children, have been the result of ingesting lead-containing paints. Lead-containing paints may deteriorate and the debris may become airborne. Lead-contaminated soils and dust may be present, contamination having resulted from auto emissions of decades past. Dust and soil may also contain industrially generated lead, and occupationally exposed workers may carry lead-containing dust home in their clothing or on their shoes.

There is a move at the present by the Department of Housing and Urban Development (HUD) to abate, or remove, badly deteriorated, exposed lead-containing paint from HUD residential housing. It has been estimated that 75 percent of all older houses have lead (0.5 percent and greater) in the paint, and there is a chance of significant deterioration in many of these homes.[41]

Polychlorinated Biphenyls

Production of polychlorinated biphenyls (PCBs) in the U.S. began in 1929. These compounds are thick, oily liquids, non-flammable, and an excellent insulator. PCBs were a viable replacement for combustible insulating fluids in transformers and other electrical equipment. Not only did they cut down on the potential for fires, but PCBs allowed for the manufacture of smaller, less expensive capacitors. Insurance companies began requiring the use of this non-flammable substance in vital locations.[42] PCBs have also been used in fluorescent light ballasts and occasionally in the manufacture of adhesives, paints, carbonless copy paper, sealants, newspaper printing inks, and caulking compounds.[42,43]

After PCBs found their niche in the electrical industry, studies indicated that PCBs can cause reproductive defects and are suspected liver carcinogens. Skin contact with the viscous liquid may result in eye/skin irritation and acneform dermatitis. Animals also have demonstrated liver injury from this suspected carcinogen. Infants born to exposed mothers have had decreased birth weights and skin discolorations. Of greatest note, however, is that PCBs have been found to contain trace levels of dioxins, one of the deadliest compounds known to man. Dioxin is a by-product of burning PCBs. If a PCB-containing transformer blows up or catches fire, dioxins are likely to contaminate the area.

PCBs are persistent in nature. They resist degradation, and they are retained for extended periods of time in human body fat. As they spread readily through the food chain via fish, birds, and mammals, PCBs are now thought to be present in the "fat tissues of all humans." A major source of contamination in humans is the consumption of fish from contaminated lakes and rivers where transformer fluids have been dumped or migrated through the soils and groundwater.

In 1968, PCBs were accidentally mixed with rice oil in Yusho, Japan. Over 1,200 people developed symptoms, including acne, headache, vomiting, diarrhea, fever, neurological disorders, and jaundice. In 1970, large-scale production reached its peak, then production began to slow down due to the Japanese incident. The succeeding years saw PCB sales limited to sealed systems.[44]

High levels of PCBs were discovered in the Great Lakes and other U.S. surface waters in 1976. That same year a law was passed to phase out the manufacture and distribution of all PCBs which were not enclosed or containerized. Later regulations mandated that transformers, located in areas where public exposure might occur, must be out of service by 1988. All other enclosed systems were to be subject to a routine inspection and maintenance program.

Between 1929 and 1977, it is estimated that 1.2 billion pounds of PCBs were produced in the U.S.[45] The EPA estimated in 1980 that 440 million pounds of PCBs were still present in the environment or landfills.[44]

Dioxins

Dioxins are not manufactured directly for commercial use. They are impurities, formed in the production of many herbicides (i.e., 2,4,5-T) and wood preservatives made from chlorophenols. Although they are considered one of the most toxic substances known to man, reports of dioxin exposures have yet to document any deaths. Dioxins are not suspected, but known carcinogens.

In 1948, 2,4,5-T was registered in the U.S. as a pesticide. It was to be used to selectively kill undesirable weeds and brush along highways and railways; in rangeland and forests; and in wheat, rice, corn, and sugarcane fields. It was also used in Vietnam, under the name of Agent Orange.[46] Between 1965 and 1970, the U.S. Defense Department sprayed 10.7 million gallons of Agent Orange, at a rate of three undiluted gallons per acre, much stronger concentrations than used in the U.S. By 1977, Vietnam veterans began contacting the VA with health problems that associated with their exposures to the defoliant in Vietnam.[47]

In 1979, a later-to-be controversial study revealed a relationship between 2,4,5-T exposures and spontaneous abortions in Alsea, Oregon.[48] Vietnam veterans were reporting dermal problems, and there were increased numbers of cancer mortalities over the statistical norm. The media jumped in, and a ban was placed on the use of 2,4,5-T herbicides.[47]

In 1983, dioxins made headlines when the town of Times Beach, Missouri, was declared a disaster area. The federal government offered to buy all the homes and businesses after the test results showed high levels of dioxin in the soil. A waste hauler had purchased 55 pounds of dioxin from a chemical plant in 1971, mixed the dioxin with waste oils, and contracted to spread it on unpaved roads throughout Missouri to act as a dust-control. The result was an expensive cleanup of the soil.[49]

Dioxin has been found around inactive industrial sites, in municipal incinerators (where it has been produced as a by-product of burning various wastes), in toxic waste dumps, on roads and pastures, and around areas that have been sprayed with dioxin-containing chemicals.[49]

DDT[50]

The Nobel Prize in medicine was awarded in 1948 to a chemist who patented DDT for use as a pesticide. DDT was first synthesized in 1877 but had no apparent use. DDT replaced a number of extremely dangerous chemicals then being used for pest control, including arsenic, mercury, fluorine, and lead. Its initial use was to kill clothes moths, skin lice, and malaria-carrying mosquitoes. Later, its uses were expanded to the control of insects which caused sleeping sickness, plague, typhus, and encephalitis. Its low cost enabled its use in pest control in agriculture and forestry. Its impact on agriculture soon became evident in increasing worldwide food supplies and fiber (e.g., cotton production).

In the early 1900s, DDT was discovered to be retained in human fatty tissue for extended periods of time. Therefore, exposures add to the body burden and are retained, resulting in a long-term buildup. The effects of short-term, high levels of exposure were found to result in headaches, dizziness, confusion, sweating, tremors, and convulsions. Long-term exposures may result in liver damage and central nervous system depression. More important, animal laboratory studies indicated evidence of possible liver carcinogenicity. Although it has never been connected with human liver cancer, the threat persists.

In 1948, 2,800,000 cases of malaria were reported in Ceylon. By 1962, following the large-scale use of DDT to kill the mosquitoes which transmitted the malaria parasite, the number of human malaria cases had been reduced to 31. That same year, as a result of Carson's *Silent Spring,* DDT spraying was ceased in Ceylon. Public debate also led to its ban in the United States in 1972. Sixteen years later, the reported incidence of malaria in Ceylon had returned to 2,500,000 cases. This raises an issue of questionable benefits resulting from its ban. It is still being phased out in the United States.

ENVIRONMENTAL CRIMES/CRIMINALS

An awareness of what could have transpired in the past and what may transpire in the future is a must when considering possibilities. Environmental crimes may be committed out of ignorance or with knowledge and intent.

Ignorance of hazardous waste and subsequent mishandling have led to numerous law suits and million dollar fines. In some states, media coverage alleges that illegal dumping has become big business; hazardous waste is being dumped on highways, in sewers, into ground cover, in empty lots, in streams and ponds, down old wells, and the list goes on. Some hazardous waste dump sites have been mismanaged, either with intention or for lack of foresight. City and state officials are accused of document alterations and cover-ups. Ambulance chasers are becoming dump-truck chasers. Frequently, hazardous waste is found in a field or rented property where the responsible party is long gone. Hazardous waste disposal involves big money, and where there is big money, crime will be its partner. Creative dumping can afford a challenging investigation for any site investigation.

Illegal Hazardous Waste Site Management

In Jersey City, 1989, bail was revoked on two owners of a dump site. They had been convicted of racketeering and bribery for illegally dumping demolition debris in two New Jersey towns. Yet, while out on a $100,000 bail during an appeal and on an order by the judge to cease their illegal operations, they continued to operate the dump that later erupted into flames. The fire, located under Interstate 78, was of such intense heat that six lanes of the interstate sagged. Estimated repairs were $6 million, and the state expects to spend $4.4 million clearing debris from the site. Both responsible parties are serving 17-year prison sentences.

In New Jersey, 1991, the director of a municipal sewage plant was charged with dumping 21 million pounds of pollutants into the Hudson River while he was managing a neighboring town's sewage plant. He was apparently attempting to set up his own business, claiming to have developed a more efficient treatment process to minimize sludge. Having tampered with monthly discharge reports to the regulatory agencies and with wastewater samples, he was charged with 38 counts of illegal wrongdoing.[51]

In Rhode Island, 1989, two brothers pleaded "no contest" to 715 counts of violating state solid waste laws while operating an illegal landfill. The state court levied a $2.8 million fine against three companies, owned by the brothers. One brother was given five years probation. The other received one year.[52]

Chemical Waste Management, Inc., one of the country's biggest hazardous waste incinerator managers, admitted to mislabeling toxic waste to evade safety regulations and suspended operations during an investigation by the U.S. government.   They are being charged with criminal misconduct.

Illegal Dumping

In Sedalia, Missouri, 1981, Alcolac, Inc. lost a $50 million liability suit for discharging hazardous wastes from its plant.   Nearby residents complained of ongoing problems with nausea, headaches, and dermatitis. Alcolac had been the maker of constituents which are used in hair shampoo, floor wax, and paint.[26]

In Hopewell, Virginia, 1973, Life Sciences Products, Inc., working out of a converted gas station, was identified as the source of air and water contamination.   Significant quantities of Kepone, a pesticide, were found in the air 16 miles from the plant, and in the water 64 miles downstream. The two owners were charged with 153 violations of the federal Water Pollution Control Act with potential penalties of $3.5 million each.   They pleaded "no contest."   The corporation was charged with 153 violations and was fined $3.8 million.   The corporation dissolved.   The previous producers, Allied Chemical, were then charged with crimes stemming from their own misconduct in the original production of Kepone.   Allied pleaded "no contest" to 940 counts of violating federal water pollution laws and was fined $13.24 million, which was later reduced to $5 million.[53]

In an affluent Westchester suburb in Harrison, New York, 1988, at least 1,500 truckloads of hazardous chemical-tainted waste were dumped over seven months in a pricey neighborhood lot, changing it into what appeared to be a battlefield.   In time, the area began to smell, and a thick, black liquid oozed into neighboring yards.   Officials were contacted, but there was no action.   When the county Department of Health took samples, it found everything from heavy metals (i.e., arsenic) to lethal gases (i.e., hydrogen sulfide).   The town was sued by one of the homeowners, and the operator was fined $6,500 for "dumping without a permit."   A year later, the county district attorney said, after having conducted an "exhaustive" study, he could not find sufficient evidence of criminal wrongdoing.   The residents alleged that all records of complaints had disappeared and city documents had been altered.   There also appeared to be ties to organized crime.[54,55]

Officials Accused of Criminal Negligence

On April 22, 1992, a buildup of gasoline ground contamination resulted in an explosion which killed more than 200 people in Guadalajara, Mexico.[56] The incident also resulted in damage to 1,422 homes, 450 businesses, 600 vehicles, and five miles of street.[57] A series of activities, beginning with a leaking underground gasoline-carrying pipeline, led to the incident. Each contributed to the next.

The ground around the leak became saturated, and gasoline vapors migrated into cracks in the sanitary sewers of Guadalajara. The sewers provided an avenue by which the gasoline could travel freely, spreading to other areas of the sewer system.[58] Residents reported to city officials the presence of a strong odor of gasoline in the city sewer. The reports were investigated but no action was recommended. An ignition source or spark and then an explosion followed.

Nine government and Pemex oil company officials were charged with negligent homicide.[58] The mayor and eight others were charged with criminal negligence. The cost for reconstruction efforts are expected to exceed $30 million.[57]

COSTS AND DAMAGES

The EPA has identified over 1,245 hazardous waste sites which are in dire need of attention. This number grows monthly, and states have their own listings. In 1986, the federal list included 500 sites. Fifteen years later, this number has more than doubled.

Superfund sites are prioritized and placed on the National Priority List. The prioritization is based on anticipated impact on the environment and natural resources. Then, Superfund money is used to cover the costs of cleanup until liability can be established. Sometimes, the guilty party has gone out of business, and the U.S. government ends up paying the entire bill.

When Superfund money was allocated in 1980, it amounted to $1.3 billion. By 1986, the funds had increased fivefold to $9 billion. Yet, most Superfund sites are estimated to cost around $25 to $30 million for cleanup. At this rate, should the existing sites not increase in total number, the cost will ultimately exceed $35 billion. Only 84 of the nation's 1,245 most polluted sites have been cleaned up.[59] Superfund monies are intended for cleanup of extremely large sites with considerable impact on the environ-ment, with the money to be reimbursed by designated responsible parties. All known sites are not included in the federal Superfund. Some are picked up by state superfunds, some are being monitored, and not all are known. An industry-sponsored study, in the early 1980s, found 4,802 contaminated sites nationwide, while a government-sponsored study estimated 50,000 sites. Either way the numbers are greater than those listed. The question remains—where are the others located?

Cleanup costs born by the private sector run anywhere from $100,000 to $500 million per site. These figures are a mean. They cost as little as a few hundred dollars for removal of a leaky waste drum, or they may run into the billions. The estimated cost for cleanup of 10,000-plus toxic waste dumps is $500 billion and will take over 50 years to remediate.[60]

Victims of hazardous waste mismanagement are claiming damages in the billions. They often involve multiple plaintiffs, aimed at multiple defendants. Many of the suits are settled out of court, as legal uncertainties and attorneys' fees add fuel to the already high costs. As of 1992, the insurance industry had spent about $1.3 billion; $1 billion, 90 percent of the total bill, went to lawyers' fees.[59] Defendants not only are afraid of unfavorable verdicts, but also they want to avoid establishing legal precedents that would make it easier for other victims to prove causation and joint liability.

Due to the latency period for identifying sites, it is oftentimes difficult to track offenders. Property changes hands, and one site may be subject to environmental impact from several different, unrelated owners. Dump sites have numerous waste contributors, some of which may have long since gone out of business or declared bankruptcy. Small, well-intended businesses have been held responsible when they dispose of their waste at a dump site which was poorly managed and allowed wastes to migrate beyond the waste site. The generators end up paying their share of the damages.

For instance, some 20 newspapers had been named "responsible parties" in abandoned waste dumps targeted for cleanup.[23] Almost all of these newspapers were "duped by contractors" who claimed to have legitimate places to dump their waste. The contractors were taken at their word, paid to dispose of the waste, then disappeared. Toxic waste is a "cradle-to-grave" responsibility, and the newspapers were charged with cleanup costs when the site was discovered.

The courts have expanded the notion of liability so that "anyone with any connection" to the company that improperly disposed of hazardous waste can be sued for the entire cost of the cleanup—if the guilty party does not have the money. This is referred to as "deep pockets." Whoever has the money pays the bill. Banks which go beyond passive ownership may be sued, especially on a repossession. In other words, the borrower gets into financial trouble, defaults on his loan, and leaves his liability concerns behind with the lenders or lien-holders.[61]

Municipalities are being held liable for their contribution. As of 1990, of the total 1,226 dumps listed on the National Priority List as Superfund sites, an estimated 20 percent are municipal landfills; some cases involve dump sites gone awry whereby the municipalities had transported household hazardous waste to mismanaged landfills. For instance, in Los Angeles, a consortium of corporations brought suit in late 1989 against the California Department of Transportation and 29 cities that transported household solid waste to a 190-acre landfill in San Gabriel Valley. These companies had already agreed to help finance over $65 million in cleanup efforts, but they felt the municipality should contribute their fair share.[62]

Uncle Sam's follies may cost into the billions. Cleaning up radioactive and chemical waste at the nation's nuclear weapons plants and military installations presents "technical challenges equal to the Apollo moon landing and space shuttle programs." In 1998, the military had an estimated 3,000 aging, soon-to-be decommissioned, nuclear weapons plants; 6,000 hazardous waste dumps, over 600 military installations; and 7,200 contaminated properties, formerly owned by the military. The cleanup costs could exceed $130 billion.[63]

Lenders can be held responsible if they foreclose on an offending company or get involved in management. Individuals who own just a few shares of a troubled company may be held liable—if that person had been actively involved at a shareholders' meeting.[61] "Any bank that goes beyond passive ownership of a lien has a potential exposure," says Thomas Kline, a Washington lawyer.[5] A company can be required to pay cleanup costs, even if its actions were lawful at the time the waste was dumped. Everyone, guilty and innocent, gets involved and shares the burden of liability and cleanup costs.

Cost-benefit studies are becoming an important tool in cleanup decisions. Impact does not always warrant the cost of the cleanup. For instance, in the Hopewell incident, where a local riverbed is contaminated with Kepone, the cleanup costs were estimated at $100 to $500 billion dollars[53]—a sum that could cost the U.S. taxpayers an estimated average of $4,348 per worker.

SUMMARY

Environmental pollution by man dates back to the turn of the century. By the 1940s, increased usage of chemicals and modern technology resulted in unregulated disposal of hazardous materials in the waterway and soil. It was not until the 1960s that the results of unrestricted chemical usage and disposal began to surface—most of which was amplified by the media. Public opinion was impacted, and regulations were created as new problems became apparent.

The U.S. EPA was voted into law in 1970, and todays' society abounds with environmental laws. The end result is criminal penalties in some instances for knowingly polluting the environment, and costly cleanup expenses/litigation costs from being associated, directly or indirectly, with a contaminated site.

Once again, the only defense is to be aware of the possibilities, and reduce the risk through a state-of-the-art environmental site assessment. Enter into all property investments with caution, and remember that even residential property is not immune to environmental pollution.

REFERENCES

1. Whelan, Elizabeth M., Dr.: *Toxic Terror*. Ottawa, Illinois, 1985. p. 13.
2. EPA: *United Nations Conference on Environment and Development*. Washington, D.C.: U.S. EPA/Office of Inspector General, January 1992.
3. Whelan, Elizabeth M., Dr.: *Toxic Terror*. Ottawa, Illinois, 1985. p. 21.
4. Ibid. p. 31.
5. Casarett, Louis J., Ph.D. and John Doull, M.D., Ph.D.: Origin and Scope of Toxicology. *Toxicology: The Basic Science of Poisons*, MacMillian Publishing Co., Inc., 1975. p. 4.
6. Ibid. p. 5.
7. Zapp, John A., Jr.: Industrial Toxicology: Retrospect and Prospect. *Patty*, John Wiley & Sons, New York, NY, 3rd ed., 1981. p. 1468.
8. Ibid. p. 1470.
9. Whelan, Elizabeth M., Dr.: *Toxic Terror*. Ottawa, Illinois, 1985. p. 196–7.
10. Ibid. p. 197.

11. Jay, Anthony and David Frost: *The English.* Stein & Day, New York, New York, 1968.
12. Whelan, Elizabeth M., Dr.: *Toxic Terror.* Ottawa, Illinois, 1985. p. 218.
13. Ibid. p. 218–9.
14. Levin, Adeline B.: *Love Canal: Science, Politics, and People.* Lexington Books, Lexington, Massachusetts, 1983. p. 13.
15. Whelan, Elizabeth M., Dr.: *Toxic Terror.* Ottawa, Illinois, 1985. p. 63.
16. Ibid. p. 63.
17. Ibid. p. 222.
18. Ibid. p. 224–5.
19. Ibid. p. 12–3.
20. Collins, Carol C.: *Our Food, Air, and Water: How Safe Are They?* Facts on File Publications, New York, New York, 1984. p. 208.
21. Rolbein, Seth: Plumbing the Mysteries of the Foul Area. *Bostonian Magazine,* Dec. 1990. p. 114(8).
22. Maugh, Thomas H.: Toxic Waste Disposal a Growing Problem. *Science,* Vol. 204, May 25, 1979. p. 819.
23. McNeil, Mary: Environment and Health. *Congressional Quarterly,* Washington, D.C., 1981. p. 33.
24. Ibid. p. 28.
25. Sun, Marjorie: Ground Water Ills: Many Diagnoses, Few Remedies. *Science,* June 20, 1986. p. 1490.
26. Taylor, Ronald: Why Pollution Watchdogs Can't Bite. *U.S. News & World Report,* Feb. 10, 1986. p. 76(1).
27. Spencer, Cathy: This Land Was Our Land. *Omni,* April 1990. p. 24.
28. Juffer, Jane: Dump at the Border. *The Progressive,* October 1988. pp. 24(6).
29. Dolan, Maura and Larry B. Stammer: Clandestine Toxic Waste Exports to Mexico on the Rise. *Los Angeles Times,* May 9, 1990. p. A1.
30. Tomsho, Robert: Dumping Grounds. *The Wall Street Journal,* Nov. 29, 1990. p. A1.
31. Cohn, DVera: Environmental Group Ranks Toxic Polluters. *The Washington Post,* Aug. 11, 1989. p. A10.
32. Kennedy, Michael: By 'Old Man River,' New Health Fear. *Los Angeles Times,* May 9, 1989. p. 1.
33. Peters, Ted: Not in My Backyard! The Waste-Disposal Crisis. *The Christian Century,* Feb. 15, 1989. pp. 175–77.

34. Feder, Barnaby J.: In the Clutches of the Superfund Mess. *New York Times,* June 16, 1991. p. F1(L).
35. Moses, Jonathan M.: Insurer Payouts Over Superfund Flow to Lawyers. *Wall Street Journal,* Apr. 24, 1992. p. B1 (SW).
36. Levin, Adeline G.: *Love Canal: Science, Politics, and People.* Lexington Books, Lexington, Massachusetts, 1983.
37. Natale, Anthony and Hoag Levins: *Asbestos Removal and Control: An Insider's Guide to the Business.* Source Finders, Voorhees, New Jersey, 1984. p. 8.
38. Ibid. pp. 9–10.
39. Ibid. pp. 10–12.
40. Ibid. pp. 14–15.
41. Schwartz, Joel and Ronnie Levin: Lead: Example of the Job Ahead. *EPA Journal,* 19:1, Mar/Apr 1992. p. 42–44.
42. Whelan, Elizabeth M., Dr.: *Toxic Terror.* Ottawa, Illinois, 1985. p. 139.
43. Collins, Carol C.: *Our Food, Air, and Water: How Safe Are They?* Facts on File Publications, New York, New York, 1984. p. 36.
44. Whelan, Elizabeth M., Dr.: *Toxic Terror.* Ottawa, Illinois, 1985. pp. 142–3.
45. Ibid. p. 139.
46. Ibid. p. 176.
47. Collins, Carol C.: *Our Food, Air, and Water: How Safe Are They?* Facts on File Publications, New York, New York, 1984. p. 32.
48. Whelan, Elizabeth M., Dr.: *Toxic Terror.* Ottawa, Illinois, 1985. p. 177.
49. Ibid. p. 208.
50. Ibid. pp. 68–70.
51. Gold, Allan R.: New Jersey Sewage Official Quits After Being Charged in Dumping. *New York Times,* February 17, 1991. p. 49(L).
52. Time for Illegal Dumping Believed to be Biggest Ever. *The Wall Street Journal,* November 9, 1989. p. C6(E).
53. Frank, Nancy: *Crimes Against Health and Safety.* Harrow and Heston, New York, New York, 1985. pp. 38–9.
54. Byon, Christopher: There Goes the Neighborhood. *New York Magazine,* January 15, 1990. pp. 34(8).
55. Byron, Christopher: In the Dumps. *New York Magazine,* March 18, 1991. p. 12.
56. Anguish and Anger in Guadalajara. *Time,* May 4, 1992. p. 17(1).
57. Mexico Blames Oil Trust and City for Blasts. *New York Times,* April 27, 1992. p. A3(L).

58. Nine Officials Are Held in Mexican Explosion. *New York Times,* May 2, 1992. p. 4(L).
59. Moses, Jonathan M.: Insurer Payouts Over Superfund Flow to Lawyers. *The Wall Street Journal,* April 24, 1992. p. B1(SW).
60. Simon, Ruth: Deals that Smell Bad. *Forbes,* May 15, 1989. p. 49(2).
61. Andresky, Jill: Cover Your Assets. *Forbes,* March 24, 1986. pp. 117–8.
62. Corum, Lyn: Spreading the Cleanup Costs. *American City and County,* September 1990. pp. 81(4).
63. Satchell, Michael: Uncle Sam's Toxic Folly. *U.S. News & World Report,* March 27, 1989. pp. 20(3).

Chapter 3

A Proper Beginning

INTRODUCTION

A complete understanding of the client's needs and a systematic plan of attack is vital to expedite an assessment and avoid confusion. The paper shuffle can easily end in a maze whereby the beginning is not obvious, and the end may seem to be somewhere in Never-Never Land.

First, the client's need must be assessed. Albeit a cloud of confusion or well-defined scope of work, each will be different.

Second, with an understanding of the client's need, a structured framework will help organize and maintain control over the process. This step is easy to ignore, particularly by those who have performed numerous surveys and think they have the routine committed to rote. On the other hand, a survey can become particularly confusing when one person or a team of people are working on several different site assessments at the same time, and each participant is assigned a task, a part of the whole. Consistency may be sacrificed, and information may be reported piecemeal.

Third, support agencies and other sources of information must be contacted immediately. Although some may respond over the telephone, many will require a letter of request and two to six weeks lead time. Your job gets placed on the production line, and you must await your turn. Some sources offer assistance, then forget the request or lose the request in their own paper shuffle. They may take a little longer than anticipated, and sometimes they need to be reminded. The paper shuffle will have the greatest impact on the amount of time it will take to complete the survey.

Finally, develop a sketch of the property. This last step, although not necessary, can be helpful.

All four steps are discussed in depth within this chapter. The methodology is not set in stone. It is only a start, one of many approaches that can be developed. These basic steps are the reader's guide to obtain direction and begin to organize the information necessary to determine the possibilities that hazardous substances may impact the property under investigation.

INTERVIEW THE CLIENT

A client's initial contact is generally by telephone. They always ask price and required amount of time to complete an assessment. Some will ask what is involved, while others will know exactly what they require. Prior to answering their most important concerns, however, your job will be to determine the purpose, scope of work, and property details.

Purpose of the Site Assessment

The purpose of a Phase I site assessment depends on the client's association with the property. As discussed in the previous chapter, the client may be a: 1) seller, 2) buyer, 3) lender, 4) lessor/lessee, 5) broker representing a buyer or seller, or 6) corporate shareholder.

They all seek to determine the probability that the property is or can become a liability due to hazardous substances on and/or associated with the property, and some may seek to be informed as to environmental factors which could restrict land use and development. Yet, each has a different vested interest.

Most site assessments are initiated by a buyer or a lender. Both the buyer and the lender stand to lose their investment and to incur unexpected liabilities due to a preexisting condition. Their purpose is to avoid or minimize the chances of making a "bad investment."

Many repossessed properties also are assessed. The Resolution Trust Company is one such entity. Their purpose for a site assessment is the same as the seller's. They want to know of any preexisting conditions which may impact their sale of the property. When they prepare to sell, a disclosure at the last minute as to factors which devalue the property may bring about a change in plans. More important, however, the seller may avoid liability for a preexisting condition if disclosure is made prior to a sale and the responsible party(ies) identified. The seller's purpose is to avoid last-minute surprises and forfeiture of his defense in a "liability suite." Small corporations and individuals rarely seek an environmental site assessment.

A lessor may be held responsible for a lessee's misuse of property. The broker has a duty to advise a client as to the risk potential. A shareholder involved in decision making of the corporation which is operating, buying, or selling property may be held liable, beyond the corporate veil.

An understanding of purpose will give the consultant a point of departure, a means for communicating effectively with the client concerning the required scope of work. Some clients need to be educated. Knowing the client's intent is important to the communication process.

Scope of Work

An "environmental site assessment" may also be referred to as an environmental audit, environmental evaluation, preacquisition site assessment, real estate environmental study, environmental impairment risk assessment, or any variation thereof. The client may request an assessment under the guise of another term, or a client may be requesting something altogether different. Discuss the scope of work, and get a clarification.

For the client who seems to be lost in a maze of uncertainty, explain the different phases of a site assessment and limitations of the scope of work which are being requested. The scope of work may be impacted once this information is clear to the client.

Clarification

The understood scope of work must be clear and concise. As do the various institutions, clients have differing requirements and perceived needs. Some may even require guidance. The only information a client may have is that a lender mandated that an environmental site assessment be completed at the time of a real estate transaction closing. Find out which lending institution is involved and what they require. Many of the standard government and lending institution requirements for completing an environmental site assessment are summarized in the appendices.

Client requirements vary from "go look and see" to "a five-pound manual of procedures." The time required to perform a survey will be significantly impacted by the requirements.

A client may be very specific and provide a detailed checklist of items to be included in the survey, or he may only know the purpose—to avoid liability or to keep a loan officer happy.

An assessment which is being performed to placate a loan officer can be difficult to negotiate. The client wants the cheapest product he can get.

He sees his money drawn into a vacuum for no understandable reason, while the consultant tallies up the liability issues. Cheap and thorough are not compatible. A detailed search requires more time than a token drive-by. Thus, the level of risk versus cost must be clarified.

For example, past experience dictates that what appears to be raw land may harbor a sleeping liability. The probability is not that of industrial property in an urban environment, but even pristine rural property may be or have been impacted by activities on or around the property. For additional examples see Chapter 2.

Once the risk has been explained, if the client still insists on a minimum scope of work, the consultant may opt to back out of the deal. The consultant must also take a risk and may choose not to—even though the client has been duly warned. Even if the scope of work have been dictated by the client, a mishap could bring the client running back to the consultant, insisting that he was not properly warned. Even if the consultant has a clear contract and has been concise as to warnings afforded the client, the consultant or consultant's insurance carrier could still end up paying legal fees for a defense.

Some consultants say they can guarantee "no hazardous substances on the property." This is a fool's folly! There are no 100 percent guarantees that a site is clean—unless every inch of the property has been sampled. The latter scenario is absurd. Never offer a guarantee! Those people who do probably don't have anything to lose—money or reputation.

The prevailing consensus is that an assessment should include at least: 1) a review of the geographic/hydrogeologic components of the site (i.e., environmental setting); 2) an historic records review; 3) a review of the hazardous building materials; 4) a site and area reconnaissance; 5) a regulatory agency review; and 6) interviews. There is also a trend toward the review of special resources. The depth of coverage in each topic varies, and requirements evolve. The minimum recommended components for a Phase I environmental site assessment include the following:

- Environmental Setting
  - Topography
  - Geology
  - Hydrogeology
  - Hydrology
- Historic Usage of the Property
  - Title Search
  - Aerial Photographs
  - Fire Insurance Maps

- • Local Street Directories
- • Regulatory Agency Listings
  - • NPL
  - • CERCLIS
  - • RCRA Lists
  - • ERNS
  - • State Hazardous Waste Site List
  - • Solid Waste Disposal Sites
  - • Underground Storage Tank (UST) List
  - • Leaking UST (LUST) List
- • Site Reconnaissance
  - • Current Use
  - • Prior Use
  - • Hazardous Substances Present
  - • Signs of Property Misuse
  - • Effluence and Air Emissions
  - • Waste Disposal Techniques
  - • Surface Water
  - • Transformers
  - • Surrounding Area Use
- • Interviews
  - • Owner
  - • Occupants
  - • Operations Management
  - • Local Governments

Some institutions group surveys by category in order to aid in the decision-making process as to the required depth of an assessment. Categories may include: undeveloped land; residential property; commercial property; and industrial property. The absurd notion that undeveloped land must be evaluated for asbestos in buildings or that developed land must be evaluated for endangered species has needed to be addressed by some of the institutional manual of procedures. Others clarify and differentiate. Table 3-1 restates and clarifies the minimum components, based on property types.

Special resource concerns generally involve raw land, but they may include developed land as well (e.g., an historic building which cannot be altered or destroyed or an archeological site associated with a building which cannot be expanded onto the site). Should the client require the

>

Table 3-1. **Components of a Phase I Environmental Site Assessment, Based on Property Category**

	Raw Land	Residential	Commercial	Industrial
Environmental setting				
Topography	X	X	X	X
Geology	X	X	X	X
Hydrogeology	X	X	X	X
Historic Usage of the Property				
Title search	X	X	X	X
Aerial photographs	X	X	X	X
Fire insurance maps	X	X	X	X
Local street directories	X	X	X	X
Regulatory Agency Listings				
NPL	X	X	X	X
CERCLIS	X	X	X	X
RCRA	X	X	X	X
ERNS	X	X	X	X
State hazardous waste site	X	X	X	X
Solid waste disposal sites	X	X	X	X
Underground Storage Tanks	X	X	X	X
(UST)	X	X	X	X
Leaking USTs				
Site reconnaissance				
Current use	X	X	X	X
Prior use	X	X	X	X
Signs of property misuse	X	X	X	X
Surface water	X	X	X	X
Transformers	X	X	X	X
Surrounding area usage	X	X	X	X
Hazardous substance usage	—	—	X	X
Waste disposal techniques	—	—	X	X
Interviews				
Owner	X	X	X	X
Local governments	X	X	X	X
Occupants	—	X	X	X
Operations management	—	—	—	X

inclusion of a special resources evaluation, clarify which issues must be addressed. To assist the client, determine the intended use for the property. Many of those which are requested, under varying circumstances are presented in Table 3-2.

Different Phases

A Phase I environmental site assessment (ESA) is the initial research phase for assessing a property. It is where historic information and documentation is compiled and analyzed. This is the speculative stage where all the information gathered may contain only one piece of information which could generate questions or other avenues requiring further investigation. Feelers are sent out in many different directions, keeping in mind that anything and everything is possible. Possibilities are subjected to speculation, based upon experience, common sense, and logic. Probability for property contamination—high, medium, or low—is the end result. Although sampling is rarely performed in this phase, some clients require some sampling for asbestos, a token sampling of the groundwater, air samples for radon in buildings, and/or drinking water samples for lead.

A Phase II ESA involves more detailed research and/or speculative sampling. During the Phase I ESA, speculation may indicate a moderate to high probability that there is preexisting contamination on the property or that development may have an impact on the environment. At this point, it is only a probability. Further investigation and/or sampling is indicated, requiring greater time expenditures and costs.

Additional research and information gathering, not normal in a Phase I, may involve the aid of a private investigator to track suspicious activities, or it may involve a time-consuming, in-depth audit of in-house administrative/management records. Where special resources have been researched, Phase II may also require the aid of a nature biologist to study the habitat.

Sampling complexity ranges from collecting water samples from within a small, easily accessed pond or taking the top six inches of surface soil to groundwater monitoring/sampling down to a depth of 500 feet or drilling for deeper soil samples. An asbestos building evaluation is generally included in a Phase II survey, but some clients require an abbreviated asbestos evaluation during Phase I. This should be ascertained during the clarification of scope of work.

Table 3-2.   Special Resources

Threatened and endangered species
Critical and unique habitats
Buildings/structures of historic value
Archeological resources
Wetlands
Wild and scenic rivers
Coastal dunes and beaches

Various sources.

In short, a Phase II ESA involves more time and money expenditures than the speculative Phase I. Its principal purpose is to "confirm or deny suspicions."

A Phase III ESA follows on the heels of a Phase II after suspicions have been confirmed The problem has been identified—the contaminant is known. Now, the questions remain—"How bad is it?" and "How much will it cost to clean up?" Extensive sampling is indicated. Keep in mind that the contaminant may have come from an adjacent property, up the river, or through ground migration. The possibilities are infinite, and sampling may go well beyond the property boundaries. Generally, once this stage is reached, a plan of action to reduce the liability is developed. Cleanup is the best alternative, but containment and ongoing monitoring could minimize the cost and control the liability. All factors are weighed.

A Phase III may require extensive soil sampling to determine the extent of contamination. Groundwater monitoring may also be indicated where migration has been extensive. Sampling of ponds and sediment may be required, or vegetation sampling may be indicated where an airborne contaminant may have entered into the food chain (e.g., fluorine contamination in grazing pastures).

Many Phase IIIs become part and parcel of a cleanup. For instance, formaldehyde contamination of the soil has been confirmed on the premises of a cosmetics manufacturing plant. The property is 100 feet above a major aquifer which supplies water to over seven hundred thousand people. The soil is highly porous and serves as an avenue to recharge the aquifer with rainwater runoff. The potential that the formaldehyde will contaminate the aquifer is high. The owners may opt to put in a groundwater monitoring well to determine if the aquifer has been compromised; if it hasn't, removal is begun immediately, avoiding costly core sampling. They will take samples during the cleanup to confirm or deny completion.

The differences between the various phases is not all black and white. As the extent of coverage completed during Phase I ESAs varies from one to the next, the same applies even more to the other phases. In most cases, a buyer will terminate the process at the Phase I, and the seller can easily end up holding the bag.

A Phase I may also be referred to as a Level 1, Category 1, or Preliminary Survey. Roman numerals and numbers may be interchangeable, but the level of care always starts with "one."

Limitations

A comprehensive Phase I environmental site assessment is limited to the availability/completeness of historic data and to physical obstructions that mask visual clues. Activities performed on the sly are not subject to historic discovery. Eyewitnesses may not be willing to talk, or they may not be accessible. An inability to properly interpret the collected data may also be a limitation. Trying to track the past becomes more difficult with time. Evidence disappears. Stories become distorted. Records are lost.

A building or other such ground cover (e.g., asphalt roads, surface water, or a shed) may conceal an area which shows signs of contamination. For instance, a shed may have been built on top of sinking ground cover—a disguise to what really is hidden below. In such cases, only damage to the property and invasive sampling would identify a problem—neither of which is feasible without other indicators.

A partial Phase I environmental site assessment will be limited accordingly. Many times, just one little obscure piece of information may cause the consultant to embark down a few more trails, not originally anticipated, in order to discover an unknown. The chances for such a discovery are minimized with an abbreviated scope of work.

Details About the Property

Where is the property located? Get the city and address, if there is an address. Zip code information, if not given by the client, will have to be obtained at a later date, when initiating a regulatory agency records review. Some may give a generalized description. They may provide street coordinates, landmarks, or a survey lot and block descriptions. The

"...A tract of woodland, beginning at a stone mound near the SW corner of John Knights pasture; thence S 71 W 1366 1/2 varas to a stone mound; thence S 19 E 216 varas with East line of "University Tract"; thence N 71 E 1366 1/2 varas for Southeast corner near SW corner of John Knights Field; thence N 19 W 216 varas to place of beginning, containing...fifty eight acres of land less one acre which is herein reserved and located on, around and including the cave known as the "Bat Cave" and said one acre to be surveyed, located upon and set [apart] at the will of the grantors herein, or their assignees by deed or gift. Also the grantors reserve for the use and benefit of the owners of said one acre of land the right of ingress and egress to and from said "Bat Cave" said fifty eight acres herein was conveyed to J.J. Dimmitt on the 23rd day of July 1975 by Wm. K. Foster and wife, Nannie Foster, by deed of said date, and filed for record in the County Clerks office of Williamson County, Texas, on the 24th day of July 1875 and recorded in the records of Clerks office in Vol. 16 and page 324."

Figure 3-1. Legal description of a plot of land.

latter information can be used to locate the property on a plat. Others will even offer a legal property description. These may or may not be helpful. Figure 3-1 is a sample legal description from the late 1800s which the owners have yet to identify. The owners have the deed and cannot locate the property.

What type of property is it? Is it raw land, farmland, or grazing pasture? Is it residential, commercial, or industrial?

What is the present use? It may be abandoned farmland or the hub for a large manufacturing operation. A manufacturing operation may involve an extensive chemical/process audit which includes examining current waste practices and regulatory compliance records.

What is the intended use? A residential investment with no further intentions to develop the land will involve less complex considerations than an intent to install a commercial complex on rural property.

What is the size and condition of the property? A 1-acre open field on flat land is easier to inspect than 100 acres of heavily vegetated, rugged terrain.

Get information of the size and number of buildings. When were they constructed, and what structural materials were used? An old steel shack on a concrete foundation is easier to assess than an industrial complex with three- and four-story buildings, all constructed at different times and of different materials.

The client's response to the above questions will be necessary, along with the purpose and scope of work, to provide the needed information to ascertain how much time the job will take. Consultants generally have a set rate per hour for their time. With the time projection and hourly rate, cost may be calculated.

Once the terms have been agreed upon, reconfirm the property location. Get names of contacts in order to gain access to the property and buildings on the property, and request pertinent records be made available regarding substances known to be associated with the property.

PLAN AND ORGANIZE

Once there is an understanding of purpose and scope of work, an investigative checklist of components should be created and a method developed for keeping the information all together. A checklist is evolved. Each time an assessment is performed, the checklist gets larger. An observation, something yet to be considered, is a good investigator's stock-in-trade.

A properly organized management plan will avoid endless hours of searching all recesses of the office, home, and automobile. Keeping the voluminous components all together and organized is like driving a car which will only go in reverse. It's not impossible, but a systematic approach and diligence will improve the process with the passage of time and experience.

A Tailored Checklist

A checklist should serve as a tool to keep track of: 1) that which has been completed; 2) that which must be completed; 3) assigned component tasks; and 4) deadlines. It is to be used as a guide; if there is more than one person performing the job, each participant should receive his own checklist from a designated, single team leader.

An Organized Management Plan

Once the checklist has been developed, the investigation could result in mountains of documents, data, sketches, and notes. Organize a method of keeping track of these. A common, single resting place for all the information may consist of a three-ring binder, organizer expansion file, or paper file box. Be sure to clearly label the name of the property if there is more than one assessment being performed. If a map or plat is too large to be placed in the designated resting place, reference its location. As the information is entered into its appointed location, it should be so noted on a composite checklist which should always remain with the common resting site for the paperwork.

Color coding folders is another alternative. File folders can be purchased in numerous colors, and each job or category of investigation may be color coded.

START THE PAPER SHUFFLE

Standard requests for assistance from other parties should be first on the agenda. Some documents and information may take weeks to obtain. This alone could serve as the greatest holdup in completing an assessment. Start on the requests as soon as possible.

A Title Search

All site assessments involve a title search, and a title search is best performed by a title search company or an experienced individual. It is possible for anyone to perform a title search, but learning the ins and outs can be futile. The frustration level starts with the retrieval of 28-pound ledgers, shelved 10 feet overhead. Uncertainty and confusion follow. One day in the county courthouse will dispel any thoughts one may have to cut corners. The cost of having an experienced person perform the search is well worth the expense. Depending upon the state and extent of the search requested, it may cost anywhere from $150 to $350. Like so many other things, experience guides one through the path of least resistance.

A search may be completed within a few days, but some of the larger firms may require two to three weeks. Degree of difficulty may further extend the amount of time required to complete the search. The following are a few of the factors which constitute a difficult title search: 1) property which has changed hands once every two years; 2) property which is part and parcel of several different deeds; 3) property which is in a county which was incorporated and broken off from another county (e.g., requiring visitation to several county courthouses for one title search); and/or 4) property which has been owned by common named owners (e.g., Joe Jones). Some county courthouses have the more recent title information listed on computer. Recent is five to ten years.

Some title search companies/individuals are being required to maintain "errors and omissions" professional liability insurance. The insurance is expensive and will add to the cost of a search but lend a degree of assurance to the credibility and completeness of the search.

Small companies or individual consultants may be as good as or better than the larger firms. They generally have a track record prior to starting their own business and don't survive unless they continue to provide a quality, conscientious service. Oftentimes, an individual maintaining a sole-proprietorship also provides a more personable service, at a reduced rate.

FOIA Requests

The acronym, FOIA, stands for "Freedom of Information Act." An FOIA request is generally required by most federal/state governments and some local agencies. Once it has been decided how extensive an inquiry is going to be, an FOIA request should be completed and the request clearly stated, along with the details necessary for the agency to retrieve the correct information. The response may take anywhere from two to four weeks. The more complicated requests take six to eight weeks. For instance, a request for aerial photos from the Department of Agriculture in Salt Lake City takes a standard six weeks, assuming the information provided is adequate. The most frequently requested FOIAs include regulatory agency listings, building permits/certificates of occupation, health/safety and environmental compliance records, and discharge permits.

An example of an FOIA which may take extensive turnaround time is a request for information concerning PCB content in specific transformers identified around the site. Information about PCB-containing transformers may be required of the local utility company. Sometimes the information is readily available on computer. More often than not, it will require the deployment of a worker to look at the transformer and take a sample. The sample goes to a laboratory, and this may take up to several weeks.

FOIA management is becoming routine business. Many government agencies have a designated individual whose sole responsibility is to respond to and/or coordinate FOIA requests, and many of them charge a fee. For instance, regional EPA offices have a designated "FOIA officer." They generally charge for computer time and number of printout pages.

On the other hand, some local agencies respond within a few days and require only a verbal request. Not only do they provide the appropriate information at no charge, but they respond in writing as well. This is, however, rare. Don't expect it!

Documents

Some of the more complicated ESAs (e.g., purchase of industrial property) will require an audit of documents which may be obtained from the owner or user of the property. Gathering these documents may take some time, and the person assigned to this task will appreciate some lead time. Furthermore, some of the information may be forwarded for your review prior to the site visit. Documents which may be on your list include: 1) building blueprints; 2) asbestos inspection reports; 3) environmental site assessment reports; 4) permits; 5) registration records; 6) material safety data sheets; 7) safety and health survey reports; 8) RCRA records; and 9) records of regulatory violations. These will be discussed in later chapters.

DEVELOP A SKETCH OF THE PROPERTY LOCATION

After developing a checklist, collect pertinent maps, then sketch the area onto the maps. This technique provides a frame of reference, and a sketch helps the thought processes. Considerable information can be presented schematically.

Maps

Obtain a street map of the area and a property record map for the site. The street map may be any map with the streets, rivers, lakes, and relative position of your property to the surrounding properties. Ideally, the map will show a minimum two-mile radius around the property to be investigated.

A Chamber of Commerce, Department of Transportation, or commercial street finder map will do. The map will be used as a basic tool for taking notes, prior to and during the site visit. The consultant may prefer one which also has the relative block numbers. This information will be necessary when attempting to identify regulated hazardous material sites which are located by zip code and street address. A drive through the neighborhood to look for each address is an unpleasant alternative. Commercial street finders are not made for smaller cities, and the latter alternative is sometimes the only option.

All properties will have a property record map which gets updated annually. These property record maps are in the form of a plat map or unrecorded tax map. A plat is prepared of incorporated property (e.g., a residential development), and an unrecorded tax map is not incorporated (e.g., rural, undeveloped land). Both can be located at the tax appraisal office, and the incorporated property plat can be obtained from the county courthouse. A walk-in visit is generally required, and expect to pay a minimal fee for copies.

Property record maps are blueprint-sized schematics depicting property boundaries, dimensions, and present owners. Some property record maps have addresses, and the surrounding property information may also be helpful. For instance, an adjacent property has what appears to be an old convenience store/gas station. The property record map shows ownership in the corporate name of Gasoline Alley Convenience. This indicates a probable existing or obsolete gasoline station which can be checked during the area reconnaissance.

A property tax appraisal is an abbreviated summary of property acreage and sizes of buildings. It will provide a sketch and dimensions of buildings on the property. Although not always accurate, appraisals will provide a basic reference point. The appraisal may be picked up at the tax appraisal office, along with the property record map.

Once the maps have been collected, copy the street map and enlarge the section of the property record map, while maintaining the integrity of the boundaries. A couple of copies each will allow for notes and corrections. These are to be used in sketching the site and surrounding area.

Sketch the Area

This step is not necessary and may be inconvenient if the property is at a considerable distance from the office, but if proximity will allow, this

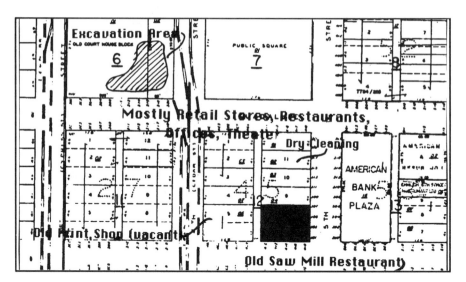

Figure 3-2. Property map used for quick sketch/notes concerning the usage of and noteworthy items on adjacent properties and vicinity. (Items should be noted which may require a closer look during the site/area reconnaissance.)

step can be well worth the abbreviated trip. Visualization of adjacent and surrounding property uses, activities, and structures is simplified. Property structures and relative positions are available for easy reference, and the composite picture is on two drawings. See Figures 3-2 and 3-3 for examples.

With the site maps in hand, visit the site and surrounding area(s). Don't plan on spending an excessive amount of time doing this. A more thorough site reconnaissance will be performed at a later date. It may be helpful to deploy an assistant to perform this duty. A second pair of eyes with a difference frame of reference and experiences may be helpful. Challenge the assistant's diligence. Give the assistant a checklist of items and make it clear that there may be more than those on the list. A checklist only gives direction!

The purpose of this trip is to establish a visual reference and to identify areas which may require further research. Finding out that additional research is needed at the time of the actual site reconnaissance

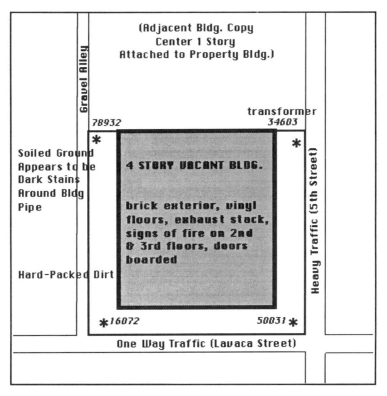

Figure 3-3.   Quick sketch/notes taken during drive around the property. (Items noted should provide direction when planning the actual site reconnaissance.)

may result in time delays and a duplication of document reviews. The client already wants the report completed yesterday, and the extra time spent generating an initial impression will have been time well spent.

Sketch the property. Depict property boundaries, building boundaries, surface water, unmarked streets and fence lines, apparent land use, evidence of effluence and air emissions, locations of transformers, and activity. Information concerning the PCB content of transformers may take time. This should be requested as soon as possible.

Drive around the area; sketch the apparent land usage, existing commercial activities, and industrial activities by type; and note strange/questionable buildings and/or landmarks of the site and surrounding areas.

SUMMARY

Get a good start and keep your records organized. A methodical approach will clear the mind and allow for a more concise investigation. Begin each Phase I environmental site assessment with a four-step guide.

Step 1: Assess the client's purpose and scope of work.

Step 2: Plan and organize by developing a checklist and a system to keep track of the voluminous amount of material gathered.

Step 3: Initiate information requests. This should include, but not be limited to, a title search, "Freedom of Information Act" letters requesting information from governmental agencies, and other documents which will take some time to collect.

Step 4: Develop a sketch of the property and surrounding areas—if proximity allows for an abbreviated drive through. This step can be a time-saver but is not necessary.

The intent of this chapter has been to clarify and provide direction. The succeeding chapters detail specifics.

Chapter 4

Environmental Setting

INTRODUCTION

The environmental setting is a physical description of the land on which the property is located. The physical characteristics assist in the speculation as to the potential for migration of contaminants to the groundwater and to, or from, the surrounding areas.

The level of diligence in an investigation should be escalated where migration potential of a contaminant to a major aquifer is significant. A site may have soils which confine and prevent migration of hazardous substances. The closest drinking water source is a well outside a one-mile radius, and the water source is 400 feet down with a layer of impermeable, unfractured slate (flat rock) as a barrier. The concern for a site as such is not as great as one involving an environment where the property is directly over a recharge zone to a major aquifer where surface contaminants may easily migrate to the groundwater.

The information contained within this chapter provides the reader with the basic concepts for understanding the relationship between an environmental setting and its impact on the spread potential of hazardous substances. Hazardous substances may spread through soil/rock formation, surface water, groundwater, and air.

Should a more in-depth understanding of the soils and groundwater be indicated, a geologist or hydrogeologist should be consulted. For instance, if the investigator determines that there is probable soil contamination on an adjacent property which could result in a costly impact to the property being evaluated, the investigator may seek additional expertise. A possible problem has been identified, and the soil is highly variable, difficult to predict migratory flow. Then, a geologist/hydrogeologist could project the probability for that contaminant to migrate to where it could have a detrimental effect on the property and its immediate environment.

Environmental factors include the relative location (geography), land contouring (topography), soil characteristics (geology), surface water characteristics (hydrology), subsurface water/soil characteristics (hydrogeology), and floodplain influences. All are a basis for potential impact on the migration of hazardous substance contamination in a given environment.

GEOGRAPHIC DESCRIPTION

The relative location of the property provides information concerning proximity to population centers. There are numerous sources for geographic maps.

Each state department of highways has a complete set that covers the entire state, including rural areas. Each city Chamber of Commerce will have maps of the entire town and some of the surrounding areas. Commercial street directories (e.g., Rand McNally Street Direction Finders), which can be purchased wherever maps are sold, are available for large population centers and the surrounding areas (e.g., Dallas Metroplex). All can be purchased for a nominal fee, and those which contain block numbers will prove useful later when plotting locations associated with the property.

A parcel of land is not an isolated entity. Its relative associations and activities may impact or be impacted by other properties. For instance, raw land located adjacent to an industrial complex may be impacted by the latter's environmental pollutants.

Likewise, an industrial activity located ten miles from the nearest residence is unlikely to either be affected by or affect the other. For instance, an industrial site may be near a water reservoir which the neighboring community relies upon for drinking water. Poorly managed hazardous wastes could end up in the reservoir—due to its proximity.

TOPOGRAPHIC CHARACTERISTICS

Topography is land contouring information, a delineation of relative elevations of land surfaces. Knowledge of the ground topography may be used to predict directional movement of soil contaminants. If the soil is known to be contaminated in a given area, migration potential to other areas will be impacted by ground contours which influence the direction of flow.

Maps are prepared by the U.S. Geological Survey and can be obtained from the U.S. Geological Survey, city planning departments, and retail stores. The most commonly used map is the U.S. Geological 7.5 Minute Series. The minutes refers to the scale. A 7.5 Minute Series spans 7.5 minutes of longitude and 7.5 minutes of latitude and is on a scale of 1:24,000, 1 inch to 2,000 feet. As can be observed in Figure 4-1, the most prominent information is the depiction of elevation levels, within contour lines. Rivers and lakes are delineated on the maps as are some major population centers, roads, marine shoreline features, mines, and caves. However, the information does not stop with topographic features. There is more which could be helpful when identifying other land features. Some of these are presented in Table 4-1.

Probable pathways and direction of flow of soil contaminants are impacted by the rise and fall of the land. Although the ground formations below the surface do not always lend themselves to the same contours as that which is observed on the surface, the surface and subsurface contours are generally similar. A geologist can further interpret the topographic maps based on their knowledge of how the earth is formed.

GEOLOGIC CHARACTERISTICS[1]

Geology is the interpretation of soils and rock near the earth's surface. Soil and rock types will determine the extent of a contaminant's migration, once again, providing the investigator a means by which to predict impact.

Soil maps may be obtained from the U.S. Geological Survey, or from the Department of Agriculture Soil Survey. The latter is generally used to provide information as to the suitability of large areas for general land use and should only be used if there are no other sources available.

The U.S. Department of Agriculture publishes Soil Survey manuals. These are published by county, but not all counties have them. Some may be out of publication. Some may have had the data collected but not compiled into a manual, and others may not have had the money to spend for a soil survey. The best place to start is the U.S. Department of Agriculture in the county where the property is located. They will provide the requested data, if available, of a copy of the soil survey for that county if one has been printed and it is available.

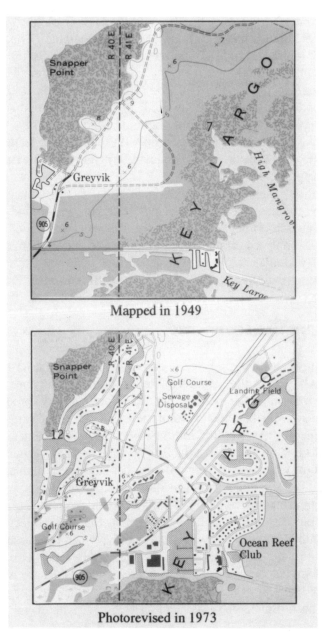

Mapped in 1949

Photorevised in 1973

Figure 4-1. Topographic Map Depicting Key Largo, Florida. (Shows ground elevations and changes over time.)

Table 4-1.   Features Depicted on Soil and Topographic Maps

Land Features	U.S. Soil Survey Maps	U.S.G.S. Topographic Maps
Contours		
Soil type	X	—
Elevations	—	X
Land features	—	X
Coastal features	—	X
Mines and Caves		
Mine dump	—	X
Pits	X	X
Quarry	X	X
Tailings	—	X
Parks	X	X
Oil/Gas Pipelines	X	X
Power transmission lines	X	X
Railroads	X	X
Roads and highways	X	X
Structures		
Aboveground tanks	X	X
Airports	X	X
Cemeteries	X	X
Dams	X	X
Dumps	—	X
Fence lines	(occasionally)	X
Oil/gas wells	X	X
Pits	X	X
Water wells	X	X
Windmills	X	X
Submerged areas		
Gully	X	—
Swamp/marsh	X	X
Vegetation	—	X
Water features		
Lakes, ponds, and reservoirs	X	X
Marine shorelines	—	X

Partial extraction from the respective map locations.

Data available from the soil surveys includes the types of soil(s) and rock; the steepness, length, and shape of slopes; the size of streams and the general pattern of drainage; and the kinds of native plants or crops. Each profile extends from the surface down to the parent material.

Each publication has a series of soil maps, presented on aerial photographs, in the back of each manual which is published by county. The scale is small (1:20,000), and the maps are marked to denote soil type(s) as depicted in Figure 4-2. Other designated markings include man-made features (e.g., roads, railroads, and pipe lines), water features (e.g., wet spots, rivers, and lakes), and other pertinent information (e.g., rock outcroppings, gullies, and dumps). Table 4-1 contains a more detailed list of features provided on these maps.

Soil type information delineates soil permeability which serves as an indication as to the potential for water and associated contaminants or liquid material to migrate downward to the groundwater, aquifers, and lower strata. Permeability is measured in inches per hour and is based on water's ability to migrate downward through saturated soil. Permeability rates range from very slow, less than 0.06 inches per hour (e.g., certain types of clay), to very rapid, greater than 20 inches per hour (e.g., sandy soil). See Table 4-2 for a relative description of the permeability rates.

If there is no potential for contaminants, the point is mute and the soil type provides nothing more than land use information. However, if a potential for contaminants does exist, the soil permeability will be relevant. For instance, an oil refinery is on a site where the soil permeability is 20 inches per hour. The threat of a chemical contaminant migrating downward is enhanced.

The steepness of the slope, also contoured in the topographic map, is given in degrees. It will indicate the potential direction of flow, not only through the soil, but over the surface of the soil. A 30-degree slope poses a greater possibility for migration horizontally than a 2-degree slope.

The size and general pattern of the drainage is indicated by markings on the aerial photographs in the back section of the manual. They are marked as intermittent, perennial, canals, or ditches. Lakes, ponds, marshlands, springs, and wells are also indicated.

The kinds of native plants will give an indication as to whether vegetation should be expected. If the area is void of vegetation and the publication indicates grass and foliage, the ground may be contaminated.

Figure 4-2.   Soil Survey Map, Depicting Austin, Texas Area.

SURFACE WATER HYDROLOGIC CHARACTERISTICS

Hydrology is the study of the occurrence, movement, and quality of water above, on, and beneath the earth's surface. Surface water is another mode for transporting hazardous substances from one site to another.

Moisture evaporates from the ground, forms clouds, and returns to the earth's surface in the form of precipitation (e.g., rain, snow, or hail). The first precipitation wets the ground and vegetation and begins to infiltrate the surface soils. Infiltration rate depends upon vegetation, soil type, and intensity/duration of the precipitation. When the rate of precipitation exceeds the rate of infiltration, overland flow occurs. Excess also percolates downward to the groundwater and then laterally to sites of groundwater discharge, feeding into the surface waters. See Table 4-3 for relative available freshwater content of the earth's surface and Figure 4-3 for a depiction of the impact of hydrologic cycle on the spread of contaminants.

Surface water includes lakes, rivers, ponds, creek beds, and streams. Lakes and rivers may be located on area maps and in the Soil Survey maps.

Table 4-2.   Permeability of Soils

Very Slow	less than 0.06 inch/hr.
Slow	0.06 to 0.20 inch/hr.
Moderately Slow	0.2 to 0.6 inch/hr.
Moderate	0.6 inch to 2.0 inches/hr.
Moderately Rapid	2.0 to 6.0 inches/hr.
Rapid	6.0 to 20 inches/hr.
Very Rapid	more than 20 inches/hr.

Ponds, creek beds, and streams are sometimes identified on topographic maps, but they will most likely require visual confirmation. Confirmation may be through an on-site visit or by aerial photographs.

Most lakes are man-made. They have been installed with a purpose. Lakes may be used as a water reservoir for a community, in which case, boating may be disallowed. Most, however, are intended for recreation.

Rivers are aboveground conduits for flowing water. Lakes vary in flow rate and depth throughout the year, and they generally have a direction of movement. Rivers may serve as a means for transporting contaminants to and from a property. Industrial effluence is a consideration and may travel miles from the point of source (e.g., an overflow relief valve, pouring into the nearby river).

Creek beds are depressed, aboveground formations which connect to form a conduit for water collection and migration. They may or may not normally contain water. Some may flow over ground fissures (e.g., karst limestone) where the water seems to disappear. These are evident when there is considerable rain with water collection and movement. Some creek beds dry up during a dry spell. They may, however, serve as a collection basin for contaminants, even without the presence of water.

Streams are small rivers. They usually contain water, and the water typically flows in one direction. It moves at various rates, depending upon the amount of water and the size of the passage. Streams may serve as a means for transporting contaminants to and from a property. Industrial effluence is, once again, a consideration.

Contaminants may be picked up by a body of water and transported to other areas, or they may be dissolved and enter into the surface water, such as a pond, and remain as a localized contaminant.

Table 4-3.   Freshwater Volume from the Hydrosphere

Ice sheets and glaciers	5,800,000 mile^3
Groundwater	960,000 mile^3
Lakes and reservoirs	37,000 mile^3
Soil moisture	20,000 mile^3
Vapors in the atmosphere	3,400 mile^3
River water	300 mile^3

Heath, Ralph C.: Basic Ground-Water Hydrogeology, U.S. Geological Survey Water-Supply Paper 2220. p. G-3.

HYDROGEOLOGIC CHARACTERISTICS

Hydrogeology is the study of groundwater and associated soil and rock formations. As it varies in depth from a couple of feet to thousands of feet and has a direction of flow, groundwater may serve as another means for chemical migration. Contamination of potable groundwater, on the other hand, must be avoided. Thus, depth and usage data must be investigated as well.

Groundwater is contained within a myriad of spaces created by sand and silt (e.g., between particles of clay, within fractures in rock, and in underground caverns). The spaces found in subsurface openings beneath the surface of U.S. soil alone are estimated to include a volume of 125,000 cubic miles. Visualize a continuous cave beneath the surface of the U.S., 186 feet deep. This is the speculated volume of the all subsurface openings, most containing groundwater. Only 14 percent of all groundwater is freshwater. The remaining spaces contain saltwater, gas, and crude oil.[2]

The first occurrence of fresh groundwater ranges from near the surface to 3,000 feet below the surface, and the soil/rock formations may restrict migration or enhance it. The thickness of saturated sediments may be as much as 8,500 feet thick (e.g., certain areas of the Mississippi delta).[2]

Relevant groundwater characteristics include depth, flow direction, usage, and flow rate. This information is obtained from the state government agency which is responsible for managing its water resources. State publications concerning groundwater are the fastest, easiest source. Although some are identified on the Soil Survey maps, many well locations are not that straightforward. States maintain their own well maps, but these

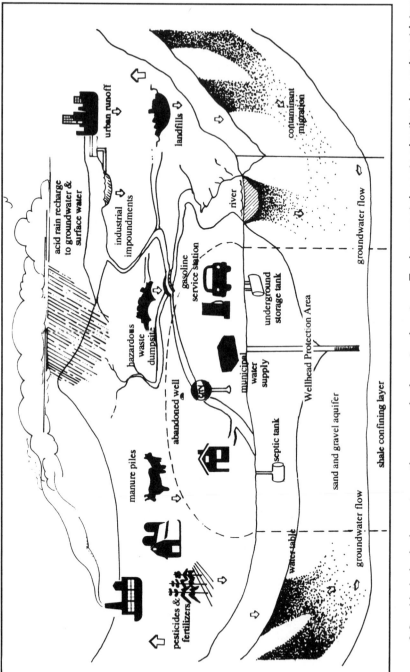

Figure 4-3. Hydrologic impact on the spread of contaminants. Environmental contamination is under stricter controls in the "wellhead protection areas." (Source: Texas Water Commission: "A Wellhead Protection Area." Texas Water Commission, Austin, Texas, July, 1990. pp. 6-7.

may also be incomplete. As a last resort, each state has its own file of registered private wells. Installed private water wells around the vicinity of the site will have records, completed by the driller, as to the depth and type of soil by water quality and quantity, and direction of groundwater flow. Yet, this information is not always available or complete for a given area.

Sometimes records are sparse, and an educated guess can be sketchy at best. One well may not provide adequate or reliable data. The one well may have been a small pocket of water, confined within a limited area. The same pocket may not be found 10 feet away from the first drill hole. To complicate matters, well logs may be incomplete. A well may be brackish, have an unpleasant odor, or contain a visible mineral deposit. It may be abandoned, and there is no further reporting. Once again, a state publication is the easiest, most reliable source—if available. See Figure 4-4 for a sample of published information.

Groundwater occurs in two different zones, unsaturated and saturated. The unsaturated zone consists of a layer of soil to a maximum depth of one or two yards and an intermediate zone which varies in thickness from a few feet to thousands of feet. The soil layer supports plant growth, and the porosity and permeability tends to be higher than those of the underlying material. The intermediate zone generally has reduced porosity and permeability. The saturated zone consists of a capillary fringe and the groundwater. The capillary fringe is where water may rise into small pores in the rock or soil, resulting in upward water movement of unconfined groundwater.

Unconfined groundwater is directly influenced by atmospheric pressure. Its depth is influenced by atmospheric pressure, and the upper surface is referred to as the "water table." Groundwater which has restricted movement, however, is confined within a given space. It tends to be under great pressure, and if the confining layer is drilled into, the water will rise rapidly to the surface through the hole which has become a pressure relief penetration into the restricted groundwater. Its water table is at the base of the confining region.

The depth of the water table and extent of confinement will have a bearing on the chances for contamination through soil migration. The quantity and quality will give direction as to the potential impact a contaminant may have on the water if it were to become contaminated. The possibilities must be evaluated in each assessment.

Well	Owner	Driller	Date completed	Depth of well (ft)	Casing Diameter (in.)	Casing Depth (ft)	Water bearing unit	Altitude of land surface (ft)	Below land-surface datum (ft)	Date of measurement	Method of lift	Use of water	Remarks
							Travis County—Continued						
* YD-58-43-105	City of Austin	--	--	Spring	--	--	Kce	675	--	--	Flows	P	Spring in Northwest Park. Measured flow 10 gal/min on Feb. 16, 1973.
* 106	W. F. Robinson	W. Watson	1927	395	5	248	Kce	733	--	--	C, W	D	Show of oil in the Edwards Limestone. Well D-133 in 1957 Travis County report. 3/4
107	Koger Properties	--	--	Spring	--	--	Kce	740	--	--	Flows	P	Estimated yield 10 gal/min on Feb. 9, 1974.
* 201	Fred Parsons	Wesley Hunt	--	400	6	150	Kce	674	93.80	Oct. 17, 1940	C, G	D, S	Well D-149 in 1957 Travis County report. 4/
* 203	John Teagle	--	--	484	6	--	Kce	721	174.60 126.37	Feb. 4, 1940 Nov. 18, 1958	N	N	Well D-148 in 1957 Travis County report. 2/4
204	R. R. Sansom	Albert Neans	--	750	--	--	Kce	694	52.76 151.05	June 4, 1940 Aug. 4, 1948	N	N	Well D-144 in 1957 Travis County report. 2/4
* 303	B. F. Payton	B. F. Payton	1940	1,456	6	460	Kce	633	21.18 56.70	July 24, 1941 Mar. 14, 1978	N	N	Well E-41 in 1957 Travis County report. 2/3/4
304	C. J. Graves	--	1941	41	30	41	Kgn, Kgt	615	38.80 24.10	June 23, 1950 Dec. 28, 1972	N	N	Dug well. Well E-51 in 1957 Travis County report. 4/
* 305	C. R. Anderson	--	1920	22	36	22	Kgn, Kgt	640	4.10	Apr. 12, 1972	J, E	D	Dug well.
306	R. E. Joseph	--	--	23	36	23	Kgn, Kgt	625	13.80	do	Cf, G	S	Do.
* 307	John Wilder	--	--	23	36	23	Kgn, Kgt	600	9.10	do	J, E	D, S	Do.
* 308	G. B. Heath	--	1963	27	36	27	Kgn, Kgt	560	5.10	do	J, E	Irr	Do.
* 309	Elmo Mertzschin	--	1971	33	6	33	Kgn, Kgt	540	--	--	J, E	Irr	--
* 401	North Austin State Hospital	Hugh McGillvray	1895	1,975	--	--	Kcho	635	1	Sept. 1941	N	N	Destroyed. Reported flow 104 gal/min when drilled. Stopped flowing in 1938. Well H-19 in 1957 Travis County report. 3/4/5
402	J. C. Campbell, Jr.	--	--	184	10	--	Kgac	675	135.26 124.40	Oct. 17, 1940 Dec. 6, 1950	C, W	N	Well H-22 in 1957 Travis County report. 2/4
* 403	Texas Department of Public Safety	Texas Water Wells, Incorporated	1962	353	10	300	Kce	680	63	Apr. 20, 1962	N	N	Cemented from 300 ft to surface. Reported drawdown 23 ft after pumping 24 hours at 300 gal/min on Apr. 28, 1962. 3/
* 404	Duggers Florist	--	1920	27	--	--	Qter	650	12.20	Apr. 20, 1971	J, E	D, Irr	Dug well. Well H-18 in 1957 Travis County report. 4/
* 405	Austin Parks Department	--	--	Spring	--	--	Kce	590	--	--	Flows	N	Seiders Springs. Discharge: Sept. 4, 1971, 150 gal/min; June 7, 1942, 30 gal/min.
* 501	Walling Estate	--	--	442	5	--	Kce	718	181.76 182.41	Oct. 17, 1940 Apr. 15, 1953	C, W	S	Well H-24 in 1957 Travis County report. 2/4

Figure 4-4. Table of Groundwater Depths. (Source: Texas Department of Water Resources: "Occurrence, Availability, and Quality of Ground Water in Travis County, Texas." Texas Department of Water Resources, Austin, Texas, Report 276, June 1983. p. 131.

Private Wells

Public and private well water may become contaminated by chemical migration into the ground. Some wells may become contaminated, and the owners do not become suspicious until a group of people become ill with no apparent cause. The taste or odor of the water is altered. The color is altered, or a sample is taken and analyzed for a specific contaminant thought to be in the water.

Although water quality is checked routinely, these evaluations don't include an evaluation of hazardous substances unless there has been a special request. Even then, the substance may not be identified unless they know what contaminants they are seeking. There is not one single test which covers all hazardous chemicals. A laboratory can test for priority pollutants, heavy metals, or any given chemical which is suspected. It cannot, however, tell with just one test that there are no contaminants. Contaminated water may go undetected for years due to the specificity required to tag a contaminant in the drinking water. Such situations eventually get found out the hard way (e.g., elevated cancer rates within a community).

The quality of the water, soil types penetrated, depth to the top of the water table, and sometimes productivity (e.g., 100 gallons per minute) are recorded in the drillers' logs. These logs are grouped and filed by area. Yet, forewarned is foretold. Clarity as to the specific location of each logged well may be elusive. Some records pinpoint the exact site on an area map. Others generalize to within a 100-foot radius.

Aquifers

Over 50 percent of the U.S. drinking water is supplied by aquifers.[3] An aquifer is a water-containing layer of rock, sand, or gravel that will yield usable supplies of water. It may be just beneath the surface or hundreds of feet down, and the water-containing layer may be a few feet or hundreds of feet thick. Major and minor aquifers are generally mapped as in the example in Figure 4-5, and the maps are available to the public through the state agency which manages the water resources.

Aquifers are a source of drinking water either for small communities using private wells or for large communities which may use the aquifer as a sole source for their drinking water. A sole-source aquifer, as defined under the Safe Drinking Water Act of 1974, is "an aquifer of critical value as the main or only supply of drinking water for a specific area." Some

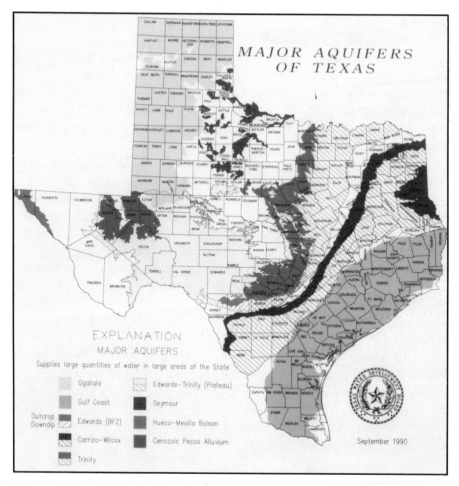

Figure 4-5. Major Aquifers in Texas. (Source: Texas Water Commission, September 1990.)

large municipalities rely solely or partially on aquifers for their drinking water. Thus, contamination of a major sole-source aquifer could have a devastating impact on large populations. Contaminants diluted in groundwater are difficult to remove, and removal could take decades. Groundwater remediation is the most expensive, time-consuming form of all forms of cleanup.

Aquifers are fed from surface water sources, cavities, and precipitation percolating downward from the surface. The area where water percolates from the surface to an aquifer is referred to as a recharge zone. Yet, some areas over an aquifer do not permit easy movement from the surface downward. The geologic characteristics of the ground may restrict movement. Aquifers are typed on this basis.

There are three types of aquifers: 1) unconfined (water table); 2) confined (artisan); and 3) leaky artisan. They are depicted graphically in Figure 4-6. Water table aquifers are the most sensitive. They are the easiest to contaminate. Contaminant-bearing water moves downward through an unsaturated zone of soil or rock to the water table.

Checks and measures are installed, in each state, to protect these vital resources. Monitoring wells are installed at various locations so the water can be inspected and sampled routinely. The intent is to identify significant changes or trends in the water quality and/or quantity.

Municipal groundwater samples are analyzed for conductivity, alkalinity, pH, trace heavy metals (e.g., arsenic), nutrients (e.g., nitrates), radioactivity, and total organic constituents. Unknowns may, however, go undetected unless there is a reason to suspect their presence (e.g., pesticides in agricultural areas). In other words, changes in the water quality may go unchecked if a specific hazardous substance which is not part of the routine analyses (e.g., pesticides in an urban environment) migrates into the water supply, and there was no reason to suspect its presence in the first place. For this reason, special attention should be given in those areas where contaminants have a high probability for impacting a major aquifer.

100-YEAR FLOODPLAIN

The 100-year floodplain is a demarcation of areas where there exists a probability that the area will flood within a 100-year time period. These areas are generally cutout ravines through the property. They may serve as a means of transport for hazardous substances at various times when the water level is up and deposit the material downstream when the bed dries out later.

100-year floodplain maps are available for all U.S. property, incorporated and unincorporated. See a sample in Figure 4-7.

Maps may be obtained from the city planning department or the Federal Emergency Management Agency (Flood Map Distribution Center, 6930 (A-F) San Tomas Road, Baltimore, Maryland 21227-6227). Indexes

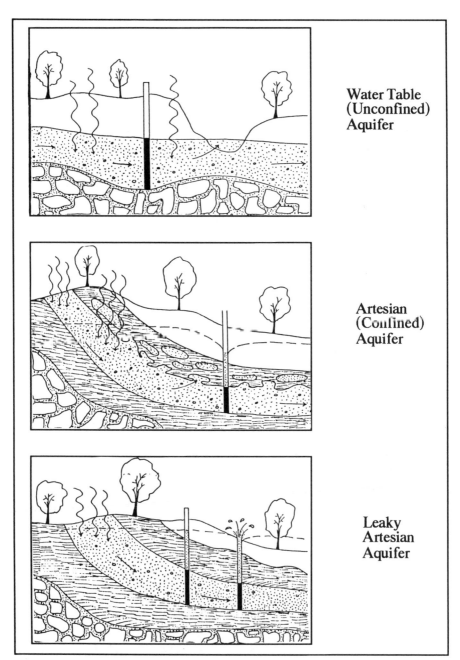

Figure 4-6. Types of Aquifers.

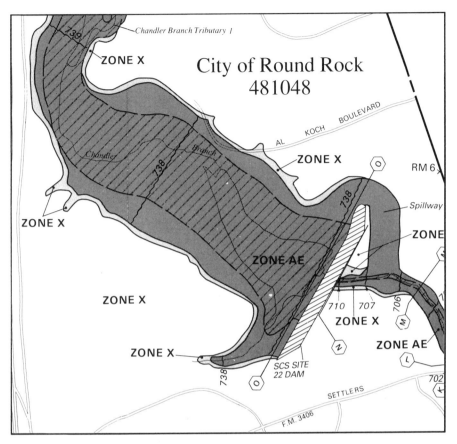

Figure 4-7. 100-Year Flood Plain Map.

and order forms are free.

INFLUENCES AND RELATIONSHIPS

The primary concern in determining the potential impact hazardous material will have on an environment is contamination of the water sources on which man relies. Depletion or poisoning of the water supplies could be devastating.

Sources of contamination include polluted surface waters, land disposal of solid or liquid wastes, stockpiled materials leaching into the ground, holding ponds and lagoons (e.g., brine associated with the oil industry), leaking sewer lines, leaking septic tanks, leaking underground storage tanks and/or pipelines, spills, ground contaminants of materials associated with various industries, exploratory wells and shafts, graveyards, de-icing salt usage, animal feedlots, fertilizers and pesticides, sumps and dry wells, and drainage holes associated with agriculture. Contamination may migrate from municipal landfills, spills around railroad tracks and roads, illegal dumping of waste, and streams containing hazardous substance.

Improper closure, or discontinued use and abandonment of underground storage tanks, water wells, and/or oil/gas wells can provide another means for leaking and contamination of the groundwater. The methods of choice for closures are the use of a specialized oil mud (a gel-like material) and bentonite cement to fill the void.

Groundwater quality may be endangered if an abandoned well connects with another source of drinking water. An abandoned well may become a receptacle for hazardous waste or human excrement. Failure to properly seal the abandoned water well may result in contamination of another water source. Often, people who construct a new well try to "save" money by not properly closing, or plugging, the old well. They don't realize, however, that the new well, their source of drinking water, may become contaminated by the old one a quarter of a mile away from a new well.

Septic tank pollution occurs when a drainfield receives more water from the septic tank than what the drainfield is designed for; when the soil cannot provide the filtration needed for removal of nitrates, phosphates, pathogens; or when hazardous substances are part of the wastewater. If the drainfield becomes saturated, liquid wastes will migrate downward toward the groundwater and surface on the ground above the drainfield. This is called effluent, untreated wastewater. It still contains large numbers of harmful bacteria and viruses. Usually, a foul odor will be present in areas where effluent has surfaced.

Automotive service stations generate waste and wastewater during daily operations. The wastes which are generated include spilled gasoline, automotive (e.g., motor oil, transmission fluid, brake fluid), coolants from radiators, and solvents for cleaning parts (e.g., degreasing fluids). There are several means by which these wastes are disposed of, legally and illegally. They should be sent to a recycling plant, but they didn't or don't always get that far. The waste might be disposed of in an abandoned well, down a latrine hole, in a storm sewer, or in a pit. Some have simply dumped drums of waste in someone elses pasture land.

There is no end to the possibilities and the complex nature in the relationship between an environmental setting and migration of hazardous substances. The investigator must manipulate these possibilities.

Many of the research methodologies for investigating the possibilities that a hazardous substance does pose a threat are discussed in this book. They should serve as tools and must not restrict other avenues of investigation.

SUMMARY

A property is not an entity unto itself. It impacts and is impacted by all that is around it. The environmental setting must be clarified in order to determine the potential impact of one property on another or to project the possibilities for existing soil contaminants to migrate from the surface to potable or groundwater which is ultimately that which must be protected. Be aware of the possibilities!

REFERENCES

1.   Werchan, Leroy E. and John L. Coker: *Soil Survey of Williamson County Texas.*   Soil Conservation Service, U.S. Department of Agriculture, 1980.
2.   Heath, Ralph C.: *Basic Ground-Water Hydrology.* U.S. Geological Survey Water-Supply Paper 2220. p. 1.
3.   U.S. EPA: *A Summary of the New Regulations for Underground Storage Tanks.* U.S. EPA, Washington, DC, September 1988.
4.   *The Underground Subject.* [Product Bulletin] Texas Water Commission, 1989. pp. 4–7.

Chapter 5

Historic Usage of the Property
and Surrounding Area

INTRODUCTION

Property usage information is a preliminary means for projecting the potential for hazardous material contamination of that site. Undeveloped property will not have the same likelihood of exposure as the site of an oil refinery. A residence will not generate the same volume or type of waste as an auto repair shop. Grazing pastures will not have the pesticide exposures associated with farmland. Historic records provide a means for tracking property usage.

A minimum historic records review should include a title search, aerial photographs, fire insurance maps, local street directories, zoning records, and building permits. Other methods for investigating past land usage include certificates of occupancy, commercial directories, newspapers, mining/natural resources records, and waste management permits.

Present management and usage records of hazardous materials may be tracked through an on-site administrative records review. This should not be confused with an environmental risk/records audit. The differences are discussed herein.

TITLE RECORDS

In accordance with recommended job start-up methodology, a title search was initiated when the client first requested the assessment. A minimum search generally goes back 50 years or to 1940, around the time of World War II, when the generation of hazardous wastes began to escalate. Some title searches go back to raw land which could be, in the New England states, as far back as the 1500s. To a title search firm, raw land means sovereignty (i.e., when the land became incorporated). In the latter cases, to overstate the obvious, a search could become quite extensive and costly. With this in mind, others may require searches going back to raw land or 100 years—whichever comes first.

A title search provides "a means to identify previous owners" which may indicate prior business activities via the owner's name. If a business was associated with the property at one time, the previous owner(s) may have purchased the property under the corporate or business name. For instance, a prior owner under the business name of Billy Bob's Service Station would likely have installed underground gasoline storage tanks for a gasoline station.

On the other hand, if there is an individual's name, do not assume that a business did not exist at the location during the time of this person's ownership. The title search is merely one possible means to identify prior business activities at a site.

The title search will also provide information on easements. An easement is the acquisition of rights to use the property; and it may include a gas/oil pipeline, underground utilities/services, or mineral rights. For instance, the owner may use the land for cattle grazing and an oil company may own mineral rights and require an easement to use the land for drilling activities.

Once a business has been tagged for further investigation, confirmation may be sought elsewhere—within other records of historic value.

AERIAL PHOTOGRAPHS[1]

Aerial photographs have become a valuable tool for studying the surface of the earth and its environment. The U.S. Geological Survey uses them for land contouring. The state departments of highways uses "aerials" to make road maps. The U.S. Department of Agriculture uses them to track land usage and crop patterns. More recently, the U.S. EPA has been using them for tracking industrial activities, for research, for enforcement activities, and for setting standards.

In environmental site assessments, aerial photographs are used, in conjunction with other historic information, to determine prior land usage. The image may depict a large concave area, devoid of vegetation. This may be a gravel pit or quarry. An image of large cylinders may be aboveground storage tanks. Ground impressions of old structures are more visible from an aerial photograph than from the ground. These photos should be used, in conjunction with the other research, either to substantiate or add information.

There are problems with interpreting aerial photographs. Most of them are taken from over 2,000 feet from the earth's surface, and only large objects (e.g., buildings) are apparent. A cleared area of land may appear as a smudge. Several dots may be 55-gallon drums which are not always clearly apparent. Buildings generally have well-defined forms and shadows. Size can be measured, and height can be approximated by shadows.

A good rule of thumb is that "if it has a defined form and structure, it is man-made." Form and structure includes straight lines, circles, and a sense of order. Roads, buildings, and plowed fields have well-defined form and structure. Unless cut away by man, hills do not have well-defined form and structure. Trees are irregular in shape, but when planted may form a straight line. Thus, unknown structures should be subjected to further research.

Stereo glasses permit 3-D visualization of a site. Two photos of the same location, taken within minutes of one another, are placed side by side to be looked at through special magnifying glasses. The photos are aligned next to one another with the site location under each of the eyepieces. The photos require further adjustment while the site location is being viewed through the glasses. This process is not advised, unless both photos are readily available, and the investigator needs elucidation of the content. Most aerial photographs are done with a 30 percent overlap, in which case, the adjacent frame photo may be readily available.

Aerial photographs are available through various state and federal agencies. Of note are those produced by the U.S. Geological Survey, the U.S. Department of Agriculture, and state departments of highways. They may be purchased directly from the pertinent agency; or they are available through libraries, history centers, and some private collections. Many cities maintain old aerials for historic interest, in their public libraries, history centers, or city planning departments. Each state has its own private collection, donations from state and federal agencies. Information as to where each private collection is maintained may be obtained from the U.S. Geological Survey.

A road map with the site clearly delineated is necessary when searching for a specific area in a composite of aerial photos. If you send away for the aerials, a map is a must, particularly when dealing with some of the major sources. There are generally an associated fee and anticipated response time.

Major sources should be consulted for availability, prices, and turnaround time. The following are major sources:

U.S. Geological Survey
Earth Sciences Information Office
507 National Center
Reston, Virginia 22092
Comments: Clearing house for information as to the state affiliates which maintain collections of maps from all sources.

U.S. Department of Agriculture
Agricultural Stabilization and Conservation Services
Salt Lake City, Utah
Comments: Aerial photos are available for various areas throughout the U.S. There is a fee, and it takes 4 to 6 weeks turn-around time. Detailed information as to the exact location must be provided, and the negatives maintained on-site date back to 1950.

National Archives and Records Service
Cartographic Archives Division
General Services Administration
Washington, DC 20408
Comments: Negatives date back to 1935 at the earliest.

Most aerial photographs are black and white. They came into extensive use in the late 1930s, but they may date back to the early 1920s. In the early 1960s, color aerials came into use. Color infrared aerials, which were developed in the late 1960s, may provide additional details and substrata information.

Infrared images respond to heat sources. All live materials give off heat, and underground pipelines generate more heat than the ground. Infrared will show an underground heat-generating source that is not normally visible to the naked eye.

Aerial photographs are created in different scales. Most are in the scale of 1:24,000 (1 inch is equal to 24,000 inches or 2,000 feet). The ideal is 1:2,000, or 1 inch to 500 feet. The latter is not normally available. It may, however, be enlarged fourfold. This may be done with an enlarger by the owner's of the negative, or by enlarging on color copy machine. Color copies reproduce with almost the same clarity and detail as the original photo.

It is ideal to collect aerial photographs for every year, back to raw land. Yet, every year is impractical, and back to raw land is impossible. Other than occasional photos taken from air balloons, aerial photos were not available until after the mid 1920s, and these are rare. So, the best efforts can only go back to the middle 1930s, when each agency requiring aerials had them performed as much as 7 to 10 years apart. In order to obtain aerials for every year, the researcher would have to go through numerous sources. An attempt to collect over 50 aerial photos can be time consuming, expensive, and possibly impossible. Thus, a reasonable limit must be set.

Some researchers seek one aerial for every 5 to 10 years, going back at least 50 years. Others use one major source (e.g., the state aerial collection agency) and gather what they can. Discrepancies and questionable findings may require aerials of specific time periods. Each situation will vary. Even raw land evolves over time. Changes should be noted and recorded.

For instance, an aerial photo taken in 1964 depicts ponds and oil drums. The aerial for that same location, taken in 1990, shows grasslands and vegetation. Further investigation is indicated. See Figures 5-1 and 5-2.

FIRE INSURANCE MAPS

Fire insurance maps were originally designed to assist fire insurance agents in assessing fire risk and determining the fire spread potential associated with insured properties. A map may be inclusive of an entire town, or it may be one of a composite of several sections of a city. Cities for which multiple sheets have been produced have a map with an index to streets and special features (e.g., schools and churches). They generally include the more populated areas of a town and do not include rural environments. See Figure 5-3.

These historic maps, typically a 1:600 (1 inch is equivalent to 50 feet) scale, are valuable sources of information. Land use and structural changes in buildings are documented for the years of coverage. They detail street addresses, land usage, occupants, gas storage areas, raw material pilings, and types of products manufactured and/or stored. Other features include type of construction (e.g., brick, stone, or frame), roof composition (e.g., asbestos), number of floors, wall construction (e.g., cloth lined), width of the street(s), and location of fire protection devices (e.g., fire hydrants, water mains, wells, and fire alarm boxes).

The earliest fire insurance map was published in 1790, a plan of Charleston, South Carolina. Then major population centers were added, to be followed by small communities. The smaller towns date back to the late 1800s. Updates were completed as often as once a year for the larger cities and once every five years for slower growing population centers. Although

Figure 5-1.   Aerial Photos (samples).

Figure 5-2. Aerial photographs of apartment complex site which had to be vacated due to seepage from a prior municipal landfill. (The top photo, taken in 1990, depicts a 135 unit apartment complex. The middle photo, taken in 1980, depicts an open field. The bottom photo, taken in 1966, depicts a landfill. All are on a 1:1000 feet scale.)

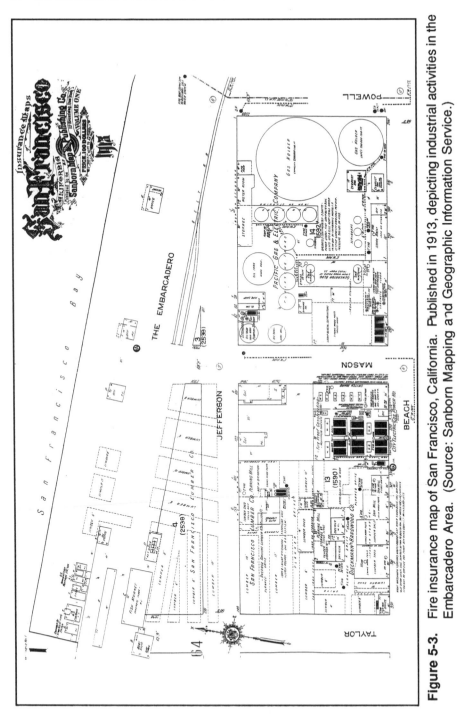

Figure 5-3.   Fire insurance map of San Francisco, California. Published in 1913, depicting industrial activities in the Embarcadero Area. (Source: Sanborn Mapping and Geographic Information Service.)

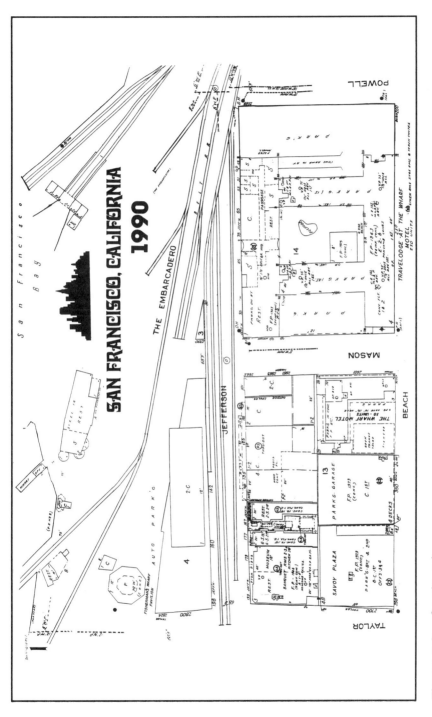

Figure 5-3. Continued.

many different firms were contracted to complete these maps, one stands out. Not only did they complete most of the maps archived today, but they collected many of those which were completed by others. This firm is the Sanborn Mapping and Geographic Information Service, formerly the Sanborn Map Company. Today, they update 40 major U.S. cities on an annual basis, and these maps are used to record land use and structural change over time.[2,3] Others are completed contractually, at less frequent intervals.

The Sanborn Map collection dates back to 1867. The present collections depict commercial, industrial, and residential sections of over 12,000 cities and towns throughout the United States, Canada, and Mexico. The originals were in color. The legends have color codes with symbols and letter coding.

In the early 1930s, production of fire insurance maps by Sanborn, the leading publisher, at the time, reached its peak, with publications describing houses on every street in more than 12,000 towns and cities. By the mid-1950s, every city in the United States, including those in Alaska and Hawaii, with a population over 2,500 had been mapped by Sanborn. Then around 1960, the requirements for fire insurance evaluations, using maps was replaced by other methods.

Many of the maps which are available through local collectors have been reproduced on black and white microfilm. Collectors include public libraries, history centers, and major universities. The single largest and most comprehensive collection of fire insurance maps available for purchase is housed in Sanborn's own archives which contain over one million maps.

The Library of Congress presently maintains over 700,000 maps, most of which were originally submitted to the library through Sanborn's Copyrighting Procedures. They have issued duplicate sets of most of the originals to each state for cities within that state, usually to a historic center or major university. Names and addresses of recipient institutions and a listing of those which are available are found in the following:

Ristow, Walter W.: *Fire Insurance Maps in the Library of Congress—Plans of North American Cities and Towns Produced by the Sanborn Map Company.* Library of Congress, Washington, DC, 1981.

Prints and microfilm negatives can be ordered from Sanborn Mapping and Geographic Information Service for a nominal fee. Prints range from 11″ × 14″ to 18″ × 24″, and 35-mm archival-quality negatives mounted on aperture cards. To request print copies, identify each site by street address and cross street, if available.   Indicate the format desired and the time span(s). Expect a couple of weeks turnaround time.   For more information regarding ordering procedures and services available from Sanborn, write:

Sanborn Mapping and Geographic Information Service
629 Fifth Avenue, Dept. OSC
Pelham, NY 10803

LOCAL STREET DIRECTORIES

Local street directories are published annually by private enterprise and may generally be located in the city library or historic center serving the property area. These directories are similar to telephone directories, but they provide listings by address.   They are a source of information concerning who or what business was at a given location for a given year, assuming they had a telephone. The information includes initial date for phone services at that location, how far back in time the present resident/business has been listed, whether the listing was a business listing, and much more. There are generally listings for every year, going back as far as the late 1800s. However, be aware that an address for a given location may have changed over the years. These changes are sometimes noted or can be tracked down in the directories.

With the proper address, the types of business listed at a given address may be identified. For instance, according to the title records, a given location may have been owned by Jim K. Jolly in a given year. However, the local street directory for that year indicates a phone number for Casey's Auto Repair Shop. The land was apparently leased or used by the owner to conduct a small commercial business, possibly generating hazardous chemical waste (e.g., oils, leaded gasoline, and solvents). A sample street directory, published by Cole's Publications, may be reviewed in Figure 5-4.

ZONING RECORDS

Zoning records provide general information as to how property land use has evolved, present uses, and future projections. An area which has always been zoned single-family residential will not pose the same concerns as property which is zoned industrial.

Generally, zoning will escalate to encompass less restrictive land usage. Therefore, if your area is zoned residential-single family, there is

.83 453-5212
.91 451-8582
NP
.89 454-5376
.90 453-9659
.90 453-9659
NP
¤ 454-7346
NP
– 454-2586
.85 453-0456
ITS
¤ 467-2271
NP
.69 452-9878
.69 453-2506
.75 452-6288
NP
¤ 459-9165
– 323-5140
.88 453-4558
.90 • 459-7592
.90 459-7592
.80 452-2227
NP •
NP
¤ 453-2753
NP
.91 452-6590
NP
– 451-1774
.61 453-8344
.74 459-9504
¤ 451-9334
.91 451-2955
– 451-6376
NP
– 451-7545
.90 450-1805
.90 454-1350
.90 454-1350
NP
– 451-9316
.84 451-2641
NP
.89 453-1169
.59 459-6887
¤ 452-4734
¤ 452-4734
.91 451-9350

78702
CT 10 $E..D13
21
– 499-0014

78734
CT 17.35 $A..D 2
W30
HI .83 261-6090
ice .83 261-6560
2 BUSINESS

R 78758
CT 18.17 $C..D18
31
.90 • 467-7781
.90 • 467-7781
.86 458-2835
¤ 452-2038
¤ 452-2109
.86 458-2835
.91 323-5363
NP
.91 459-5370
.91 459-5370
.87 454-1349
.90 454-1349
.91 454-1378
.75 451-2738
ch .70 451-2514
.79 458-6738
y ¤ ⊙ 451-2514
.89 454-9749
.87 • 453-8924
.91 • 450-1369
.89 452-2447
NP
.89 454-8102
.89 • 454-8102
– • 459-1765
.70 451-1841
.82 • 454-3945

12 William J Albright .80 288-4972
14800 ★ **Life Works** .91 **288-6808**
NO # Joe E Buckner .87 288-0097
NO # John Luton .91 288-3934
NO # Greg Markley .85 288-4079
NO # Glenn W Mitchell .86 288-5080
NO # John W Payne .90 288-5003
NO # S J Rodolf .85 288-4079
NO # M E Stanczak ¤ 288-4057
9 RESIDENCE 1 BUSINESS

● CROSSDRAW DR 78731
New Street–1973.
7500– 7599 CT 17.05 $A..D17
● RAND McNALLY 148–H31
7503 Frank A Laboon .75 345-2230
7504 Edward A Feille Jr ¤ • 346-7044
7506 James H Watkins .74 345-5930
7507 NP
7508 E Generes Dufour .73 345-2146
7509 James A Varney .89 346-9650
7510 Gustav Gutman .85 • 345-1614
7512 Dr Quintin J Smith .73 345-3107
7514 Joe T Jerkins .81 • 345-2603
★ **Group Tours** .91 **343-8578**
7516 B F Dewberry .74 345-3153
Dan Dewberry ¤ 345-1979
7517 W Bruce Woolcott .79 345-8916
7518 Robert H Stratmann .87 345-3916
7519 NP
7520 W P Gannaway .73 345-2501
15 RESIDENCE 1 BUSINESS

● CROSSING PL 78741
New Street–1984.
1500– 1899 CT 23.11 $E..F18
● RAND McNALLY 209–K19
1705 Condominium
Roy Vincent Alanis .89 385-5529
Cindy Bedsole ¤ 389-1750
Craig Bennett – 389-0477
Nolan O Bewley .88 389-2640
Mingcheng Chang ¤ 389-1646
Jeff Cuban ¤ 385-8971
G R Davila ¤ 385-2504
Harold Eggers Jr .90 385-3670
Anthony Festi – 385-3234
Sylvana Garibay ¤ 389-3324
S H Goetz .91 385-4450
Gail Guerrero .85 385-4052
Carlos F Gutierrez – 389-2329
Fred Harvey .90 389-3209
Steven Herzfeld .85 385-5658
Spencer Higgs ¤ 385-7057
Chihli Hsu .88 389-1646
Krista Johnson ¤ 389-1750
Joel S Kelly .90 • 385-1122
Colleen Krohn .91 389-0477
Sumei Kuo – 389-1646
J Leclour-Robinson .90 385-5403
Victor Lennhoff ¤ 385-7027
Morgan Lindegren ¤ 385-0188
Mike McCanlies .91 385-8134
B S Metcalfe .89 389-2272
Tim P Rafferty ¤ 385-4071
Daniel Sanchez – 385-4939
Philip J Schwartz .90 389-0432
B A Siemsen ¤ 385-3382
John Siemsen .91 • 385-7304
John Steiner ¤ 389-2616
Eric Stockton .86 385-5663
Martin Thomas .90 385-5403
B G Turner .91 385-1272
Alvaro Vela ¤ 389-2329
William Webb .88 • 385-5663
Betty Williams .91 385-4828
Betty L Williams – 385-6739
Rob Wilson – 389-3324
Steve Witt – 385-1888
Ming Yu ¤ 389-1646
★ **American Restoratn** ¤ **385-0000**
★ **Andrews Paintng Co** .91 **385-1066**
★ **Eggers Group Inc** .90 **385-3670**
42 RESIDENCE 3 BUSINESS

● CROSSLAND DR
New Street–1990.
● RR39 78726
11000–11299 CT 17.10 $A..C16
● RAND McNALLY 127 E37
● RAND McNALLY 127–E37
11004 ★ **Scott Felder Homes** .91 **258-6832**
11004 ★ **Weekley Homes** ¤ **219-0995**
11007 Edwin L Bronaugh .91 • 258-6687
11009 Ronald Rohrbach – 331-1722
11012 Bill Seward .91 335-3286
Celia Seward .91 335-3286
11013 Charles C Tomich .91 • 335-5481
11014 Ken Potter – • 335-3698
11019 Charles E Hoover .91 • 250-1678
11021 Mac Powell .91 335-9197
Brian Powell .91 335-8987
11023 Raymond E Moore – • 335-5887
11025 Steve Omrani .91 335-3923
11026 Richard Spalding – • 219-0783
11028 Thomas R Brandt ¤ • 331-0486

Kenneth Greene .91 • 331-5289
11201 Peter Vercolen ¤ • 219-1550
11202 Kerry Afflerbaugh ¤ 331-5744
Martin Afflerbaugh – 331-5744
11203 Claude Bookout .91 • 335-5494
11204 Kevin Ward – • 331-8610
11205 Liijin Lo ¤ 331-7867
Wingcheung Tam – • 331-7867
11206 J E Muyshondt ¤ 335-4186
11209 Doug Davaz ¤ • 219-8582
11211 Paul Carlson .91 • 258-1723
11216 J L Owens – 335-2834
11218 Donald Payette .91 • 335-6485
11220 Dan Evans .91 • 335-6460
11222 Richard Ridder .91 • 258-7932
56 RESIDENCE 2 BUSINESS

● CROSSMEADOW DR 78750
New Street–1966.
7500– 7699 CT 17.10 $A..C16
● RAND McNALLY 148–G31
7600 Thomas ORourke .85 346-6942
7601 Earl A Tyson .82 346-0655
★ **Gnrl Vision** .87 **346-0005**
7602 NP
7603 Brad Heath .91 338-0018
Darshann Heath .91 338-0018
7604 R L Dodson .79 • 345-1663
7605 Earl Sanders Jr .70 345-1719
7606 Tony R Pulliam .67 • 345-1659
7607 Isom A Sheffield ¤ 345-8692
7608 Roger Schultz .67 345-0277
7609 C L Marcus .73 345-3714
7610 C E Webb .91 338-4932
12 RESIDENCE 1 BUSINESS

● CROSS PARK DR 78710
New Street–1986.
8200– 8799 CT 18.34 $B..D19
● RAND McNALLY 170–M28
8225 ★ **Chiles Cafeteria** .90 **928-8353**
★ **US Postal Info&Rts** .89 **929-1253**
★ **US Postl Zip Code** ¤ **929-1255**
★ **US Postal Cstmr As** .90 **929-1252**
★ **US Pstl Clms&Prmts** .89 **929-1284**
★ **USPS Express Mail** .89 **929-1267**
★ **USPS Special Dlvry** .89 **929-1238**
★ **USPS Registry Sect** .91 **929-1220**
★ **US Bulk Ml Accptnc** .89 **929-1271**
★ **USPS Main Ofc Wndw** .90 **929-1241**
★ **USPS Emplmt Info** .90 **929-1139**
★ **USPS Passport Info** .89 **331-7737**
★ **USPS Passport Info** .90 **477-7907**
★ **USPS Passport Info** .90 ⊙ **929-1241**
★ **US UT Station** .90 **471-8867**
★ **US Postmaster** .89 **929-1283**
★ **USPS Dlv Grwt Coor** .89 **929-1426**
★ **USPS Mgr Bg&Equip** .90 **929-1500**
★ **USPS Admin Ofcs** .91 ⊙ **929-1252**
● 78754
8305 ★ **Cardio Metrics** ¤ **834-0605**
★ **Leons Carpet&Tile** .87 **834-9811**
★ **Leons Carpet&Tile** .91 **834-8891**
8309 ★ **Tex St Florists** .87 **834-0361**
8314 ★ **Lk Trvs ISD Tax** .88 **832-8092**
★ **MISD Tax Office** ¤ ⊙ **832-8092**
★ **Tax Info&Records** .87 **834-9138**
★ **Travis Cntrl Apprs** .87 **834-9317**
★ **Travis Cntrl Apprs** .87 ⊙ **834-9138**
★ **Co Tx Apprsl Dist** .87 ⊙ **834-9317**
8329 ★ **Wstnghs Elec Supp** .88 **832-1211**
8330 ★ **Hisco** .91 **834-9773**
8341 ★ **Arthur Valve&Fttng** .90 **832-5057**
8402 ★ **Charter Hosp Austn** .86 **837-1800**
8403 Cntl Pk On Wlnt Ck
See Building Drty
8504 ★ **Marshall Industris** .86 **837-1991**
8505 Building
★ **Grn Leaf Whlsl Flr** .88 **835-9303**
★ **Magic Valley Dist** .91 **339-8577**
★ **Tex St Brd Phrmcy** .87 **832-0661**
★ **Thomas Schl Flrstr** .91 **837-8666**
110 ★ **St Pharmacy Bd** .87 ⊙ **832-0661**
8508 ★ **Airborne Life Sppr** .91 **873-0033**
★ **Intrntl Bio Mdcl** .91 ⊙ **873-0033**
★ **Narco Bio Systms** .91 ⊙ **873-0033**
★ **A J Segars** .91 ⊙ **873-0033**
★ **Telecare** .91 ⊙ **873-0033**
8601 Building
★ **Fine Art Prints** .91 **835-2998**
★ **Tejas Busness Syst** .90 **834-8777**
100 ★ **WEI** .88 **835-5570**
100 ★ **Windberg Enterpris** .88 ⊙ **835-5570**
200 ★ **Windberg Studio** .90 **834-1015**
8605 ★ **Carbon Implants** .90 **837-9900**
8613 ★ **Clinical Path Labs** – **320-1600**
★ **Clinical Path Labs** .90 **320-1604**
★ **Clinical Path Labs** ¤ **873-1630**
★ **Clinical Path Labs** ¤ **873-1625**
★ **Clinical Path Labs** ¤ **339-1275**
8701 ★ **Aus Semiconductor** .89 **339-1188**
★ **Comprotek Services** .89 **832-9151**
★ **Impact Printhead** .90 ⊙ **832-9151**
★ **Imperial Litho-Grp** .90 **339-7116**
59 BUSINESS

11605 Sleshi Tebedge .91
T Workineh .91
11606 Michael Kutsch .86
11607 Guy Jakthong .85
G P Nichols .85
11608 Steve Berres –
11609 Homer C Flynn .79
11610 Mathew Ryan ¤
11611 David Meyer .91
11613 Ed Gattis ¤
11700 G B Alexander Jr .87
11701 H C Kinzler .82
11702 NP
11704 R F Andrews .86
– MOURNING DOVE DR INTS
20 RESIDENCE 1 B

● CROSSWOOD DR
7000– 7199 CT 24.14
● RAND McNALLY 227–F16
– HILLSIDE OAKS INTS
7000 A Rodriguez Jr .78
7001 Natalya Johnson .88
Lisa Smith .88
7002 Richard Ramirez Jr .81
7003 Jerry Yasuhara – •
K Yasuhara – •
7004 7006 NP
7008 Alicia Ford –
Virgil C Ford –
7010 Jorge L Rodriguez .89
7012 Joe Martinez .91 •
7014 NP
7016 Fran Rademachir –
Hugh Rademachir –
7017 NP
7018 Richard R Adams .88 •
7019 Norma Bayliss .90 •
7020 Carl Albert Marley .91
7021 Gary W Winston .78
7022 Chester Clifton –
Todd Clifton –
7023 7025 NP
7100 Juan Pedro Solis .91 •
7101 Douglas M Smith .91 •
7102 Gerald L Briggs .78
7103 Barbara Foreman .84
7104 Marie Brown ¤
7105 NP
7106 Clinton J Willman .91
7107 Henry B Talbott .79
7109 James N Shaw .78
7110 K C Bredahl .91
7111 Martina Lopez ¤
7112 NP
7113 Lavern Mitchell .84 •
– MATTHEWS INTS
37 RESIDENCE

● CROW LN
6200– 6299 CT 24.02
● RAND McNALLY 228–G16
6201 ★ **Bug Dudes Day Care** .84
6204 William E Smith .84
6210 ★ **Safway Cesco** .81
★ **Safway Scaffolds** .68 ⊙
★ **Safway Steel Prdct** .86 ⊙
6216 A Nancy A McKee .86
6224 NP
– NORTH BLUFF INTS
3 RESIDENCE 4 B

● CROWLEY TRL
New Street–1986.
6300– 6599 CT 17.20
● RAND McNALLY 129–J37
6301 NP
6303 Steve Peterson .91 •
6305 6307 NP
6401 M J Saurage .91 •
6403 Greg Smith ¤
6405 Dana Harsh –
Shelby L Schroeder ¤
6407 Lee Knight ¤
6409 Dennis Dimaria .86
6411 Gerrodeau Mast .91 •
6413 Nancy Hoffman –
Kalab Tye –
6415 NP
6417 Neil Read ¤ •
6501 Jerry Knight .88
Sherman Vanmeter .86
★ **Jerry Knight** .88
6503 Bennie Ruiz .87 •
6505 Cuong Duy Nguyen .87
Luan Duy Nguyen .87
Luan Duy Nguyen ¤
Nghiem Doan Nguyen .87
Pho Van Nguyen .87
6507 Corey Ziegel .91 •
24 RESIDENCE 1 B

● CROWN COLONY DR
New Street–1982.

Figure 5-4. Local Street Directory Sample. *Cole's Directory for Greater Austin and Vicinity.* Cole's Publications, Lincoln, Nebraska, 1992-93. p. 201.

not much likelihood of the area having been zoned industrial at any one time, but this is not always the case. The planning department will have a map of the areas under its control, and the zones will be clearly delineated. It will also have recent projections for rezoning.

Rezoning of residential to commercial or commercial to industrial will have an impact on future potential contamination. Although contaminants may not be generated on a given site, they may migrate from another and possibly provide a conduit for the associated properties' contaminants to enter into a major aquifer. For instance, a resident installs a water well and the driller did not comply with proper drilling precautions. A contaminant migrates to the hole and down through the confining rock layer.

The city planning department will have zoning and expansion plans for incorporated areas. However, if an area is outside a city in a rural community, it will be classified "unincorporated." There is no zoning for unincorporated property.

BUILDING PERMITS

Building permits are generally available through the city planning department. These permits are filled out by the builder, owner, or owner's representative; and filed by street address. A permit must be filed whenever any changes in a building are anticipated. Changes include usage of the building. There may be plans to change a building from an apartment complex to an office building. This intent must be followed with a permit.

Plans and building specifications generally accompany each building permit but are maintained for a limited time—with a few exceptions. Plans and specifications where the building is large are generally maintained for an indefinite time period. These plans are kept so they may assist fire fighters when developing a strategy for managing a fire. The plans and specifications are also helpful when assessing structural materials, a topic to be discussed in the next chapter.

CERTIFICATES OF OCCUPANCY

Certificates of occupancy are generally available through the city planning department. These certificates are filed according to building address, and they contain the owner's name and the building usage information. A certificate of occupancy may also include the name of a lessee who is not named in the deed information.

HEALTH/SAFETY AND ENVIRONMENTAL COMPLIANCE RECORDS

Regulatory compliance records are oftentimes overlooked in environmental site assessments. This may be due to the required additional time and expense. It may be due to the low probability of generating any more information than that gathered by other means, or it may simply be a site which has had no industrial activities which, in turn, would not have a compliance history. Yet, this is available and is another source of information.

Safety and Health Records

The Occupational Safety and Health Act (OSHA) is a federal regulatory agency which enforces workplace exposures to employees. It has been in effect since 1970. The first list of health hazards included only ten substances. This has grown to over 350 chemicals in the more recent years, and the list is ever increasing.

All agency records are maintained for at least twenty years, and requests are made through the Freedom of Information Act (FOIA). Administrative and copy fees can be excessive where there are several files on a given location or business. Older files are archived and may take time to locate.

Compliance visits are generated in one of three different ways. A worker may complain and/or express concern regarding workplace exposures to health and/or safety hazards. All complaints are confidential, but the records are a matter of public record. A complaint may have been generated through the sincere concern of the worker and his inability to approach management with his concerns for whatever reason, or he may be a disgruntled employee trying to cause problems.

Most visits are random. Out of each industry type, OSHA will generate a number of visits. Although the visit may be fairly innocent, many managers feel that OSHA will always find a problem. This is OSHA's job. However, the compliance officer judges the situation(s) to be minor or "serious and willful," depending upon his evaluation of the work environment and the attitude of the management. A "serious and willful" citation could accompany a maximum fine of $20,000, and insurance/bonding companies frown seriously upon firms receiving one.

A visit may be a follow-up visit to evaluate whether the company has come into compliance. This, again, may reflect the attitude of management.

Keep in mind also that if a site visitation does occur, the compliance officer cannot see all or know all. Things do get missed! Do not make the mistake of assuming that if a hazardous substance has not been named by a compliance officer that there are none, especially where the information conflicts with other data.

For example, an investigator visits a plastic container manufacturing plant. Management makes a statement to the consultant that the plant received a clean bill of health from OSHA two weeks prior to this visit. The investigator later finds that an activity, which was part of normal business, was not being performed during the OSHA visit. During a discussion with one of the employees, this information was disclosed. An employee had previously been required, as part of his job, to toss a flammable solvent on the ground around the machinery. This was done in order to cut costs and allow the cleanup of machine-generated grease on the floor. The solvent was subsequently squeegied out the back door onto the soil. After the worker received first degree burns, this practice changed. They now use a toxic, non-flammable chemical to accomplish the same end result. OSHA was unaware of these procedures.

These records are only a portion of the larger parcel. Further investigation may be indicated.

State and Federal Environmental Records

The U.S. Environmental Protection Agency (EPA) handles environmental health hazards (i.e., stack emissions from industrial plants, air pollution of the community air, pollution of the ground/groundwater, effluent from industry, and pollution of crops and livestock by industry). It was made into law in 1970, and the agency began operating in 1974.

Each state has been given the option of handling all or a portion of the federal EPA requirements. States vary as to what agency manages the different details. Either one agency or several may be involved. Records and file maintenance will vary from state to state, and some state laws will exceed federal regulations.

Once a commercial or industrial activity has been identified as having operated on the property, past or present, the investigator should contact the pertinent agency for information concerning registration and citations. A search can usually be done by company name. Registration records provide information as to what is or was being discharged into the environment. Citations provide information as to non-compliance with discharge restrictions or administrative procedures.

WASTE MANAGEMENT PERMITS

Waste may be handled by in-house treatment and then discharged or hauled away. In-house management of waste may involve, but not be limited to, neutralization of a chemical, surface impoundments, incinerators, evaporative ponds, biological degradation, landfills, and air scrubbers.

Sanitary Sewage Discharge Permits

Sanitary sewage discharge permits are required of certain commercial and all industrial wastewater generators. The organization most affected by discharge will be the local water/wastewater management agency. Permits will frequently give the constituents of the discharge and sometimes the volume. This information can be used should you suspect ground/groundwater contamination.

Each agency sets its own standards by which the local operators are required to comply. This may involve routine monitoring of certain records which are reviewed by the agency on a routine basis, and it may involve compliance monitoring or random routine checks. An operator may refuse to report a discharge, hoping he will not get caught. Generally, where there is industry there will be some form of discharge.

Storm Water Discharge Permits

Storm water discharge permits are required any time industry discharges into the storm drains. This water eventually discharges into surface waters. Contamination of surface waters can lead to the destruction of aquatic habitat and to the contamination of groundwater and drinking water sources.

Stream and Lake Discharge Permits

The U.S. Army Corps of Engineers (Corps) is charged by Congress with regulating the nation's water resources. Any activity which will discharge, fill, or dredge material into a freshwater stream, lake, or adjacent wetland requires a permit and must be reviewed for compliance.

Air Emission Permits

Air, or stack, emissions are handled by state and local agencies which are designated by that state government to manage air pollution. The total air burden of a hazardous substance is the issue, not a measurement of an acceptable standard or standard emission rate for a given industry. A large industrial complex or numerous air waste generating sources in an urban environment will contribute a much larger total burden than a large plant in a small rural community. Many states require industry which has any type of process involving gaseous emissions to seek air pollution permits.

Gaseous emissions could be generated by incinerators, local exhaust stacks, or open burning of materials. Hospitals and international airports generally have incinerators, as does heavy industry, with by-products they wish to dispose of in-house. Local exhaust stacks may be associated with various operations in the semiconductor industry, paint shops, fiberglass operations, and so on. Open burning of allergy-causing bush, tree limbs, and woodland scrap can cause community complaints. And the list goes on.

ON-SITE PAPER DETECTIVE

Property which is presently used for industrial purposes will general require some form of a records review. The purpose is to tag hazardous substance usage and determine whether in-house management of these materials may result in environmental contamination. An attempt to track records on obsolete activities may be like chasing a red herring. So, the investigator may have to confine efforts to the present.

Some consultants automatically include an in-house records audit in all industrial assessments.   Insurance carriers require risk audits when issuing environmental insurance packages, and occasionally the client requires a complete records audit as they may intend to purchase the business with the property and want to know into what operating liabilities they may be investing. These audits are time consuming and expensive. A partial review may be feasible and informative, but should an extensive records audit be indicated, recommend this as part of a Phase II.

The easiest, most informative records to review are the chemical inventory records, material safety data sheets, Community Right-to-Know records, and process flow charts. These are discussed herein, along with a few others which are typically included in the assessment.

Chemical Inventory Records

Most manufacturers maintain a chemical inventory. If done properly, the manufacturer will have a chemical inventory list which is generally located with the MSDS manuals

Otherwise, the inventories may be maintained by the purchasing department, shipping and receiving, the safety and health manager, or the person who formulates the processes. Some may have these records spread throughout the plant in the various departments. Locating these elusive papers may be a challenge.

Keep in mind you may also wish to go back several years to when MSDSs were not a requirement. The chemical inventory records may be a last resort, and they may already have been archived.

Material Safety Data Sheets

Maintenance of product material safety data sheets (MSDS) have only recently been required for commercial and industrial activities.   The requirement was created by OSHA, and the law requiring the maintenance in-house of MSDSs became effective for manufacturing in 1986, for non-manufacturing activities (excluding construction) in 1988, and for construction in 1989.

OSHA requires an MSDS on all chemicals, hazardous and non-hazardous, used and/or sold by a particular manufacturer. The material safety data sheet is a product data sheet with information regarding the constituents of a particular product. These sheets are required to be made available to the workers who may potentially be exposed to them.   Generally, a manufacturer will maintain a centralized file of MSDSs.   Along with a list of the components and their associated flammability, reactivity, and health hazards, the data sheets give information as to what the decomposition products are, which chemicals they should not be mixed with, how to handle and store the products, and what to do in case of an emergency. See an example of the information contained within these data sheets in Figure 5-5.

Many material safety data sheets, including those which involve non-hazardous chemicals, are created with a concern for the liability of the manufacturer.   Therefore, in the recommendations for proper handling, most data sheets will tell you to use proper ventilation.   They do not define proper ventilation.

The MSDS will give you information as to the chemicals currently being used by the manufacturer at that property.   Some composites consist of less than 20 MSDSs, but many are bound by volumes (e.g., several volumes of three-inch binders).

Community Right-to-Know Records (SARA Title III)

The Community Right-to-Know Law, Superfund Amendments and Reauthorization Act (SARA), Title III, is a more recent law.   It requires that industry provide a listing of all chemicals which are maintained on-site. Information on the forms will divulge chemical names and descriptions, physical state, associated hazards, daily usage, amount stored and where, peak quantity, and NFPA hazard rating.   The intent is to provide information for emergency response activities.   For instance, fire response teams may use the information in case of a fire.   They can determine the location and type of hazards potentially involved, potential hazards to the response team, and potential hazards to the community.

The information must be submitted annually, and it will be up to the different states to enact the law on their own.   The states were to have complied by March 1, 1992.

Transport Manifests

Whenever hazardous chemicals are shipped in certain amounts/volumes they must be manifested.   All manifests must be

TRAFFIC MARKER PAINT
MATERIAL SAFETY DATA SHEET

I. PRODUCT IDENTIFICATION

Manufacturer:	Noname Corporation	Telephone:	800/111-1007
Address:	P.O. Box 007	Product Name:	Traffic Marker Paint
	Cross Over, Missouri	Date Prepared:	15 February 1993

II. HAZARDOUS INGREDIENTS

CAS No.	INGREDIENTS	% by WEIGHT	ACGIH-TLV	OSHA-PEL	UNITS
64742-89-8	Lt. Aliphatics	15	100	100	ppm
64742-48-9	V.M.P. Naphtha	8	300	300	ppm
108-88-3	Toluene	4	100	100	ppm
1330-20-7	Xylene	2	100	100	ppm
14807-96-6	Talc	14	2	2	mg/m3
1332-58-7	Kaolin	16	10	10	mg/m3
471-34-1	Calkcium Carbonate	14	10	15	mg/m3
1344-37-2	Lead Chromate	5	0.05	0.05	mg/m3

III. PHYSICAL/CHEMICAL CHARACTERISTICS

Boiling Point:	174 - 325° F	Specific Gravity:	> 1.0
Vapor Pressure:	N.A.	Melting Point:	N.A.
Vapor Density:	Heavier Then Air	Evaporation Rate:	Slower Than Ether
Solubility in Water:	N.A.		
Appearance and Odor:	Bright Yellow and Smells Like Paint Thinner		

IV. FIRE AND EXPLOSION HAZARDS

Flash Point:	20°F
Flammable Limits:	LEL - 0.9 % UEL - 6.0 %
Extinguishing Media:	Carbon Dioxide, Dry Chemical, Foam
Special Fire Fighting Procedures:	Full protective equipment should be worn, including a self-contained breathing apparatus.
Unusual Fire and Explosion Hazard:	Isolate from heat, electricity, sparks, and open flames.

V. HEALTH HAZARDS

Routes of Entry:	Ingestion, Inhalation, Skin and Eye Absorption
Toxicity:	Moderately Toxic
Acute Overexposures:	Irritation of the eyes, skin, and respiratory tract. May cause central nervous system depression. Extreme conditions may result in respiratory distress, unconsciousness, and death. Symptoms of overexposure include headache, dizziness, nausea, and loss of coordination. Eye contact symptoms include redness accompanied by an itching and/or burning sensation.
Chronic Overexposures:	Chronic exposures to lead may result in damage to the blood-forming cells, nervousness, urinary and reporductive system problems. The symptoms include abdominal discomfort/pain, constipation, loss of appetite, a metallic taste, nausea, insomnia, nervous irritability, weakness, muscle and joint pains, headache, and dizziness.

Figure 5-5. Material Safety Data Sheet

First Aid Emergency Procedures:	Chronic exposures to chromates may result in an increased risk for respiratory cancer. If ingested, drink profuse amounts of water, and consult a physician. If eye and/or skin contact, flush with water.
Suspected Cancer Agent:	In accordance with OSHA, IARC and NTP, chromium VI compounds are suspected cancer-causing agents.

VI. REACTIVITY HAZARDS

Stability:	Stable __X__ Unstable _____
Conditions to Avoid:	N.A.
Incompatibility:	None Known.
Hazardous Decomposition Products:	Carbon Dioxide, Carbon Monoxide, Oxides of Metals
Hazardous Polymerization:	May Occur _____ Will Not Occur __X__

VII. SPILL OR LEAK PRECAUTIONS

Spill Response Procedures:	Remove all sources of ignition. Ventilate and remove the spilled material.
Waste Disposal Methods:	Dispose of in accordance with local, state, and Federal regulations for "hazardous materials" as defined by RCRA , 40 CFR 261.

VIII. CONTROL MEASURES

Ventilation:	Local Exhaust Ventilation
Minimum Respiratory Protection:	Organic Vapor/Particulate , where ventilation is inadequate to control the airborne exposures to the hazardous ingredients.
Protective Gloves:	Gloves Impermeable to Aromatic Hydrocarbons
Eye Protection:	Contact lenses should be prohibited when working around any chemicals. Chemical goggles with enclosed side shields.

IX. SPECIAL PRECAUTIONS

Keep away from heat, sparks, and open flames. Ventilate to avoid accumulation of vapors.

DO NOT SMOKE during use. Turn off stoves, electric appliances, tools, and all sources of ignition.

Properly label all conveyance containers with the product name and pertinent warnings, and keep container closed when the product is not in use.

DO NOT APPLY TO TOYS OR OTHER CHILDREN'S ARTICLES, FURNITURE, OR ANY INTERIOR SURFACE OF A DWELLING OR FACILITY WHICH MAY BE OCCUPIED OR USED BY CHILDREN, AND DO NOT APPLY ON ANY EXTERIOR SURFACE OF DWELLING UNITS (e.g. window sills, porches, stairs, or railings which children may come in contact with).

This information pertains only to this product as it has been formulated and is based on that information which was available at the time of its preparation. Addition of additives or other mixtures may alter the composition and thus the hazards.

Figure 5-5. (continued)

maintained by the originator. The Department of Transportation began mandating manifests in 1980, but the originators of the material are required to maintain these records for only three years. The manifest will contain not only information as to the type of chemical shipped, but also the amount and where it was taken. There have been cases of falsified receipts in disposal activities. Waste disposal in a Class I dump is expensive. Transporters have been known "to get lost and end up at the wrong dump."

Process Flow Charts

Process flow charts diagrammatically describe the use of the chemicals, their contributions to the process(es), the amount used, and their destination. A flow chart will afford an easy-to-read sequence of events and usage of each of the chemicals. See Figure 5-6.

Safety and Health Audits

If a manufacturer has had a safety and health audit, it will have been completed by corporate auditors, the manufacturer's insurance company, or an outside consultant. These reports, generally completed by an industrial hygienist or safety engineer, are informative, direct, and may provide valuable information. Some even disclose the in-house process description for the time the survey was performed.

Purchasing Records

If all else fails, purchasing should have maintained records. The records will have not only chemical purchases, but also paper, mechanical parts, and other unrelated items. Reviewing these records could be extremely frustrating and time consuming. Yet, these too are likely to have been archived, and past information may be accessible for review. This step could involve a tremendous volume of work with very little to show for one's efforts.

I. Polycrystalline ("Poly") Silicon Production
$Si + HCl \rightarrow SiHCl_3$

II. Single Crystal Ingot Growth
    a. Czochralski, or
    b. Float Zone

III. Ingot Evaluation
    a. Cropping, Grinding, Chamfering, Flatting, and Seed Slicing
    b. X-Ray Diffraction
    c. Etching
        1. Sirtl Etch
           $HF + CrO_3$
        2. Dash Etch
           HF, HNO_3, CH_3COOH
        3. Secco
           $HF + K_2CrO_7$

IV. Slicing
    a. Ingot Mounting
    b. Wafer Sawing
    c. Wafer Washing
        $NaOH, CH_3OH$
    d. Wafer Lapping
        Ethylene Glycol, Morpholine, or Cr+6
    e. Edge Rounding
    f. Wafer Etching
        HNO_3, HF, and CH_3COOH

V. Polishing
    a. Wafer Polishing
    b. Carrier Stripping
        Methylene Chloride, MEK, or Cellosolve
    c. Polish Cleaning
        HF, Oxidizers (e.g. H_2O_2), or Cleansing Agents

VI. Final Processing
    a. Final Cleaning
        Ammonia
    b. Tray Cleaning
        Freon
    c. Final Packing

Figure 5-6. Process Flow for Semi-Conductor Ingot and Water Manufacturing. (Initial process in Silicon Wafer Manufacturing.)

Corporate Management Records

Records of safety meetings may be helpful. They generally review recent accidents and/or potential problems associated with safety and health concerns. Once again, this step could also involve a tremendous volume of work.

REFERENCE MANUALS/DOCUMENTS

There is a never-ending source of reference manuals and documents. Those listed herein are the more frequently used sources. The items discussed are by no means a complete list of all possibilities.

Commercial Directories

Some towns have directories which list commercial activities by name and location. This is a source of information which may require a voluminous amount of work with data already gathered from other, easier to access records. The city Chamber of Commerce is the most likely source.

Newspapers

An incident involving a property or property owner may have been of such note that newspapers did a write-up on the event. The major newspaper articles are often indexed and retrieved in the local libraries. Newspapers that are distributed on a large scale, nationally, will be indexed in university and public libraries. For small city news articles, there is generally no indexing either at the public library or by the publishers.

Where indexing is available, suspicious events of potential public note in a given time frame may be checked, using the address, company name, and/or responsible party's name. Computer indexing started around the middle 1980s. Prior years are indexed in Periodical Indexes.

Where indexing is not available, dates must be known and a visit to the newspaper publishing office is necessary. They have copies or microfiche/microfilm that can be reviewed. Yet, this involves a time-consuming search of each paper around the time of a suspicious event.

Industrial Process References

An industrial process reference may aid in the identification of industrial process descriptions and hazardous wastes that are generated. This should be reviewed prior to the on-site inspection/evaluation of work practices. Most industries follow a similar sequence of events in their processes, and these processes are generally known and published for your review. Process descriptions can be evaluated, based on industry standards.

The U.S. EPA Forms and Publications Distribution Center in Cincinnati, Ohio, has information sheets on various types of manufacturing. These range from leather product and cleaning agent manufacturers to chemical and printing industries. The topics covered include an industry overview, hazardous wastes generated, and effective waste minimization techniques used within that industry. These publications are easily accessed and a good source to begin identifying potential environmental exposures associated with a given industry.

A commercial/industrial reference is provided in Chapter 10 to assist the reader, give direction. This information is provided as a starting point.

MINING/NATURAL RESOURCES RECORDS

A source of groundwater contamination which will require a separate records search is the use of the land's natural resources. This includes mining for minerals, oil/gas activities, and water well drilling. Each state has an agency charged with maintaining records and regulating natural resource extraction from the ground. The investigator may obtain this information from that state agency which manages the water resources. They will most likely manage the water resources and know who handles mining and gas/oil extraction sites. All this information should be plotted on an area map with the locations delineated relative to the site. Should any seem noteworthy and the sites are accessible, they may be further evaluated during the site reconnaissance.

Mining

Mining encompasses the extraction and processing of rock, ore, and minerals. These operations are often overlooked, because they are generally located in sparsely populated areas. Although most of the early mining activities were underground, most mining performed today is on the surface (i.e., quarry, open pit mining) or through solution injection and retrieval from the ground.

Some of the more common sources of environmental contamination in mining are mine drainage, surface storage of materials, dewatering activities, wellhead contamination, and tailings (i.e., solid wastes derived from on-sire processing). Liquid and slurry wastes are disposed of in ponds, sumps, lagoons, and injection wells; or they are discharged into surface waters. The spent liquids are transported to these spots via pipelines or ditches. In the ponds, suspended solids settle out in the ponds, and the liquids either evaporate or are discharged to surface water. The remaining solids are later dredged out or abandoned. In unlined ponds, contaminants may migrate into the soil, down to the groundwater. Liquid wastes which are too toxic to dispose of in surface water (e.g., uranium wastes) are disposed of in injection wells.

The type of mining activity which becomes identified may or may not be associated with hazardous substances and potential environmental contamination. This information should be clarified and the process evaluated.

For instance, gold extraction generally involves a process whereby mercury is used to scavenge uncollected gold from the final slurry wash after which the mercury gold-alloy is subjected to heat. The mercury is boiled off and recycled. The mercury-tainted slurry goes into a holding pond. If not managed properly, mercury residue may be left behind in an unlined pond and/or be discharged into surface water.

The potential for groundwater contamination is considerable. A records search for mining activities in the vicinity of rural property is highly recommended.

Oil/Gas Wells

Oil and gas wells may serve as a conduit for groundwater contamination. As the gas/oil yield declines in drilling operations, brine (i.e., saline water, usually high in dissolved solids) is pumped to the surface with the gas/oil. This brine may render groundwater undrinkable.

The first wells date back to the late 1800s when brine typically discharged directly into gullies an streams. Later, unlined (then lined), evaporation pits were used. It was thought at the time that the salts would evaporate with the water into the atmosphere. However, the minerals remained and brine seepage from pits became evident with the passage of time as brine reached the groundwater. Overflow during the rainy seasons also became means for migration. Consequently, since 1969, brines have been injected into deep well or reinjected back into the ground from whence they came. Disposal into these wells is very expensive, and midnight dumping incidents may result.

Logs can generally be obtained from a state designated agency which has been assigned to manage the records (e.g., Texas Railroad Commission). The agency maintains records of oil and gas wells, generally identified on a large map. More recent ones which have yet to be entered onto the map will be recorded. Management and information retrieval methods of marked maps and well files vary by state.

The designated agency which manages gas/oil logs will also have records and maps of pipelines which run through one property to another. However, if the pipeline remains on the same property, it may not be identified in the agency records but instead on the property easement records. The identification of wells within vicinity of the property is a sound practice.

Water Wells

Water wells improperly abandoned can be a big source of ground-water pollution. Abandoned wells which have not been properly plugged or capped find other uses. An improperly abandoned well might end up being used as an inexpensive means of hazardous waste disposal, a disposal site for brine, or a convenient place to dispose of human waste.

Another source of contamination is inadequate completion of a well by not installing a cement surface casing and/or cementing intervals where poor water quality exists. Interval cementing is to prevent interaquifer mixing, particularly where one aquifer is of poor quality or already contaminated with hazardous substances.

Ground penetrations may disrupt the natural ground barriers which may serve to isolate the groundwater. Where the water has a natural barrier which protects it from the downward migration of contaminants, penetration may provide an easy conduit or channel from one layer of soil to the next, as may the oil/gas wells. Contaminants in one layer may have been stopped from downward movement—until the underlying layer was penetrated.

Mark the location(s) of all water wells within the vicinity of the property on a map. These wells should be inspected on the site reconnaissance.

SUMMARY

Historic usage of the property and surrounding areas provides a point of departure for the investigator to speculate as to what hazardous substances and/or activities may require further investigation. There are numerous sources of information, some easier and more informative than others. Not all topics need to be addressed, and some may be addressed only in certain incidences. The minimum recommended historic records review, to be used for all site assessments, includes the following:

- Title Records
- Aerial Photographs
- Fire Insurance Maps
- Local Street Directories
- Zoning Records
- Building Permits

Don't be limited to the sources presented herein. Likewise, some of these topics may be a waste of time, depending on the situation. Other subject searches may be requested by the client. Other sources may be used as a means to confirm information and intuitive concerns. Site assessment methodologies and research approaches evolve.

The records provide the investigator with additional information so special attention might be afforded to certain areas or even be added to the list of topics to be addressed for the site reconnaissance. These records are another tool, another piece of the puzzle, so the investigator can project probability for soil and/or water contamination of the site and/or surrounding areas.

REFERENCES

1. Johannsen, Chis L. and James L. Sanders: *Remote Sensing for Resource Management.* Soil Conservation Society of America, Ankey, Iowa, 1982.
2. Ristow, Walter W.: *Fire Insurance Maps in the Library of Congress—Plans of North American Cities and Towns Produced by the Sanborn Map Company.* Library of Congress, Washington, DC, 1981.
3. *The Use of Historic Sanborn Maps in the Identification and Analysis of Properties and Structures Containing Potential Environmental Hazards.* [Letter from J.C. Cherubini, Director of Marketing and Sales], Sanborn Mapping and Geographic Information Service, Pelham, New York, May 7, 1990.

Chapter 6

Regulatory Agency Listings

INTRODUCTION

Hazardous waste contaminants in the environment migrate and may impact areas which are distant to the source. Thus, it becomes necessary to identify, not only on-site sources of contamination, but the surrounding area sources as well. Many of the sources have already been identified, and the circumference of potential impact is speculative, based in part on past experiences with hazardous substance migration in the environment.

Federal, state, city, and local regulatory agencies track sources of use and/or misuse of hazardous materials and maintain this information which is accessible to the public. The information is part of a database or kept on file. All this is accessible to the public.

The circumference of potential impact is the distance from a source which may be affected by migration. However, potential impact distance may vary, depending on the environmental setting. A hazardous substance spill on low permeability soil a half mile from the site will not have the same potential impact as the same spill in surface water, located upstream from the property under investigation. Yet, a minimum recommended search distance is typically based on the type of listing.

Most site assessments include a minimal database review and search distance. Those minimums are listed in Table 6-1, but the investigator should neither be limited to the minimum type of search nor the minimum search distance. The minimum listings to be searched are discussed within this chapter, along with other types.

Search limits should be plotted on an area map (e.g., a 0.5 mile and one mile radius around the property) and the listings located/identified by type on the map (e.g., CERCLIS listed by an identifying number with a red circle on the CERCLIS site). This methodology helps the investigator visualize the relationships between an identified potential source and the property, while permitting a means for determining distance.

105

Table 6-1. Minimum Search Distances

Type of List	Radius from Site
National priority lists	1 mile
State priority lists	1 mile
CERCLIS	0.5 mile
RCRA lists	
Treatment, storage, and disposal facilities	1 mile
Large and small generators	0.5 mile
Transporters	Property and Adjoining Properties
Emergency Response Notification System	Property Only
Landfill and/or solid waste disposal sites	0.5 mile
Underground storage tanks	Property and Adjoining Properties
Leaking underground storage tanks	0.5 mile

Various sources.

FEDERAL LISTINGS AND DATABASES

The EPA does not have a one-source clearinghouse for information concerning environmental activities. Their basic purpose is to manage, track, and control hazardous materials to minimize exposures to people and the environment—a job delegated to several different divisions within the agency. Information is available through tracking systems within these divisions.

Most of the information can be obtained through some of the many databases which are generally maintained within the regional EPA offices. As many states manage their own EPA programs, a state-designated agency maintains some or all of the databases as well. State printouts may look different, but they contain the similar information. They will also provide more up-to-date listings.

EPA and the state-designated agency generally require a letter requesting a printout of the database or a file search for records. The method for making this request, referred to as an "FOIA," is discussed in Chapter 3. Such a request may take ten workdays or longer to obtain, depending upon the size of the database requested (e.g., a request for

RCRA listing for the state of New York may take up to six to eight weeks). An invoice for computer time and number of printouts will accompany each response.

For those who choose to avoid the administrative treatise and waiting period, many of the larger cities have privately owned, environmental information services which—for a fee—will retrieve the needed information in an abbreviated time frame. These services do obtain their information from the EPA and state agencies, passing it on to their clients on a routine basis. The cost is a little more than going direct to the source, but the ease of usage and time savings is sometimes worth it. Watch for age of data!

National Priority List

The National Priority List (NPL) is also referred to as the Superfund List. This is a list of "identified"—abandoned and not abandoned—hazardous waste sites which pose an imminent threat to life and the environment. Those on the list are prioritized, according to the anticipated impact. They receive attention and are subject to remediation (i.e., cleanup) according to where they fall on the list of priorities. Remediation may involve removal, treatment, and/or containment. Although the minimum search distance from a property is one mile, chemical migration from some sites have been recorded to impact surrounding properties as far as five miles away. The minimum is based on that which is typical and should not restrict the investigator's search.

> Minimum Search Distance for NPL Sites: 1 mile

The Superfund list is managed by the EPA and authorized by the Comprehensive Environmental Response, Compensation, and Liability Act (CERCLA), enacted December 11, 1980. A Hazardous Substance Response Trust Fund of $1.6 billion was authorized over a 5-year period. This act was amended by the Superfund Amendments and Reauthorization Act (SARA), enacted October 17, 1986, allocating a Trust Fund of $8.5 billion over a 5-year period to manage the projects. Later, CERCLA extended the Trust Fund to September 30, 1994 with an additional $5.1 billion authorized. The total of monies authorized, as of publication of this book, stands at $15.2 billion.

The Trust Fund pays the costs not assumed by responsible parties for cleaning up hazardous waste sites or handling emergencies that threaten public health, welfare, or the environment. It also pays for activities leading up to reimbursements by the responsible party(ies). An example of a site proposed for placement on the list is the Refuse Hideaway Landfill in Middleton, Wisconsin. A summary description follows:

> The Refuse Hideaway Landfill encompasses 23 acres of a 40-acre parcel of land in a rural area in Dane County, Wisconsin. It is off U.S. Highway 14, 2 miles west of Middleton and 4 miles east of Cross Plains.
>
> Municipal, commercial, and industrial wastes were disposed of at the privately owned unlined site between 1974 and 1988. The landfill owner reports receiving full barrels of glue and paint; spray paint booth by-products and paint stripper sludge; and spill residues containing methylene chloride, acetone, and other solvents. Based on volume calculations, the landfill could hold up to 1.2 million cubic yards of waste.
>
> The Wisconsin Department of Natural Resources (WDNR) closed the site under court order in 1988 when volatile organic compounds (VOCs) were discovered in private wells southwest of the site. The owner closed the landfill according to the Wisconsin Administrative Code in late 1988, covering it with 2 feet of clay, 18 inches of general soil, and 6 inches of topsoil, and seeding the cover. In January 1989, the owner declared bankruptcy.
>
> A WDNR inspection conducted in 1990 revealed that the cap is eroding. Tests conducted in 1991 by a WDNR consultant detected vinyl chloride, tetrachloroethene, methylene chloride, 1,2-dichloroethane, and trichloroethene in groundwater down gradient of the site, including two private wells. Several of these compounds were disposed of at the site, according to the owner's records. An estimated 14,600 people obtain drinking water from public and private wells within 4 miles of the site. The nearest well, within 0.5 mile of the site, is a private well and is contaminated. Wells are also used to water cattle. Some contaminated wells have been outfitted with treatment systems and others are being taken out of service. WDNR's 1991 study indicates that the plume of contaminated groundwater extends as far as 3,800 feet southwest of the site.
>
> In 1991, WDNR started to operate a system to collect methane gas and leachate.

Potential sites are identified by states, municipalities, companies, and private citizens. Each potential is assigned a number; a federal or designated state official investigates the property, assigning each site with a hazard ranking system (HRS) score, according to the following formula:

$$\text{HRS Score} = \sqrt{\frac{S^2 \text{ groundwater} + S^2 \text{ surface water} + S^2 \text{ soil} + S^2 \text{ air}}{4}}$$

The categories which are used to perform the assessment are based on points given for the likelihood of release, waste characteristics, and environmental threat. The HRS categories for getting listed on the NPL can be reviewed on Table 6-2 as this information provides a generalized sense as to the methodology used by the EPA for making a determination.

If the score exceeds 25 or 30 points, the site is added to the NPL in the Federal Register. Cleanup studies are performed; the assessment, which may take up to 3 years to accomplish, is published and becomes subject to public comment for 60 days. A site-specific cleanup plan is formulated, averaging 1 to 1-1/2 years; and cleanup is initiated. Actual cleanup may take anywhere from 1 to 6 years, and groundwater cleanup may take several decades.

During the preceding steps, the EPA legal staff attempts to identify the potentially responsible party(ies) (PRP) to encourage them to pay for the cleanup. A PRP may be the present owner, a previous owner, or parties identified to be contributors to the problem. Once the PRP is identified, the EPA legal staff attempts to negotiate a settlement. Then, sues it for cleanup costs or issues orders for the PRP to perform the cleanup.

The NPL was promulgated in 1983, and updates occur semi-annually. The status of each is published. Yet, if a site is listed, this is no assurance that a problem exists at the present. A site remains on the NPL indefinitely, even after a cleanup.

As of October 1992, there were 1,236 active sites on the federal Superfund List. A total of 105 sites have been remediated as of this date.[1]

Should further information be desired concerning an NPL, contact the Enforcement Section for Remedial Actions in the EPA Region where the site is located or the Superfund Docket and Information Center (SDIC) which maintains CERCLA-related documents. The SDIC address is:

U.S. EPA
Superfund Docket & Information Center
OS-245
401 M Street, SW
Washington, DC 20460

Table 6-2.   Hazard Rating System Categories for the National Priority Listing

GROUNDWATER

Likelihood of Release	Waste Characteristics	Targets
observed release vs. potential release *containment* *net precipitation* *depth to aquifer* *travel time*	toxicity/mobility hazardous waste quantity	nearest water well population resources wellhead protection

SURFACE WATER

Σ Drinking Water Threat + Human Chain Threat + Environmental Threat

Likelihood of Release	Waste Characteristics	Targets
a. Drinking Water Threat		
overland/flood component observed release vs. potential release *[potential by overland flow: containment runoff distance to surface water]* *[potential by flood: containment flood frequency]* **groundwater to surface water component** observed release vs. potential release *contaminant* *net precipitation* *depth to aquifer* *travel time*	toxicity/persistence/mobility* hazardous waste quantity	nearest intake population resources
b. Human Food Chain Threat		
observed release vs. potential release *[similar to a.]*	toxicity/persistence/mobility*/ bioaccumulation hazardous waste quantity	food chain affected population
c. Environmental Threat		

Likelihood of Release	Waste Characteristics	Targets
observed release vs. potential release [similar to a.]	ecosystem toxicity/mobility*/bioaccumulation/persistence, hazardous waste quantity	sensitive environments

SOIL

Σ Resident Population + Nearby Population Threat

Likelihood of Release	Waste Characteristics	Targets

a. Resident Population Threat

Likelihood of Release	Waste Characteristics	Targets
observed contamination	toxicity, hazardous waste quantity	resident individual, resident population, workers, resources, terrestrial-sensitive environments

b. Nearby Population Threat

attractiveness/accessibility, area of contamination	toxicity, hazardous waste quantity	population within 1 mile, nearby individual

AIR

Likelihood of Release	Waste Characteristics	Targets
observed release vs. potential release, Gas: gas containment, gas source type, gas migration potential, Particulate: particulate containment, particulate source type, particulate migration potential	toxicity/mobility, hazardous waste quantity	resources, population within a 4-mile radius, nearest individual, sensitive environments

*Mobility applicable for groundwater to surface water component.

EPA: *The Revised Hazardous Ranking System - Background Information.* [Bulletin]. U.S. EPA/Office of Solid Waste and Emergency Response, EPA 9320.7–03FS, November 1990. pp. 5–10.

A status update may be obtained, or the entire file may be accessed. However, a request for a copy of the entire file could result in a couple of file boxes worth of proceedings and documents. Try to be specific and detail the information requested.

CERCLA Information List

The Comprehensive Environmental Response, Compensation, and Liability Act Information System (CERCLIS) contains data on potential and known hazardous waste sites. This encompasses sites with the potential for releasing hazardous substances into the environment as well as those on the state or federal NPL which are known to pose an imminent threat.

Minimum Search Distance for CERCLA Sites: 0.5 mile

Information which is provided by the database includes facility name, address, type of ownership, NPL status, and assessment status. If a site has already been scored in accordance with the NPL Hazard Ranking System and did not make the list, the printout will state "No Further Action." Other comments include:

- "Further investigation" is indicated.
- "Proposed" for inclusion to the NPL.
- "Final" proposal accepted to NPL.

Any or all of the above actions may have been performed by the EPA or contracted with the pertinent state. The CERCLIS printout will contain this information as well.

As of October 1992, there were 34,618 sites listed. This number changes daily.

A site listing on the CERCLIS does not necessarily mean it is contaminated. Likewise, the absence of a site on the inventory does not mean it is free of contaminants or should not be listed. It means that someone identified the site as potentially hazardous. Others may go unnoticed.

RCRA Databases

The Resource Conservation and Recovery Act (RCRA), or the Solid Waste Disposal Act, was first enacted on October 21, 1976. It was one of the first attempts by the EPA to control hazardous wastes, and states share the responsibility to oversee the programs.

> Minimum search distances for RCRA sites:
> TSDF - 1 mile
> LQG and SQG - 0.5 mile
> Transporters - Property and adjacent area

The law directs the EPA to establish and administer a national program for the safe management of hazardous waste. Subtitle C of RCRA establishes a means for regulating generation, transportation, treatment, storage, and disposal of hazardous materials. The intent is to track hazardous wastes from "cradle to grave." Table 6-3 has a summary overview of the facilities which are included. The number listed in the table was the number of facilities listed in this category as of June 1991.

In 1980, a database was created to more easily track information. Databases presently available under RCRA are the RCRA Information System and Biennial Review System.

RCRA Information System

The RCRA Information System (RCRIS) is a management and inventory program for hazardous materials handling. Handlers may fall into one or a combination of the following categories:

- Treatment, Storage, and Disposal Facilities (TSDFs)
- Large-Quantity Generators (LQG)
- Small-Quantity Generators (SQG)
- Transporters

A list of handlers, referred to as an RCRA Notifier's list, includes all those who have supplied identification information. It has been speculated by some that only 60 percent of all actual hazardous waste handlers are identified, and to complicate matters locating the facilities may sometimes be difficult.

Table 6-3.   RCRA Subtitle C (June 1991)

4,300 Treatment, Storage, Disposal Facilities	A facility that treats, stores, or disposes of hazardous waste. Examples: incinerators and landfills.
15,350 Large-Quantity Generators	A generator that generates 1,000 kilograms, or more, of hazardous waste a calendar month; or 1 kilogram, or more of acutely hazardous waste in a calendar month. Example: chemical manufacturing plant.
210,000 Small-Quantity Generators	A generator that generates less than 1,000 kilograms of hazardous waste in a calendar year, or less than 1 kilogram of acutely hazardous waste in a month. Example: a dry cleaner.
19,700 Transporters	A person engaged in the off-site transportation of hazardous waste by air, rail, highway, or water. Example: overnight delivery services.

*About 2,300 TSDFs also generate large quantities of hazardous waste.

U.S. EPA: *RCRA Hazardous Waste Information Management Executive Summary*. [Bulletin] U.S. EPA, Washington, DC, p. 2.

Except for the transporters, RCRA identification numbers are supposed to be site specific, not by company. Historically, however, many notifiers took their identification number with them when they moved or added another location. Thus, the reporting system broke down, and the intent to identify-by site—failed. Although this problem is being rectified, an ESA professional should be aware of the possibility for an information maze.

The RCRIS has the RCRA Notifier's list, permitting activities, corrective actions, and compliance records. Yet, the RCRA Notifier's list is the only source for information pertaining to all handlers. Other RCRA information systems are as follows:

- Permitting Activities - TSDFs
- Corrective Actions - TSDFs and LQG
- Compliance Records - TSDFs, LQG, and Transporters

Permits are required of TSDFs. They must complete and submit Parts A and B of the Hazardous Waste Permit application. Part A summarizes specific types of activities, and Part B details information pertaining to safe construction, operation, and eventual closure of a specific type of activity. Land disposal facilities must also include a plan for post-closure care and groundwater monitoring. Adequacy is judged by state and regional EPA officials.

Corrective actions are imposed upon TSDFs and LQGs by state and federal EPA officials wherever RCRA-regulated sites require cleanup due to an environmental release of hazardous waste.

Compliance records are maintained for TSDFs, LQGs, and Transporters. These are often referred to as the Compliance Monitoring and Enforcement Log (CMEL), nicknamed the "Camel" report. These records contain information concerning inspection dates, waste violations, and enforcement activities.

In brief, the RCRIS is a directional guide to provide information as to those who may potentially pollute the environment, where they are located, and compliance history. The potential for each of the identified sources within a given radius of the site should be considered. That radius may vary from 1/2 to 4 miles. Air emissions may require a 1- to 4-mile radius, whereas solid waste requires less due to its decreased potential for migration.

Biennial Reporting System

The Biennial Reporting System (BRS) collects data on the generation, management, and minimization of hazardous waste. It details data on the generation of hazardous waste from large-quantity generators (LQG) and on waste management practices of treatment, storage, and disposal facilities (TSDFs). The information is collected annually and is intended to enable trend analyses.

TSDFs and LQGs are required to submit information biennially on the quantity and type of waste generated, waste management practices, and waste minimization efforts to the state or regional EPA officials. Databases provide generation and management history, and waste minimization activities. Management practices are only provided for TSDFs.

Prior to 1980, the only way to obtain data, which is now being provided by databases, was to review the actual site records. Yet, long hours of digging through files and stacks of paper are becoming a thing of the past. Also, industrial usage of other property would not normally be available, and speculation was required to theorize the possibilities of hazardous waste migration from another property. Industrial records are entered into an easy-to-access database which is available to the public. The Biennial Reporting System abbreviates specific industrial site waste management practices which were, in years past, unmanageable.

Federal Tracking System

The Facility Index System (FINDS) contains an inventory of facilities which are monitored by the EPA. There has been an attempt to consolidate the databases and give each site one EPA identification number instead of a different number for each program. Without this system, each database assigns a different number to the same site. One location may have as many as 15 different identification numbers, and tracking a site is complicated by volume.

The FINDS list has the facility name, the physical address, a single EPA identification number, and a source. Source numbers are associated with systems. The list may include sites from the following databases:

- CERCLIS
- RCRIS
- Permit Compliance System (PCS) - Wastewater discharge facilities.
- Aerometric Information Retrieval System (AIRS) - Facilities which are monitored or permitted for air emissions under the Clean Air Act.
- Federal Insecticide, Fungicide, and Rodenticide Act and Toxic Substances Control Act Tracking Enforcement Systems (FATES) - Corporations or facilities involved in pesticide production.
- FTTS/NCDB - Industrial discharge into U.S. waterways.
- Enforcement Docket System (DOCKET) - Facilities undergoing civil, judicial, or administrative enforcement.
- Enforcement and Compliance Monitoring
- Federal Facility Information System (FFIS) - Facilities that have submitted specific environmental project budget plans.
- Chemicals in Commerce Information System (CICIS) - Chemical manufacturers who submitted chemical production information in response to the 1977 Toxic Substances Control Act inventory rule.
- State Regulated Facilities (STATE) - Facilities that are regulated by a state environmental program.

- PCB Data System (PADS) - PCB generators, storers, transporters, or permitted disposers.
- Resource Conservation and Recovery Act - J System (RCRA-J) Transporters and on-site incinerators of regulated medical waste.
- Toxic Release Inventory System (TRIS) - Facilities that release any of the more than 300 extremely hazardous substances stipulated in the reporting rule, which are in excess of threshold amounts.
- Chemical Update System (CUS) - Facilities which have manufactured or imported in excess of 10,000 pounds of specific toxic chemicals in the preceding fiscal year.

At the writing of this book, the FINDS database has been recently created and still has a few flaws. Entries may or may not have been made; therefore, the system is not to be relied upon until data entry problems have been resolved.

Information retrieval may be by alphabetical listing, identification number, city, state, and/or zip code. Any combination of these may be requested in the FOIA.

STATE/LOCAL LISTINGS AND DATABASES

Each state differs as to the agency assigned to maintain and enforce federal regulations. Where the pertinent agency is unknown, the regional EPA office will have this information. State governments are charged with enforcing the federal laws, yet each state has the option to enact a stricter requirement.

Likewise, local governments may be charged with the responsibility for enforcement of some of the state requirements. They must comply with minimum state requirements.

State Priority Lists

States manage a program similar to the national Superfund program, and each maintains a listing similar to the NPL. These lists do not include the NPL sites in that state. They identify, manage, enforce, and seek cost recoveries in a similar manner to that of the federal government—under state law.

Underground Storage Tanks

Underground storage tanks (USTs) and their associated pipes store not only petroleum but a wide range of products ranging from industrial solvents and acids to hydraulic fluid and motor oil waste. Although it is not know at this time how many are leaking, the EPA estimate, as of 1988, was over 25 percent of all USTs are leaking. Many have the potential for impacting the groundwater.

Subtitle I to the Resource Conservation and Recovery Act of 1984 required the EPA to develop regulations to protect human health and the environment from leaking USTs. Regulated under this act are the following:

- Petroleum, crude oil, and any fraction thereof.
- Substances designated as hazardous under CERCLA, excluding those which also fall under RCRA.

Some USTs are not included in the regulation. These include the following:

- Farm and residential tanks holding 1,100 gallons or less of motor fuel, used for noncommercial purposes.
- Tanks storing heating oil, used on the premises where it is stored.
- Tanks on or above the floor of underground areas (e.g., basements and tunnels).
- Septic tanks and systems for collecting storm water and wastewater.
- Flow-through process tanks.
- Tanks holding 110 gallons or less.
- Emergency spill and overfill tanks.

The law mandates minimum leak controls: leak detection, corrosion protection, and secondary containments (e.g., double lined tanks and pipes) spill/overfill prevention. The depth of involvement within each of these controls is different for new tanks/piping versus existing tanks/piping. Abandonment, or closure, requirements are also detailed for permanent and temporary closing of a tank.

Whenever an underground storage tank is to be abandoned permanently, it must be removed or filled with sand or concrete. Temporary closure (less than 12 months) involves capping all lines, except the vent line and continued leak detection and corrosion protection.

The available databases are the underground storage tank listing and the leaking underground storage tank listing. Proximity sites should be located on the map and evaluated for potential impact on the property under investigation.

Underground Storage Tank Listing

Each state maintains and manages a "product" UST registration program and database management of tank conditions. Many of these USTs contain petroleum, but others contain highly toxic substances. This law does not cover USTs containing hazardous wastes. The latter is covered under RCRA.

Registration requirements apply to all product USTs in all states and aboveground storage tanks in many states. In both instances, ground contamination may result from leaks in the container, around the pipe fittings, and from operator overflows/errors. One instance involved a trucker who backed into an aboveground storage tank while performing other duties and knocked off the supply nozzle and drove away, leaving the contents of a 10,000-gallon container to spill to the ground.

> Minimum Search Distance for USTs:
> Property and Adjacent Properties

The aboveground storage tank list is sometimes part of the UST listing. A large aboveground storage vessel may contain one million gallons of material. Large numbers of aboveground petroleum and crude oil containers are called "tank farms." The author recommends aboveground storage tanks be included as part of the investigation even though they are not included in the minimum topics to be covered. They may have a substantial impact on the environment. However, there are numerous aboveground butane tanks which when they leak will pose a fire/explosion hazard, not a groundwater concern. Thus, consider the contents when evaluating potentials.

Owners are required to register their tanks and pertinent tank information with the state agency assigned to manage the program and provide updates whenever there are any changes. Retrievable database information may include the facility name, owner, physical address, manager's name and phone number, number of tanks, tank size, substance stored, year installed, type of construction material, corrosion protection, capacity, and leak detection information.

Although enacted in 1988, registration requirements include obsolete tanks as well as those still in use and new units. If a tank is obsolete or temporarily out of service, the owner was and still is required to report its status. With this ruling comes a harsh daily monetary penalty for not reporting. Yet, the knowledgeable party may be long gone; and an obsolete, potentially leaking underground storage tank may go unreported. One source speculates that "when completed according to the federal requirements, the lists of [USTs] will contain less than 50 percent of all existing underground storage tanks and very few of the sites of tanks that ceased to function prior to 1980."[1]

In brief, the UST listing will locate underground (sometimes aboveground) storage tanks. This list provides information as to the status of the tanks and provide information which can be used to determine leak potential. Should signs of USTs be noted during the site or area reconnaissance, a failure to be listed should not be taken as an indication of obsolescence or adequate "abandonment or closing." The location may be included in the speculative evaluation of the property under Investigation.

Leaking Underground Storage Tank Listings

Leaking Underground Storage Tank (LUST) listings are available through the same state-designated agency which provides the PST list. It contains information on facilities with leaking underground storage tanks and their status and priority. Status may include one of the following:

- Notice Pending
- Remediation in Progress
- Remediation Complete
- Inadequate Response

Priorities are based on the type of impact. Groundwater impact of a major aquifer which supplies water to thousands of people would be assigned a high priority, over contaminated subsurface soil which impacts the air in a single-family dwelling. High priorities include the potential for groundwater contamination, particularly major aquifers; the potential for migrating to underground pipes (e.g., cracked sewer lines); and the potential for migrating upward to largely populated areas (e.g., cracks and fissures in the ground).

> Minimum Search Distance for LUST: 0.5 mile

Contamination of a major aquifer can impact thousands of lives. A community's water source may be shut down; cleanup, if possible, could cost millions of dollars and many years of remediation.

Some hazardous substances may migrate a considerable distance into, along, and through sewage pipes, septic tanks, and basements. There are reported instances of petroleum leaks resulting in fires and explosions in areas remote from the source (e.g., toilets exploding in homes).

Leaking USTs may also pose a potential health hazard. In April 1992, the community located around a petrochemical storage facility east of Austin, Texas, developed concerns over existing gasoline leaks and subsequent soil contamination. The petroleum "tank farm" owners were forced to move, and complaints of health effects still persist.

In brief, the leaking UST listing identifies known sites of leaking underground storage tanks. The list provides information as to location and cleanup status. An in-depth status report may require a phone interview with the compliance officer or a visit to the central files.

Community Right-to-Know Records

The Emergency Planning and Community Right-to-Know Act was created under Title III of the Superfund Amendments and Reauthorization Act (SARA) of 1986. Its intent is to provide easy access to information which may be required in case of an emergency. An emergency may include, but not be limited to, fire involving hazardous materials, emergency release of hazardous substances, and facility environmental monitoring.

An inventory must be performed and a summary of information must be reported annually by all facilities that manage hazardous materials. Over 500,000 "hazardous" chemicals which are used and/or generated are considered. This includes pure substances, mixtures, fuels, solvents, and other consumer products. Chemical information for each hazardous material is reported as follows:

- Name (i.e., chemical and common name)
- Type of material (i.e., mix, solid, liquid, gas, and/or extremely hazardous in concentrations of 1 percent or greater)
- Type of hazard (i.e., fire, pressure, reactivity, acutely toxic, or chronic toxicity)

- Amount by weight
- Peak storage quantity
- Time stored on-site and usage
- Location
- Hazard rating

These inventory sheets are filed with the designated state controlling agency, local emergency planning committee, and local fire marshall. The annual filing is a minimum requirement. Should a facility purchase, use, and/or generate any of over 300 extremely hazardous materials (e.g., greater than 100 pounds of hydrocyanic acid) in excess of a published limit, the facility must update its files immediately.

Do not confuse this inventory of hazardous substances with the in-house inventory used to list MSDSs for the Employee Right-to-Know Law. The Community Right-to-Know list is more directed to locating the material, volume, a summary of hazards, and environmental impact.

Information may be sought on the state or local level either by reviewing the files or requesting copies as per the "FOIA." Each state has a different system, but the local fire marshall maintains the records in case of a fire or other community emergency.

This reporting requirement was implemented by designated state agencies. All filings were to have been completed by 1992, with a copy sent to the local fire marshall.

In brief, the Community Right-to-Know Law is a source of information concerning reported hazardous substance inventories at a given location. Because the law has only recently been implemented by the states, records are very recent and past inventory information is not available. This is, however, a source of information concerning hazardous substances used by businesses which surround the property being assessed.

Landfills/Solid Waste Disposal Sites

Under RCRS, state governments must designate an agency to regulate landfills and/or solid waste disposal sites. The investigator will need to determine the appropriate agency to contact in the state where the property is located. Solid waste disposal sites can be a very real threat to the surrounding environments, and their potential impact on the property being assessed should be considered in all investigations.

Prior to the Solid Waste Disposal Act of 1980, hazardous waste was disposed of indiscriminately, with little or no recordkeeping, no consideration of soil types or proximity/potential impact on groundwater in locating the sites, or concern for the environment. As a result, many of these sites now pose a threat to the groundwater and have subsequently been listed on the NPL, state priority list, or CERCLIS. As of August 1987, there was a total of 808 abandoned waste sites which were listed on the NPL, 75 percent of which were documented to have impacted the groundwater.

There are several cases whereby property adjacent to an abandoned landfill was developed, or the site itself was developed. Later, the hazardous material migrated and posed a health hazard to the associated land owners. The end result was forced abandonment of homes and commercial buildings.

Even the location of a nonhazardous site, relative to the property, may be important. There have been records of landfill gases rising from an abandoned sanitary landfill up into an apartment complex which was built on the site. Subsequently, the apartments had to be evacuated.

> Minimum Search Distance for Landfill and/or
> Solid Waste Disposal Sites: 0.5 mile

Land disposal of liquid/solid waste is done by industrial waste management facilities, sanitary landfills, and waste disposal wells. Hazardous substances may migrate from any of these sites.

Industrial waste management facilities handle waste from large industrial activities. They are categorized into classes, i.e., Class I, II, and III. A Class I landfill manages extremely hazardous materials. Type of soil and opportunity for contamination to enter the groundwater and/or impact the environment is used to determine the lining requirements. Once the lining has been installed, material is brought in, checked for content and proper containerization, logged, tagged, categorized, isolated from chemicals with which it may react, and charted as to its location within the site. Past management of hazardous wastes were inadequate, resulting in improper protection of the groundwater.

A Class II landfill manages moderately hazardous materials which are generally degradable. This includes many solvents, gasoline, and heavy metals.

A Class III landfill manages hazardous materials which are not expected to leach into the ground. This includes rubber tires and metal shavings.

Sanitary landfills receive waste products from residences, small industries, and some commercial activities (e.g., grocery stores). These wastes are generally, but not always, nonhazardous. They will not accept tires, explosives, or certain hazardous materials. City restrictions may vary.

A waste disposal well, or injection well, is a deep well which serves the purpose of isolating hazardous/nonhazardous wastes. These wells are generally installed in rock formations where migration is not anticipated. This is a relatively new method of disposal and some states don't permit them, due to the types of soil.

Air Emissions Records

The federal government requires state governments to enforce air emissions standards, and sometimes the state requires the local governments to monitor their own areas. This requirement for air emissions control was mandated under NESHAPS and the Clean Air Act. Each state has its own designated air emissions control agency, its own recordkeeping requirements, and a means by which the investigator may retrieve records of air monitoring compliance.

This information may be helpful where there is a RCRA generator adjacent to the property. A hazardous substance is emitted into the air, and the material could impact the property. Although airborne hazards resulting property contamination are becoming a thing of the past, a site may have their scrubbing system go down or increase their operations such that the airborne contaminants are more excessive than that which was previously monitored.

There are also allegations that a government official may be paid to look the other way. One such case is alleged to have occurred in a small southern town where a pesticide manufacturer was on record for being in compliance and the community had the soil checked for arsenic. They found that the levels were significant, and the manufacturer proceeded to purchase all the property surrounding the plant.

Once again, anything is possible. This extensive a records search is just another tool.

FEDERAL AND STATE SPILL LISTINGS

The list of sources contained within this section is not all inclusive. There are other methods for tracking unplanned releases and spills, and they vary by state.

Emergency Response Notification System

The Emergency Response Notification System (ERNS) is an EPA database which contains information concerning unplanned releases of oil and hazardous substances by location. These releases have been reported to the federal government by the generator, a witness, or a compliance official. The EPA database includes date of the release, name of the discharger, type of hazardous material released, cause of the release, location of the incident, and amount of material involved.

> Minimum Search Distance for ERNS: Property Only

This information may be used to determine other known sources of environmental contamination. Many of this will be minor spills, but some may be significant (e.g., a train derailment involving a formaldehyde transport tank to overturn). The investigator may choose a larger search area for potential releases than being restricted to the property only.

Toxic Release Inventory System

The Toxic Release Inventory System (TRIS) is an EPA database of facilities that release any of more than 300 extremely hazardous substances stipulated in the reporting rule as being in excess of threshold amounts. These are the larger generators. This database provides a limited overview as to potential contaminants resulting from a more noteworthy spill. The investigator may choose to extend this search outside the property, particularly in areas where spills are likely to occur (e.g., an industrial community).

State Spill Databases

State agencies maintain a more nearly complete, up-to-date list of unplanned releases and spills. The pertinent state agency can be identified by contacting the regional EPA office. The state databases should be more up-to-date and complete than the federal ones.

SUMMARY

Many of the listings and databases of "known" sources of hazardous materials management may be obtained from designated state and federal agencies. The most commonly required searches are the following listings/databases:

- National and State Priority Lists
- CERCLIS
- RCRA Databases
  - Treatment, Storage, and Disposal Facilities
  - Large-Quantity Generators
  - Small-Quantity Generators
  - Transporters
- Landfills/Solid Waste Disposal Sites
- Petroleum Underground Storage Tanks
- Leaking Petroleum Underground Storage Tanks
- ERNS

Other listings which may or may not be required include the following:

- Air Emissions Records
- TRIS
- State Unplanned Release and Spill Listings

The search radius which constitutes the "surrounding area" varies from one site to the next. Minimum search distance around an assessment property are a 0.5 to 1 mile. These are recommended "minimums" and are subject to the environmental setting and circumstances. An environmental setting where migration potential is considerable may require greater search distances to identify potential contamination of an assessment property. The investigator may choose, in the latter situation, to increase the 1 mile search to a 5 mile search to 1 or 2 miles.

Information sources are abundant, beyond those listed in this book. Each situation is different and should be handled accordingly. Some sites may require additional information not mentioned here. Others where the minimum is performed may seem overdone. This may seem to be apparent before the search has been completed. Then again, there may be a few surprises!

REFERENCES

1.   EPA: *National Priorities List for Uncontrolled Hazardous Waste Sites; Rule and Proposed Rule.* U.S. EPA/Office of Solid Waste and Emergency Response, Washington, DC, 57 FR 47180, October 14, 1992.

Chapter 7

Property and Area Reconnaissance

INTRODUCTION

A site and area reconnaissance is performed in order to "observe existing conditions and activities," not apparent through other means, which may have resulted in property contamination. The investigator attempts to identify potential sources of environmental contamination, not previously identified, and to evaluate possible means by which the soil and water may become contaminated. Sometimes a reconnaissance will confirm suspicions. At other times, it will open new avenues for further investigation.

Although the process appears to be quite simple, this attitude can result in an oversight. The process will require common sense, an analytical mind, and persistence. If something appears out of place—it probably is! An old dirt road overgrown with vegetation has a reason for being and it should be questioned. Although many of these issues are discussed within this chapter, the realm of possibilities is limited only by one's imagination.

RECONNAISSANCE OF THE PROPERTY

A "site reconnaissance" is a thorough investigation of the grounds and all buildings on the property. Chapter 9 contains the methodology for evaluating buildings which should be accomplished during the grounds inspection. All activities performed in and around the buildings have an impact on the property, and the property may have had other uses than may have been derived from the historic usage background search, presented in Chapter 5.

Plan the visit. The site investigator may require special equipment. For instance, an 8-hour walk through of a densely vegetated, 200-acre lot, on a hot, humid day may require a machete, lightweight and heavy duty boots, a long-sleeved shirt, a water jug, and a backpack. If planning on performing some form of sample collecting, take the necessary equipment. Think in terms of accessibility, consolidation of supplies, and reduced bodily discomforts.

Area diagrams are a must. They include a copy of the plat and area map. Plan on getting them dirty, marking them up extensively (e,g,. locating 55-gallon drums), and taking extensive notes. See Figure 7-1.

Improper, or the lack of enough supplies can be cumbersome and inconvenient. Taking too much adds to the confusion. Taking too little may necessitate an additional trip to retrieve needed items and can be time-consuming. Always carry a clipboard and take several permanent markers or pencils. Papers are going to get wet and dirty, so use permanent markers or pencils which will not bleed and result in an ink blot for notes.

Prior to departing for the site, review collected information. Take notes and generate questions. The review should include, but not be limited to, the following:

- Environmental setting
- Historic usage of the property
- Building records
- Regulatory agency listings

The investigator should attempt a visual evaluation of every square foot of the property, but it is not always feasible to walk an entire area. To overstate the obvious, a flat, barren 1-acre plot of land is easier and less time-consuming than a 1,000-acre parcel of property with gullies and thick vegetation.

When it is not feasible to investigate every foot of the property, minimum coverage should include the following:

- Around the perimeter of the property
- All surface water routes, including dry creek beds
- All roads, paved and unpaved
- All areas which are reasonably accessible

Some of the more common techniques which are used to assure adequate coverage of "accessible land" include one or a combination of the following:

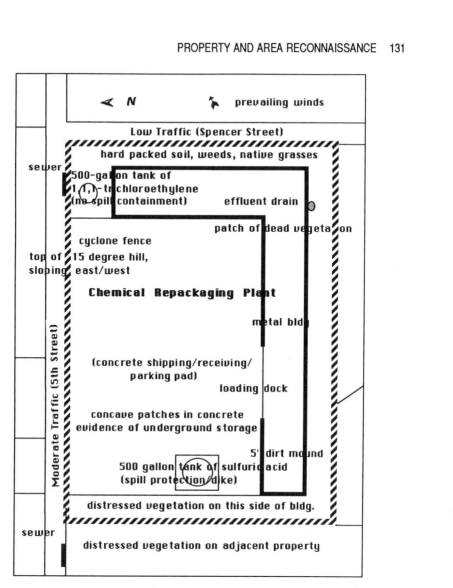

Figure 7-1.   Sketch of property grounds, notes taken during the site reconnaissance. (Notes taken of features which may influence or impact the environment.)

- Parallel Coverage - The property can be walked by following parallel patterns, with 5- to 20-feet separations from the center. The distance from each centerline should depend on the ground visibility.
- Expanding Circles/Squares - The property can be walked by starting at the center and walking outward in a methodical fashion. This may involve a walk around a high point or an assessable portion.

Property with a central focal point (e.g., a hill) with a shape conducive to this approach is the most likely candidate for this technique.

Last, prior to departure to the site, contact the person(s) designated as the contact party for the property. They will want to be kept informed if the investigator is not to be escorted, and they will require notification if the investigator needs an escort.

Once on site, the investigator must be aware of all possibilities and then some. The succeeding items are those most frequently included on the checklist, along with a few other considerations generally overlooked or ignored.

Water Wells

Today, the installation of water wells is a controlled process. 20 years ago, it was not. Now, the well-drilling operator is required by law to cement the surface casing and/or cement intervals where interaquifer transfer may occur. The intent is to prevent travel of soil contaminants from one segregated geologic layer to the next, or to the groundwater. In the past, the driller was not required to comply with any of these procedures, and older wells pose a greater threat to the groundwater than those more recently installed in accordance with acceptable practices. See Figure 7-2 for an example of a poorly installed water well.

Abandoned wells may pose a problem as well. Besides providing a "hot spot" for someone to fall into, abandoned wells may serve as an easy means for illegal dumping of hazardous materials. The well water may be associated with an aquifer which is used by others who may unknowingly drink the contaminated water. A small community, using well water, may develop an increased incidence of an exotic illness. The occurrence of miscarriages and/or deformed fetuses may increase. A rare debilitating disease may affect large numbers of a community. A rare form of cancer may prevail. Sometimes these latter scenarios are the only reason for suspicion within a given population.

There have been cases where abandoned wells doubled for a septic system. Household waste has been innocently piped out to a big hole in the ground. Although the human waste generally breaks down to a non-hazardous substance, there is a potential for conveyance of parasites and bacteria which may be in the feces. There also may have been other wastes disposed of, such as household paint products or motor oil waste.

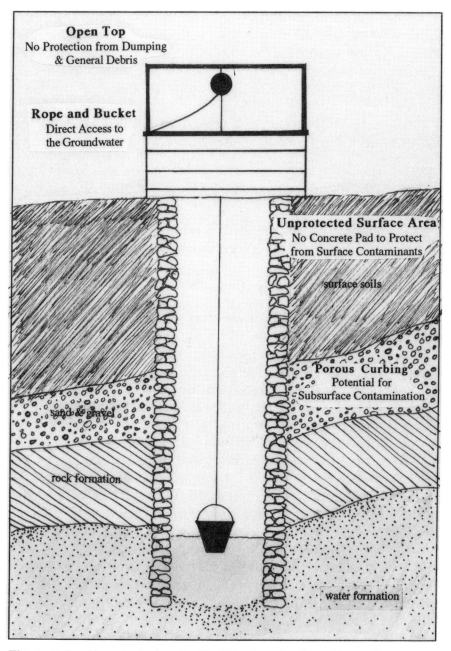

Figure 7-2. Unprotected well. Partial extraction from Texas Department of Health: Individual Home Water Supplies. Texas Department of Health, Austin, Texas. Stock No., 2-105, October, 1970. p. 18.

Some second world countries still have systems whereby the water wells are not encased and adequately separated from the community septic system. They have no more than a hole into which their household and septic waste is discharged. Next to the waste hole is an unprotected water well. These countries have a lot of problems with fecal-transmitted diseases.

All water wells should be evaluated and possibilities considered. Further research may be indicated after the site visit.

Drinking Water Sources and Quantity

The drinking water may come from personal water wells, cisterns, or city supplies. The city water source may be a lake, reservoir, river, or aquifer.

Today, personal water wells are initially analyzed for quality, and unless the owner is suspicious, the well may not get checked again. Contamination may occur subsequent to the initial check, and the owner or potential buyer may not be aware of the contaminant. If there is reason to be suspicious, the investigator may collect a sample of the water and have it analyzed for the suspect hazardous substance. This may require collection of the water in a sterile, quart-sized, glass jar with inert sealing material. Prior to analysis, information concerning the methodology for taking the sample and means for shipping it should be confirmed with the analytical laboratory which will perform the analysis.

A cistern is a water retention device, built into the ground, for collection and storage of bathing and/or drinking water. It may be a rain-collection container at the base of a roof drain spout. It may be a primitive hole in the ground, or it may be an insulated, contained bladder built into the ground. An abandoned cistern may serve as a means for contaminant disposal, or it may be physically dangerous from a safety point of view (e.g., a child falling in). Some older cisterns also contained lead sealant, a source for lead contamination of the environment. See Figure 7-3.

The city water may be on an old system, and lead solder may have been used in some of the soldered joints where there are metal pipes or there may be lead pipe present. The city will be able to provide information concerning lead content of the supply lines. Then, too, the lines leading from the supply main may have lead. Lead content in the water can be determined as per Chapter 9. If the results of a sample from a home/building exceed the acceptable limit of 15 ppb (parts per billion), this

Figure 7-3.   Old cistern found around an old frame house.

should be compared with the supply line analysis performed by the municipality.

Debris

Many properties which have yet to be developed have become a convenient dumping ground.   Dumping is generally in the form of household junk and motor oil, but industrial dumping may occur as well.

Domestic dumping may include old tires, auto parts or whole automobiles, plastic jugs, paper, roofing material (possibly containing asbestos), cleaning product containers, unused paint, and so on. See Figure 7-4.

Figure 7-4.   Domestic debris with asbestos-containing roof shingles.

Industrial dumping comes in all sizes, shapes, and forms. Containers may—but will probably not—be labeled and certainly will not be traceable. There are any number of scenarios possible. As the cost of industrial disposal increases, the temptation for illegal dumping increases.

Chemical Storage Drums

Today, all chemicals which are shipped directly from a manufacturer or distributor must be labeled with the trade name, manufacturer, and specific hazards associated with the chemical. Labels provide information as to chemicals used on-site in a manufacturing operation. Take notes, even where there appears to be no associated problem with the container(s).

Sometimes a container is not labeled. Labels may get damaged in shipment, worn away by weather, torn off through rough handling, or eaten away by chemicals (e.g., sulfuric acid dripping down the side of a glass bottle). In some of the worst hazardous waste sites within the United States, there are hundreds of thousands of such drums. Many leak, and the chemicals in two adjacent drums may not be compatible. In other words, they may leak out, mix with one another, and result in a fire or an explosion. They may also react with one another to produce a toxic gas. Some may have a residue in the lid, around the opening, which will explode when the container is opened (e.g., oxidized hydrogen peroxide crystals). See Figure 7-5.

Likewise, the drum may never have had a label. A chemical may have been transferred from a marked container to an unmarked container. The drum may only contain water, or it may contain explosives. Unmarked drums which cannot be identified by anyone should be handled with respect.

Sometimes the contents of drums are known, but their whereabouts is unknown. For instance, witnesses know that several mercury-containing drums were buried in a field, but do not know their exact location. Steel drums have a "maximum life expectancy" of 50 years, and locating suspected burial sites requires speculation and extensive soil sampling (i.e., a Phase II assessment). Some may also be detected by the use of a magnetometer.

Soil Mounds

Backfill is identified by obvious disturbances in the surface of the soil. In a field of vegetation and/or grass, newly placed backfill will not have anything growing on it. Yet, within weeks grass will grow and the site may be recognizable only by the presence of a mound. See Figure 7-6.

Containerized and non-containerized substances may have been dumped into a hole and backfilled. The method of hole preparation and soil coverage may be that of a modern day landfill with special liners and soil-type precautions, or it may involve a blatant disregard for the environment. A chemical may be poured into a hole of highly porous soil with no attempt to contain its spread, or drums with a limited life expectancy may be randomly placed into a hole.

Look for mounds which seem out of place (e.g., a 10 feet high, 20 feet wide mound in the center of a flat field with no explanation or rationale for its presence). A mound may be nothing more than the excess

Figure 7-5.   Old drum, found in pasture.

from property leveling, or it may be a small landfill of drums containing hazardous wastes. Its purpose may be explained by the owner; or, where there is no rationale for its presence, a mound will require further speculation.

Ground Depressions

Concave surfaces may be found over an area where the contents of a drum have seeped into the ground and all the containers have collapsed under the pressure of the soil or where buried debris has degraded. This area may be a small 5-foot diameter depression in the soil, or it could be

Figure 7-6.   Soil mound, concealing hazardous waste.

a hundred feet across. In the latter, it is easier to observe a depression by looking at aerial photos than walking an area. See Figure 7-7.

Where obsolete underground storage tanks may collapse, asphalt/ concrete surface covering will cave in also. There may be other signs of the existence of such a structure, or all other evidence may have been destroyed. In the latter situation, there may be no other clue as to the presence of such a tank—without the observed depression(s).

Distressed, Stained Soil

Mishandled chemicals may result in contaminated grounds. This may involve spills, container leaks, or intentional dumping. In the soil, the

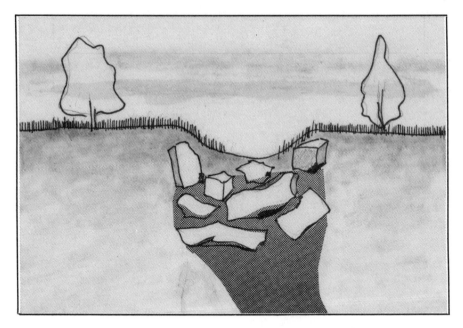

Figure 7-7. Ground depression, collapsed waste containers

contaminant may migrate into the subsurface soils, surface water, and groundwater. Some of the signs of mishandling include extreme dryness, cracking, discoloration, a distinct wet spot next to a chemical storage container or where one used to be, noticeable sheen, or residue ring. These items should be noted for possible investigation at a future date. See Figure 7-8.

Poor or No Growth of Vegetation

The lack of vegetation in an area which is typically vegetated may be due to poisoning. This may be related to an herbicide, or it may be related to contamination by a hazardous substance or material which will not allow growth. Further investigation is indicated. See Figure 7-9.

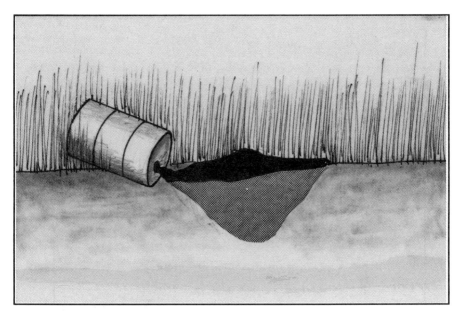

Figure 7-8. Stained soil, leaking into the ground.

Dead Wildlife

Dead animals around a water source scream of contaminated, poisoned waters. However, do not assume the water is contaminated with chemicals. The deaths may be due to disease or some other factor which may not be readily apparent. Yet, this deserves an investigation (i.e., a Phase II site assessment).

Oftentimes, fish are used in laboratories for chemical toxicity testing, due to their extreme sensitivity to toxic substances. Generally, the fish in a stream of contaminated water will die before other wildlife are affected.

Check surface waters which normally have fish. Note whether the fish are flourishing or the water is lifeless. For instance, along the Gulf of Mexico, a manufacturer was dumping heavy metal contaminants into an estuary which was spilling into gulf stream waters. During this time, catfish were dying and washing up on the beach, a fish being deposited every other foot all along the shore. Catfish are bottom feeders. They

Figure 7-9.   Wastewater sludge, used for landfill.

were poisoned by the heavy metal which had settled to the bottom of the gulf shoreline.

Consider again dead animals around a source of water. If the animals are dead and the fish are thriving, look around for other reasons that caused the wildlife to die. If the fish and the animals are dead, it's probably the water. Further research is indicated.

Evidence of Surface Water Contamination

Surface waters include, but are not limited to, lakes, rivers, streams, springs, and creeks. Use your senses to evaluate these. Look, touch, and smell!

Observe the top of the surface waters. Look for a surface sheen or a layer of apparent differentiation (e.g., a thin red layer of an unidentified muck floating on the top of the water).

Excessive soil runoff into the water supplies nutrients and mud to the water. You may not be able to see any fish in such waters, yet they would thrive quite well. The use of surface water as a viable fishing hole may provide clues as to the existence of fish. Surface algae would also indicate the probability of high nutrient levels.

Fecal material may enter into the surface water. It may enter by a makeshift human waste discharge to the surface water. It may be from large numbers of cattle, horses, sheep, and/or other farm animals. This waste will elevate the coliform bacterial growth, carry disease, and provide a breeding ground for undesirable bacteria. The odor may provide a clue.

The edges of the surface water may show signs of contaminants. If the water level has recently dropped or if there is an area where the water has been restricted from entry by diking, the edges may be observed for deposits. An oil deposit will be black and slimy to the touch.

During dry spells, creeks may not have any water. Yet, in the rainy season, the investigator should expect the creek beds to retain water—unless there is a means for water seepage into rock formations. Lack of water in a creek, during the rainy season, could be significant if the water is, or becomes, contaminated. The surface water is going deeper, increasing the possibilities of affecting the groundwater where there is known surface water contamination. Even where the soil and rock provide a very poor means for contaminants to travel to the groundwater and/or aquifers, fissures in the creek bed may provide a direct, easy access to a local private water well or to a reservoir. Material may also migrate by entering shallow, non-potable groundwater and be conveyed to other properties.

Smell and taste the surface water, but don't drink it. Taste a small amount from a wetted finger. Does it have an odor? If so, describe the odor in your notes. Be forewarned. No two people will describe a given odor the same way. Odd smells and/or tastes should be further investigated.

Surface Impoundments

According to the EPA, a surface water impoundment is a contained surface enclosure (e.g., pits, ponds, and lagoons).[1] Surface water impoundments may be used as settling ponds for separating particulates and/or chemicals from water. In industry, surface impoundments have been used to contain contaminated wastewater. In 1986, the EPA reported that there were over 195,000 waste treatment surface impoundments nationwide. The breakdown was as follows:[2]

- Oil/gas related - 65%
- Mining - 10%
- Agriculture - 9%
- Industrial - 8%
- Municipal - 1.2%
- Other - 6.8%

An additional 3,200 surface impoundments were associated with known hazardous waste management facilities for treatment, storage, and disposal purposes. Then, too, some facilities discharged their wastes directly into nearby surface waters.[2]

Cities may have surface impoundments to which initial street and soil runoff is conveyed for evaporation, leaving behind the contaminants. These contaminants may then be cleaned up and properly disposed of or have, in the past, been left behind when the need no longer existed. See Figure 7-10.

Where a surface impoundment is, or was, present, there may be hazardous substances which are, or were, improperly contained. Further investigation is indicated, and the EPA has published "A Manual for Evaluating Contamination Potential of Surface Impoundments" which provides more in-depth guidance.[1]

Aboveground Structures Other Than Buildings

Aboveground structures include, but are not limited to, chemical storage containers, chemical treatment vats, railroad tracks, sheds, and storage facilities. See Figure 7-11.

Aboveground butane storage containers generally provide a fuel source for heating and cooking. Improper connections and/or management may result in an explosion, resulting in the leveling of buildings and other structures in the immediate vicinity.

Chemicals may be contained within large metal storage containers. Find out what they contain. Look for corrosion, leaks, and spills. Check for secondary spill containment structures (i.e., dikes and concrete pads).

In a sawmill, where wood was being treated with pentachlorophenol, the surface and groundwater was becoming contaminated as the wood came off the treatment line and was stacked on the unprotected ground, next to

Figure 7-10.   Waste and debris in recreational surface water.

a stream. The soil was sandy and highly porous, and the stream was within 20 feet of the off-load stacking area.

Railroad cars frequently carry chemicals. A derailment or an unobserved leak of contents may result in the release of hazardous substances. The area around the tracks should be inspected.

Storage facilities are generally no more than an old wood shack. The structure itself may not pose a problem, yet it may be used to isolate hazardous substances from the main building. Many flammable chemicals are kept in shacks. These should be checked for content (past and present), leaks, and spills. Should any of these appear to be a potential problem, note the structure of the shack, surfacing material, and proximity to other points of interest on the property.

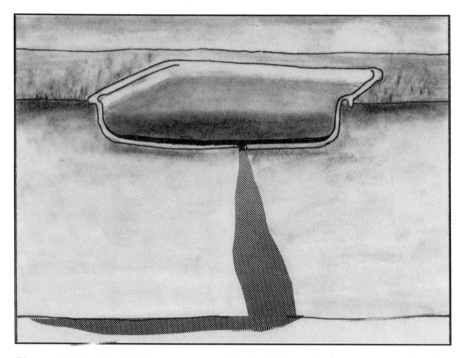

Figure 7-11. Surface impoundment with leaking liner, contaminating the groundwater.

All aboveground structures should be noted. Further investigation may be required.

Signs of Subsurface Structures

Subsurface structures include sanitary sewers, underground transformer vaults, gas/oil pipelines, and underground storage tanks. Most will have some form of visible structure which can be identified. The older they are and the longer they have been obsolete, the greater the chance that the investigator is looking for a "needle in a haystack."

Sanitary sewers should be located and plotted on the area diagram. They may be used either by those on-site or in the periphery for illegal dumping of hazardous waste, or they may provide a conduit for hazardous ground contaminants to travel from a remote site to other properties. Gasoline may enter into a crack in the sanitary sewer, travel up the line into someone's home around an ignition source, and explode.

Structures may contain hazardous chemicals which have traveled from a remote area. There may be an odor. There may be illnesses. Yet, there is no immediately apparent source, and the chemical may go unidentified without a clue as to where it came from or what it might be. This requires a little more investigation.

Transformer vaults are buried in the ground. They are compartmentalized and may have several transformers.

Gas/oil pipelines are frequently identified by a warning sign posted every 100 feet along the easement. They are also identified by long stretches of ground where trees and bushes have not grown and which are more apparent from the air. The previously trenched ground appears to have been disturbed and is frequently differentiated from the surrounding terrain. Leaks may be associated with odor or discoloration.

Either underground storage tanks may be in use at the present, or they may have been closed with the access port sealed and covered with soil or concrete. If not obsolete, they "should" have relief valves and monitoring ports, but don't assume they will. In looking for signs of existing underground storage tanks, observe the grounds. Look for closure plates, adapters for usage, attachments, and vents.

If an underground storage tank has been abandoned, the owner may have gone through proper closure procedures or may have left the tank with chemicals still in it, with or without sealing the openings. These openings are your evidence of its existence. If the owner has sealed the openings and covered the evidence, the obvious signs become more elusive. In such a case, the ground around the buried tank may show signs of settling, or additional cement may have been poured over the access ports. See Figure 7-12.

Ground which has been dug and loosely backfilled may settle creating a concave appearance on the surface. If there was an asphalt or concrete covering, this material may show signs of cracking. If a surfacing material (e.g., concrete) existed prior to an underground storage tank installation, the owner may have had to jack hammer through the material and redo the surface after installation. In the latter situation, the new surface will vary from the old. Note these observations.

Today, they protect underground storage tanks in one or several of the various methods available, and some may have a backup concrete vault. Gasoline underground storage tanks must undergo routine leak testing and

Figure 7-12.   Obsolete service station with concrete patches, evidence of dispensing station.

are reported to the EPA equivalent for the state in which the tanks were installed. Yet, there are many which have not been reported; some have been in the ground for over 50 years and others for as long as 100 years. These are probably steel, are without protection, and most likely are leaking.

Leaks may be due to corrosion, damage to the tank, or inadequate fittings. Corrosion occurs where evaporation and water settling occurs. Other factors which will affect corrosion are type of chemical stored, moisture content, and pH of the soil. Damage can occur "upon installation" where the tank is placed on a sharp, hard object; excessive weight/pressure is applied to the exterior of the tank from aboveground activities and inadequate protection; or the tank had prior damage (e.g., cracks).

Inadequate fittings may result in corroded seals, improper seals, or damaged seals/fittings.

Odors

Be particularly alert to odor; and, remember, not all hazardous chemicals smell bad. The presence of an odor which does not have an explanation should trigger further investigation.

Don't expect to smell "something" and then to go back later and investigate. When you smell something, note the type of odor, intensity, and source. If you have time, try to track it down while the odor is still present. Otherwise, olfactory fatigue will occur, and you may not be able to: 1) smell the chemical, 2) track its source, or 3) differentiate the odor from others.

Effluence from the Building(s)

Effluence is a liquid/solid material which is being discharged from a building or process structure. It may be a hazardous industrial chemical, human waste, or uncontaminated water. It may be discharged through a pipe into a well or water source, or it may be discharged through a hole in the wall to the ground outside. It may pour, or it may dribble. This is the means whereby lakes and streams have been polluted prior to passage of strict regulatory requirements. See Figure 7-13.

Effluence of any kind should be noted. Track down the source. Determine the use of all open-ended pipes which have no explained usage, even if there is no discharge at the time of the site reconnaissance. Further review and search for information may be indicated.

Air Emissions

Contaminated air may be exhausted from a building through a stack, a vent on the side of a building, or an open window or door with the air being forced outside. A system may be sophisticated and have an associated air scrubbing unit, or it may be a simple pedestal fan, blowing contaminants out the window. As with the effluence, the air emissions will require further investigation.

Figure 7-13. Effluent pipe from a building and a septic system discharging industrial waste. The top of the septic tank is visible in the upper left portion of the photo, and the drain field is in the foreground. Many septic systems are neither obvious nor visible.

Signs of Mining/Quarry Activities

Hazards associated with mining activities have to do with the type of mining in progress. For instance, granite will oftentimes have radon, and limestone will have silica. Radon is a radioactive hazard that can cause lung cancer, and silica dust can cause a debilitating lung disease.

Not only will the investigator need to know the type of mining but the processes and procedures common to the industry as well. Figure 7-14 depicts the site of an old quarry, land that has since been developed.

A common source of groundwater contamination around mines is acid-bearing water. Water which extracts minerals from the mine wastes is referred to as "acid mine drainage." Water passes through sulfide mineral components of the tailings (i.e., unused portion of the extracted, mined resource), spoil piles, or the mine/quarry itself. Then, the sulfide is oxidized to sulfuric acid. This may occur anywhere the sulfide content of the soil is high.

Figure 7-14. Remains of old rock quarry. Some of the area received soil from a remote location.

Quarry activities are generally noisy and oftentimes dusty. Past operations have used spent oil to keep down the dust and debris on the dirt roads. Some have had PCBs and other hazardous materials in the oil.

Find out what type of material is being extracted from the land and what will be done with the resulting hole. Some obsolete holes are used for the disposal of wastewater sludge—hazardous and/or non-hazardous material.

Electrical Supply System

Electrical supply systems use transformers to increase or decrease the electricity delivered to a site. These transformers contain a coolant which used to contain polychlorinated biphenyls (PCB). PCBs are a suspected liver carcinogen which is retained in the body for long periods of time. It accumulates in the body and remains in the fatty tissue for extended periods of time. Thus, it only adds to the body burden. It is not readily metabolized or eliminated.

The transformers may contain from trace amounts, 5 ppm (parts per million) of PCBs in the oil, to 5,000 ppm. It is non-flammable; therefore, it has been an excellent substance for use with electrical delivery systems. In 1975, PCBs became outlawed for use in new transformers. Yet, transformers may have a life expectancy of as much as 100 years, and the older transformers have a high probability of PCB content.

The PCB-containing oil does not pose a health hazard unless it gets into the groundwater or is inhaled, absorbed through the skin, or drunk. Leaks and spills may result in airborne exposures and/or be a source of skin contact and absorption. The PCB-containing oil is not an EPA concern unless the amount of PCB contained in the oil is greater than 50 ppm. As long as the material is contained within the transformer and there are no leaks, exposure is a low probability.

There are several types of transformers. They may be: 1) pole-mounted, 2) pad-mounted, or 3) underground vaulted.

The pole-mounted types may be clearly marked "No PCBs." They may not be marked, or they may have a sticker requiring a magnifying glass to read. The electric company that owns the transformer may have records as to PCB content. Yet, they generally do not. You may request a field evaluation by the electric department. It may come back with no more information than you had prior to the request. Where the content is unknown and there is a need to know (i.e., the transformer is leaking onto the site), a sample collection and analysis can be requested from the electric company or a sample may be taken of the leaked material. Leaks generally occur around the seals, including the seals on top of the transformer. The oil is under pressure. Damage to the integrity of the transformer may occur as well. Reports of transformers being subject to target practice are not unheard of.

The pad-mounted transformers don't always have a fluid. Temporary construction site transformers do not contain "oil," and the external cabinet is generally locked on all pad-mounted transformers. Those pad-mounted transformers which do have oil may also leak around the seals. A few drops may look like a puddle, and oil stains are generally observed around the concrete pad on which the transformer has been mounted. See Figure 7-15.

Figure 7-15. Pad-mounted transformer with "No PCB" label.

The underground vaults generally contain multiple transformers, each with different PCB content in the oil. Although some of the vaults are partially underground and accessible for visual inspection, many are under heavy manhole covers. A special tool and/or equipment may be required to open the cover. This should be done by the electric company. Once again, look for leaks and damage to the integrity of the unit.

Cemetery(ies)

Potential pollutants from deteriorated caskets include embalming fluid (i.e., formalin), metals (e.g., arsenic used for embalming during the Civil War era), salts, and microorganisms. For each body buried, there is an average of about 8 quarts of formalin per grave site. Formalin is a 38 percent aqueous solution of formaldehyde with 15 percent methanol. As it is water soluble, the formaldehyde-bearing formalin may easily migrate to the groundwater.

A theoretical situation may also be considered. The formalin has migrated horizontally to your property which is located adjacent to the cemetery. This is a country setting, and your client decides to install a water well. He penetrates the previously impermeable layers of rock and soil, and the well is not properly sealed during penetration. The well, thus, creates a means for formalin contamination of the groundwater.

Although the above scenario is not a recorded event as of this publication, there have been isolated reports of microbial diseases originating in graveyards. In Germany during the late 1800s, people living near cemeteries were reported to have a higher incidence of typhoid fever than the normal population. This was attributed to proximity to a graveyard.[3]

The investigator should also be alert to the potential for a client to install a water well on the property, adjoining a cemetery. A new well may either provide a conduit for the migrated contaminant to enter the groundwater, or the groundwater may already be contaminated. Minimum distances between a cemetery and drinking water wells are required by law in England, France, and Holland. These distances are 300, 328, and 164 feet, respectively.[3]

Other

Note any object or condition which appears to be out of the ordinary or has no explanation for its presence. This may include, but not be limited to, the following:

- Drainage pathways and erosion plains
- Evidence of old structures
- Outcroppings, stockpiles, and embankments
- Heavy equipment
- Monitoring wells
- Gas wells
- Usage of pesticides and/or herbicides
- Tire tracks in the soil

Many of these will not jump out and scream, "I am here!" They must be derived from careful observation.

RECONNAISSANCE OF ADJACENT PROPERTIES

Adjacent properties may have an impact on the targeted property. Ground contamination of one property may migrate to the grounds and/or drinking water of another. Draw a diagram of the area, and identify relevant information on your area drawing or an area map. The succeeding subjects should be addressed. See Figure 7-16.

Property Usage

Property usage is an indicator for what hazardous materials may be used in the area at the present. The property(ies) may be undeveloped or developed; the developed properties may be residential, commercial, or industrial.

Undeveloped property may be used for local dumping. Note what appears to be dumped on these properties. Note where signs of solid waste/liquid dumping are apparent.

The type of commercial/industrial usage should be specified, especially where it may be associated with hazardous substances. As will be discussed in Chapter 10, different commercial/industrial activities have different, known waste products and hazardous chemicals which are used in their processes. For instance, a chrome-plating operation will have chromic acid, and battery recycling plants will have large quantities of lead. Even the construction business generates hazardous waste. Be wary of these processes.

Remember, the adjacent properties also have a history, and it is not feasible to investigate their past—unless something indicates a probable concern. In such a case, the time to accomplish the survey could become greatly lengthened. Thus, it is not feasible to investigate the past of all adjacent properties, unless there is reason to suspect something due to observations made during the reconnaissance or from interviews.

If further investigation is indicated, recommend this be performed. However, your client may be reluctant to pay extra to have this performed just on the basis of a hunch. If, however, the recommendation is ignored, the investigator will be on record as having noted the potential problem.

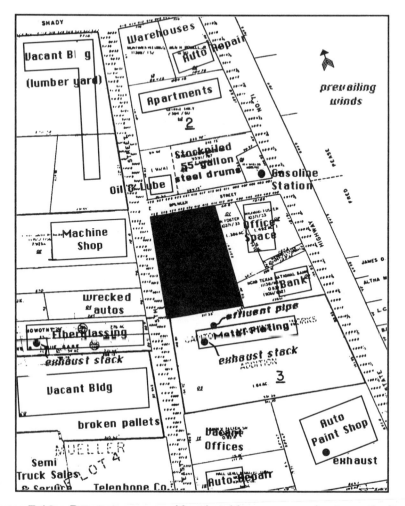

Figure 7-16. Property map used for sketching usage and noteworthy items of adjacent properties.

Storage Tanks/Drums

Note the presence of storage tanks and drums. Locate and check the integrity of all aboveground/underground gasoline storage tanks, butane tanks, chemical tanks, and drums. The underground storage tanks will be easy to identify are those associated with existing gasoline stations. Obsolete gasoline stations are not as obvious as in Figure 7-12.

Aboveground storage tanks are easily identified. An attempt should be made to identify the contents. The contents will generally be noted on the outside of the container, along with warning labels. Yet, the owner may be reluctant to allow access and/or supply information.

Sometimes underground industrial chemical storage tanks can be identified, but identification may be difficult without access to the property or information from workers/management at that location. The information may be helpful.   Yet, obtaining this information may require some additional finesse. Very few investigators go this far.

Effluent and Air Emissions

Note sources of effluence and air emissions in the adjoining areas, particularly those immediately associated with the property. The effluent from an adjoining property could contaminate the property being assessed and depreciate its value.   The composition of the effluent may not be identifiable without sampling. Note its location and the effect it appears to have on the environment.

Air emissions are generally visible. A stack is a definite indicator. Not so obvious is the pipe or hole in the wall where something other than just air is being emitted into the atmosphere. Many materials which are exhausted into the air have a color. Some appear steam-like or result in a distortion of image when one looks through it. Look for the exit hole, pipe, tube, or stack.   The type of operations being performed at this location will provide a clue as to the type of substance being exhausted. Whatever is being exhausted may impact the surface soils and water. The end result may be contaminated drinking water and pasture lands.

For example, air emissions of hydrogen fluoride into pasture land could result in dental deterioration, an inability of the livestock to properly chew the grass, and the ultimate deterioration in the health of the livestock.

RECONNAISSANCE OF THE SURROUNDING AREA(S)

The areas surrounding the site are typically evaluated through record reviews. However, some sites which could have an impact on the property are not on record. The records are based on an owner complying with registration requirements and/or citations based on discrepancies noted by a neighbor or compliance officer. A quick drive around the vicinity of the site could uncover some of the not-so-obvious activities which could impact the property. For instance, all dry cleaning operations should be on the RCRA Notifiers' list. They are not all listed.

Sketch these suspected sites on an area drawing/map. Where they may lead to probable contamination of the ground and/or groundwater, note means for the contaminant to potentially reach the assessment property. See Figure 7-17.

SUMMARY

Information gathered up to this point may be used as an aid to assist the inspector in developing a plan of attack. The property should be, at a minimum, inspected for the following:

- Water wells (e.g., obsolete well)
- Water source(s) (e.g., lake reservoir, operated by the city)
- Debris (e.g., construction waste)
- Chemical storage drums (e.g., 55-gallon steel drums with liquid contents and no labels)
- Soil mounds
- Ground depressions
- Distressed, stained soil (e.g., oil stains)
- Poor or no vegetation (e.g., no growth in the center of a grassy field)
- Dead wildlife (e.g., dead coyotes around a pond)
- Surface water (e.g., oil film on the surface of the water)
- Surface impoundments (e.g., unlined impoundment in porous soil)
- Aboveground structures, other than buildings (e.g., storage vessels)
- Signs of subsurface structures (e.g., gas/oil pipelines and underground storage tanks)
- Odors (e.g., pungent odor in the soil)
- Effluence from the building(s)
- Air emissions
- Ground irregularities
- Mining/quarry activities
- Electrical supply system
- Cemetery(ies)

Any given property does not exist separate and apart from the influence of adjacent properties. The inspection should also include a look at the adjoining areas which should include, but not be limited to, the following:

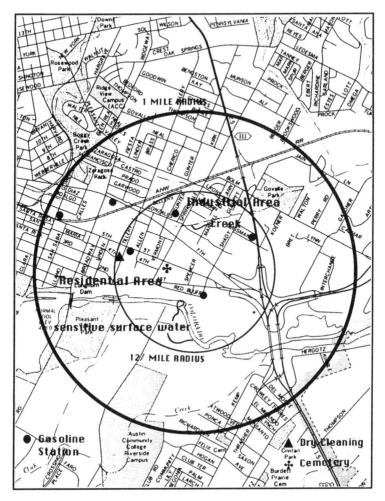

Figure 7-17. Local street map used for sketching usage and noteworthy items in the surrounding property.

- Property usage
- Storage tanks and drums
- Effluent and air emissions

More distant properties may impact the property through contaminated soils, groundwater, and surface water. Property usage should be checked for areas within a given radius of the site. A minimum 1/2 mile radius from the boundaries of the site should be visually inspected, if not by foot, by a slow moving vehicle.

REFERENCES

1. U.S. EPA: *A Manual for Evaluating Contamination Potential of Surface Impoundments.*   U.S. EPA/Office of Drinking Water, Washington, DC, 1978. p. 1.
2. Groundwater Protection Unit Staff: *Ground-water Quality of Texas—An Overview of Natural and Non-affected Conditions.* Texas Water Commission, Austin, Texas, TWC Report 89-01, March 1989. pp. 124-125.
3. Ibid. p. 112.

Chapter 8

Interviews

INTRODUCTION

Unrecorded information concerning the past usage of and activities associated with property can only be collected through interviews. People familiar with the site and surrounding areas may have witnessed, participated in, or observed that which was never recorded. This may have been an observation of one brief incident, a sequence of events, or a routine. They may be aware of what they witnessed, or they may not have any idea as to what actually occurred and its significance. They are the participants in an activity or the eye-witnesses.

An interview may be done by phone, or it may involve a visit to someone's home. Always carry calling cards! Homeowners are particularly suspicious, but even businesses may be difficult to approach. Introduce yourself and explain the purpose of your visit. Ask if they mind your taking notes! Some people are intimidated by the process. Notes are a must, but, in some instances, notes may have to be completed after the fact.

Document the interviewee's name, his relevance to the information being sought (e.g., retired employee who worked for a business which was located on the property), time, date, address/relative location of the interview (e.g., across the street from the property, at a neighboring residence), form of communication (e.g., telephone), telephone number of interviewee, and details of the conversation.

Some investigators maintain a form with normally asked questions. Do not be limited by forms. They are very general, at best, and could be a distraction. Conjure up a clear picture of the information which is important, and be prepared to rework the picture as the interview progresses.

When taking notes, be concise and accurate. Travel the path of a good reporter—don't interpret intent. Be objective and record what they say, not what your interpretation is.

In closing an interview, leave a calling card. The interviewee will need a means to contact you, and this should be encouraged. Something that a participant or witness thinks is irrelevant at the time of the interview may be recalled after the investigator's departure. For instance, a neighbor may have noticed drums being hauled away from the site on a routine basis—in the middle of the night. Although this is suspicious behavior, the witness perceived it as business-as-usual at the time of the interview. Later, however, the witness reconsiders past events based on questions posed during the interview and decides the information may be relevant. Most people want to help. Provide a means whereby you can be reached.

Also, follow-ups may be required. If the interviewee understands this, future questions are easier to handle, possibly over the telephone, where the parties concerned have been forewarned.

Any of a number of people may be interviewed. Yet, a minimum attempt should be made to interview the present owner and a couple of impartial, unbiased people associated with the property and surrounding area (e.g., a neighbor).

The objective is to identify "possibilities," generate ideas, allow more speculation than what records will allow. The interviewing process is not set in concrete.

OWNER(S)

The path of least resistance leads to the property owner. Although the owner is the easiest source of information concerning prior site usage and building structural records, the owner is biased and must be considered only one of several people to be interviewed.

An interview with the owner could be limiting where the owner is or has been responsible for questionable and/or illegal activities. Seek corroboration of information from other parties where suspicions arise.

Questions should be site dependent, based on research information gathered and observations made during a site reconnaissance. Some consultants use a guide or a screening questionnaire. See Figure 8-1.

An owner may not have answers to all of the questions but may be able to point you in the right direction. Seek names and contact information for these other parties familiar with the property(ies). For instance, a property may have been leased to a tank cleaning service prior to the present marketing business. The owner is unfamiliar with the process but has the name and contact information for the former lessee. The lessee should be added to the list of people to interviewed.

Known/Suspected	Present	Past
Property usage Uses of adjoining properties Aboveground storage tanks Underground storage tanks Landfills Obsolete/demolished buildings/structures Disposal activities on site Effluence/air emissions Vents/pipes in the ground Debris Drums Pits, ponds, or lagoons Private water wells Gas/oil wells Pesticide usage		

Figure 8-1. Items to Address While Interviewing the Property Owner.

Present

As the present owner may have some historic information on the property, the owner should be consulted on present activities and "previous" site usage. This interview should be conducted prior to and possibly after the site reconnaissance. This information may aid in giving direction for the site reconnaissance and answering questions generated as a result of the property inspection.

Owners may be helpful in clarifying the rationale for some environmental findings. For example, an overgrown building foundation is found on the property next to a clearing where no vegetation grows. The owner may know that 20 years ago the structure was used to repackage and warehouse herbicides. Although the kind of herbicides are unknown, there is an explanation for the lack of vegetation and further investigation may be initiated.

Past

Previous owners may be difficult to locate. A title search provides a good start, and the present owner may know where to locate some of the previous owners. Yet, more often than not, the more recent owner is long since gone, and the others may have either moved or passed away. If the previous owner cannot be located, someone may provide information concerning his reputation. For example, the previous owner may have committed suicide, leaving behind a trail of indebtedness and a reputation for shady dealings. One of his business activities involved hazardous chemicals which were not generated at the site but may have been dumped on the property. Such situations may alert the investigator to possible environmental contamination where the property may not appear to be associated with industrial/commercial activities which generate hazardous wastes.

SITE RESIDENTS

Site residents include single family or multi-family occupants of the property. This may include a resident employee (e.g., security guard who is given a home on the premises). They have a tendency to notice unusual activities, odors, and conditions more readily than those using the property for a business, the visiting owner, or the neighbors. For example, a family may notice that their 10-year-old son and their small terrier dog, who were the picture of health prior to moving into their home on the property, have been listless and frequently ill with flu-like symptoms since the move over a year ago. A pungent odor occasionally prevails when the wind blows from the southeast. This is worth further investigation.

SITE PERSONNEL

Site personnel, past and present, who have worked on the property in an industrial/commercial setting should be interviewed. The plant or business manager is number one on the list. Then, attempt to interview some of the employees.

The plant/business manager will be able to disclose the processes, chemicals used, and waste management procedures specific to their operation. If there is or was an industrial/commercial activity on the property, this interview is a must. As discussed in Chapter 7, on "Industrial/Commercial Activities," a general idea can be formulated as to the operations and generated hazardous materials. Yet, each operation is different. Specifics and details can only be obtained from those operating the business and their employees. For example, the plant manager of a chemical formulating complex will identify what specific chemicals were being used, how they were managed, and which means are used for disposal.

The employees are an excellent source of job specific details. Sometimes they are the only ones available to be interviewed—particularly if the businesses are no longer active. For example, a retired maintenance employee for one industrial complex was consulted for information concerning where he buried three 55-gallon drums of mercury 30 years ago. His response, "Out under 'de ol' oak tree that died 10 years ago."

NEIGHBORS

Residential neighbors generally notice strange activities on a property and are more than happy to have someone to tell their observations to. They may also have noticed normal activities which created a situation for which there appears no easy investigative tool—other than to interview someone who knows. For example, an investigator notices on a site visit that there is a large mound of overgrown dirt on the premises. A neighbor, having lived in the area for over 20 years, clarifies that the mound is nothing more than the excess soil which resulted when the ground was leveled. No further investigation is indicated.

In another example, the operator of an automotive repair shop located just outside of town died of a coronary. The property was leased, and the man had a reputation for being a reclusive, spiteful old man. He never had any employees who might have known what he did with his waste oil. Although the neighbors maintained their distance from the man, they had not once observed waste oil being hauled away. The man had dug his own latrine, and the property is over sensitive groundwater. Further investigation is indicated.

On the other hand, neighboring businesses rarely notice activities on adjacent properties—unless they are blatant. For example, an office building has 80 percent of its occupants complaining of foul odors, and eye and respiratory irritation on the days when the wind is blowing from the north. The property site is located on the north side of the building, and it houses an industrial activity. The building management staff was interviewed, and the above information was volunteered. Further investigation is indicated.

HISTORIANS/LOCAL HISTORICAL SOCIETIES

Most cities and towns have some form of historical records which are maintained by a city librarian, a specially designated historic center, or an agency already performing other functions (e.g., city planning department). They generally attempt to collect historic records and information from the local public. Many of the items/records of historic value have been donated. The designated responsible person who maintains these records is an invaluable source of information, and this person can oftentimes provide reference source information as well. For example, a fire insurance map indicates a "filling station" dated 1887. Although cars were being produced at that time, they were not being manufactured until the early 1910s. The town historian reviewed some old records and discovered that the first automobile in this city was in 1914. This rules out the requirement for a gasoline station. The question remains, "Was this a misprint or is a filling station something other than a gasoline station?"

OTHERS

A shot in the dark—anything goes. Now that the obvious sources have been exhausted, locating an individual familiar with activities on the property may be futile—unless one of the other interviews result in a name and means for contacting someone who may be more knowledgeable about activities on and/or around the property. For example, the present owner says that the previous owner left town in a hurry. The bank foreclosed on the property which was later purchased by the present owner. The loan officer is identified and interviewed. He discloses that the previous owner appeared to be connected with illegal dumping. Newspaper reporters investigated, but nothing was found. Yet, he did disappear about the time the local residents began to get suspicious. This might lead the consultant to interview the newspaper reporter who investigated the property. The list goes on.

SUMMARY

Interviews are an important part of the Phase I site assessment. Questions develop as an assessment nears completion. Keep a list of these questions, and consolidate the list. People to be interviewed include, but are not limited to, the following:

- Present owner
- Past owners
- Site residents
- Site personnel
- Neighbors
- Historian/local historical societies

The present owner is a must, and neighbors are an important source of unbiased information.

The ultimate purpose is to identify "possibilities" and "potentials" for a site to have become contaminated with hazardous materials—using the last resource. The interviews should be used as a "catch all" for information which may have otherwise slipped through the cracks.

Chapter 9

Building Materials

INTRODUCTION

Many buildings contain hazardous materials which are part of the structure or are typically associated with buildings. Construction materials contain substances which pose a potential health hazard to the building occupants if mismanaged, and hazardous substances may be released from associated structures or functional enclosures. Their presence devalues a building.

In Phase I environmental site assessments, asbestos content in buildings is always assessed, either through speculation or sampling. Asbestos has received a considerable amount of press, and it has become a "hot" topic. Lead-containing materials in the building materials and around the property, and the potential for PCB contamination of the grounds should be assessed for all property uses.

Other issues to investigate include radon in homes, pesticide usage, and high-power electromagnetic emitters. Radon is a concern in some parts of the country more than others, depending on uranium content of the soil and building structures. The potential for the toxic pesticides in a building are sometimes addressed, and exposures to electromagnetic fields from high power transmission lines is getting press.

Prior to beginning a building materials investigation, review the building records. In the interest of saving time spent on-site, an up-front records review is important.

BUILDING RECORDS

Request all pertinent building records from the building owner or representative as soon as the assessment is authorized. These records will aid in the evaluation process by decreasing the time required to sketch the structure(s), collect pertinent details, and identify/locate pipes. These documents are generally sparse, or their location is unknown. An owner/representative may require some time to follow-up on the request.

Date of Construction

Establish the date of construction for the building(s) to be surveyed. If there have been add-ons, obtain the dates for these as well. Most of this information can be obtained from building permits and certificates of occupancy which were discussed in Chapter 5 on historic usage.

The date can be compared against the dates of product manufacturing/sales, of product banning, and withdrawal from the market. Ban dates for manufacturing, importation, and processing oftentimes vary from the ban dates for use due to prestocked supplies. There is sometimes a phasing out period associated with the ban of materials on the marketplace. The "year banned" in Table 9-1 is the manufacturing ban in all cases. These dates are significant and helpful in determining probable usage of the hazardous building materials.

For example, friable (i.e., flaky, easily damaged) asbestos-containing insulation was banned from new building construction in 1974. A building constructed in later years has a reduced probability for containing friable asbestos-containing surfacing material.

Do not assume that materials which were banned were not used in a building. An existing ban on material usage at the time of construction reduces the possibility. There have been reported incidents where banned materials have been used.

Blueprints/Special Drawings

Blueprints may be available through the owner or the city planning department. Should the owner not have blueprints, try another source. All blueprints must be filed with building permits and certificates of occupancy at the city planning department. Although the plans for the smaller structures are generally disposed of within a couple months of filing, plans are maintained for the larger buildings indefinitely. These plans can be purchased.

With blueprints in hand, be forewarned that original plans are merely plans. Often, the final product may not be as it had been originally designed by the architect. In other words, it may not be the "as-builts."

Table 9-1. Generalized Usage and Banning Dates for Hazardous Building Materials

Building Material	Year First Used	Year Banned
Friable asbestos	1897	Partial Ban: 1975–1978
Non-friable asbestos	1890	Phase-out Ban
Lead-containing paint	early 1900s	Partial Ban: 1978
Leaded gasoline	early 1900s	1996
Lead-soldered water pipes	early 1900s	1986
Polychlorinated biphenyls	1929	Manufacturing: 1979

Construction alterations and add-ons are not generally included in the original blueprints, and the original prints are rarely updated. Thus, details should be confirmed during the walk-through.

If there are no blueprints available, some building owners have floor plans or schematics that are frequently updated to accommodate altered space utilization. These plans may be used for space management, fire escape plans, or locating personnel. Commercial buildings and multi-family housing complexes generally have them. Although they may not be to scale, they do provide an overview, a basic sketch from which to depart.

Architectural Records

Building specifications are records which detail material requirements and restrictions for a building. More recent specifications state that there will be "no asbestos-containing materials" installed in the building. Some residential plans will state "no lead-containing paint." Past specifications have required the use of hazardous building materials, not known at the time to be hazardous.

The architect or architectural firm that performed the work will generally maintain its own blueprints and specifications. The name of the building architect is on the blueprints, or the owner/owner's representative may know or be able to track the name.

Be forewarned! Specifications are frequently followed but not always. Contractors may misinterpret the specifications, may have missed the expensive details in the bidding process, or the owner may have add-ons.

Clearly, a review of specifications may be a waste of time. However, if the specifications clearly state "no lead-containing paint," the probability that it is present is reduced. If the building was constructed in 1982, the probability is, once again, reduced.

HAZARDOUS SUBSTANCE BUILDING MATERIALS

Building materials which contain hazardous materials may pose either a real or imagined problem to the occupants. Exposure management and control of these potentially hazardous substances and perceived problems could be costly for the owner, as is the cost for removal.

This section will discuss uses, health hazards, exposure potentials, special regulatory requirements, and "basic" sampling methodology. Although sampling is not generally included in a Phase I, some clients request it and will call the assessment a "modified" Phase I. Refer to Chapter 2 for an historic overview and abbreviated overview of pertinent regulatory events.

Asbestos removal is one of the most expensive considerations facing a building owner. Removal of lead-containing paint is in the running, and costs increase as required removal procedures become more restrictive.

Asbestos-Containing Material

Asbestos-containing material (ACM) can have a significant impact on the value of property. Wherever a building is involved in an assessment, the building materials should be considered and asbestos content speculated, if not sampled. Yet, sampling materials in large buildings is involved and generally require special training. Speculation as to the materials contained within a given building and the possible impact on the value of the building may prompt the client to seek a more in-depth evaluation of the building material. The information contained within this section should assist the investigator in this speculation process.

All materials have a percentage of asbestos. This percentage is rarely in excess of 90 percent. Thus, the material is asbestos-containing material, not "asbestos" alone.

> Asbestos-Containing Material: > 1% asbestos

According to the EPA, asbestos-containing material is any material which has greater than one percent asbestos by volume. Less than one percent is considered not detected—even if there were a couple fibers identified in the analysis. No detection means less than three fibers counted during the analysis of the material. This does not pose a significant exposure concern.

Material may be classified as friable or non-friable, and the EPA has assigned two categories to the non-friable classification. These categories are summarized in Table 9-2.[1]

Friable asbestos-containing material poses more of a potential release problem than the non-friable. Then, the percent by volume of asbestos in the material will impact the exposure levels—once there has been a release.

Uses in Buildings

The original use for asbestos in 1890 was for fireproof roofing material. Later in the 1890s, this expanded to engine gaskets and boiler insulation. Thus, all the asbestos-containing materials produced in the late 1890s were used for fireproofing and heat insulation.

In the 1900s, uses expanded to acoustical and thermal insulation, hot and cold, and by 1935 it was being used in everything from baby blankets to cement.

There have been over 3,600 commercial products manufactured since its creation.[2] The year of origin is sometimes elusive or even controversial. Yet, these dates are, for the most part, agreed on and have been widely published. Some of the products and their date of origin are listed in Table 9-3.

Most buildings have asbestos-containing material—if there has not been a serious effort to remove *all* of it. The most frequently found material having asbestos is sheet vinyl. Asbestos-containing floor tiles, also frequently found in buildings, have from 3 to 25 percent asbestos.

Other asbestos-containing materials which are frequently identified and tend to pose a potential problem are acoustical/decorative surfacing material, sprayed-on fireproofing, pipe insulation, and boiler insulation. Any of these materials may have up to 80 percent asbestos content. The acoustical/decorative surfacing is a texturized sprayed-on or trowelled-on

Table 9-2.   Classification of Asbestos-Containing Material

Friable ACM	Crumbled, pulverized, or reduced to powder by hand pressure, and >1% asbestos.
Non-friable ACM	When dry, cannot be crumbled, pulverized, or reduced to powder by hand pressure, and >1% asbestos.
Category I	Asbestos-containing packings, gaskets, resilient floor coverings, and asphalt roofing products.
Category II	Any non-friable ACM not designated as Category I.

U.S. EPA: Asbestos/NESHAP Regulated Asbestos Containing Materials Guidance. [Bulletin]. Office of Toxic Substances, Washington, DC, EPA 340/1-90-018. p. 12.

ceiling material.   The fireproofing is sprayed onto steel and rein-forced—concrete structural members of a building.   Pipe insulation may be in the form of premolded forms, corrugated paper, "air cell" material, and cementitious joint/elbow paste.   Boiler/water tanks are often insulated with preformed asbestos-containing blocks and have asbestos gasket material (as high as 100 percent asbestos).

It is speculated that about 5 to 10 percent of all ceiling tiles have asbestos.[5] Some consider ceiling tiles to be friable, and the air space above the ceiling tiles in many commercial buildings may serve as an air return plenum which can pick up debris and return it to the main air handling unit for recycling with the general air.

All other materials must be considered on a case-by-case scenario. Even non-friable, cementitious conduit may release fibers, given the proper situation.   Some such products are listed in Table 9-4.[5]

Health Hazards

Exposures to low levels of airborne asbestos can cause lung cancer and/or mesothelioma, cancer of the lining of the lungs.   The incidence of

Table 9-3.   Date of Origin of Some Asbestos Products

1890	Roofing material[3]
1897	Sprayed-on acoustical insulation[4]
1902	Pipe insulation[4]
1909	Cement cladding[4]
1910	Corrugated paper products[4]
1910	Roofing felts[5]
1920	Asphalt tiles[5]
1926	Brake linings[4]
1930	Cement[4]
1930	Caulking putties[5]
1935	High temperature, cement-like pipe elbows and joints[4]
1935	Roofing shingles[4]
1938	Transite board[4]
1945	Theater curtains[5]
1946	Drywall[4]
1950	Vinyl floor tiles[5]
1950	Asphalt[4]
1951	Electrical insulation[4]
1952	Paper laminate for electrical equipment[4]
1953	Conduit[4]
1965	Teflon[4]
Unknown	Vinyl wallpaper[5]

Composite of three publications. (See References.)

lung cancer increases three-fold when a non-smoker is exposed and 90 times for cigarette smokers. These low exposures may occur in office buildings and other public buildings where asbestos-containing material is damaged or disturbed.

Exposures to high levels of asbestos can cause a debilitating, progressive disease of the lungs, known as "asbestosis." One prominent theory as to the mechanism is that fibers become surrounded in the lungs by macrophages which attempt to remove the foreign material. Due to the size, shape, and chemical resistance of the asbestos fibers, instead of being carried away, the fibers kill the macrophages which release a poison. This poison, in turn, becomes closed off, forming a web of inelastic tissue. As this scarring increases, the lungs lose their elasticity, resulting in restrictive breathing. Symptoms may not develop fully for 7 to 9 years and may result in death as early as 13 years from the time of exposure. Yet, it

Table 9-4.   Non-friable Asbestos Products

Subdivision	Generic Name	Asbestos (%)	Binders/Sizing
Roofing Felts (Category I)	smooth surface	10-15	asphalt
	mineral surface	10-15	asphalt
	shingles	1	asphalt
	pipeline	10	asphalt
Cementitious Extrusion Panels (Category II)		8	portland cement
Concrete-Like Products (Category II)	corrugated	20-45	portland cement
	flat	40-50	portland cement
	flexible	30-40	portland cement
	flexible performed	30-50	portland cement
	laminated (outer surface)	35-50	portland cement
	roof tiles	20-30	portland cement
	clapboard	12-15	portland cement
	siding shingles	12-14	portland cement
	roofing shingles	20-32	portland cement
	pipe	15-20	portland cement

Asbestos-Containing Compounds (Categories I and II)		
caulking putty	30	linseed oil
adhesive	5-25	asphalt
roofing asphalt	5	asphalt
mastic	5-25	asphalt
asphalt tile cement	13-25	asphalt
roof putty	10-25	asphalt
plaster/stucco	2-10	portland cement
sealants	50-55	castor oil or polyisobutylene
cement, insulation	20-100	clay
cement, finishing	55	clay
cement, magnesia	15	magnesium carbonate

U.S. EPA: Asbestos/NESHAP Adequately Wet Guidance. [Bulletin]. Office of Toxic Substances, Washington, DC, EPA 340/1-90-019. p. 18.

generally takes 20 to 30 years for onset of symptoms. These higher exposures have been associated with the mining industry, and there have been reported cases in pipe insulation workers and building maintenance workers.

Although ingestion of larger asbestos fibers has been associated with stomach and colon cancer, ingestion of the smaller fibers, which are generally associated with water conduit, is not thought to be associated with any known health problems. Food, drink, or contaminated surfaces, which have been contaminated with the larger asbestos fibers, may result in ingestion.

Fiber Release/Exposure Potential

Fiber release must occur for asbestos to pose any of the previously mentioned health problems. Disturbing the material causes fiber release. Vibration and air movement in air plenum which has asbestos-containing acoustical/thermal insulation or the installation of ceiling hangers through asbestos-containing surfacing material are common occurrences. Basketballs hitting asbestos-treated cross members in gymnasiums and playful jabbing at the surfacing material with the end of a mop handle are methods of unplanned disturbance. The potential for fiber release may be high, or it may be unlikely. It is never non-existent.

When asbestos is located in the backing of sheet vinyl it is generally not exposed—unless there has been damage to the covering. This backing has as much as 80 percent asbestos and is extremely friable, easily crumbled with hand pressure. Uncontrolled removal of this type of floor covering can result in excessive levels of airborne fibers and may contaminate not only the general area but the air conditioning/heating unit and all areas associated with the system. Many floor replacement workers are not aware of this potential and inadvertently expose themselves to tremendous levels and contaminate not only the area they are working in, but the surrounding area and air handling unit as well. Homeowners don't know any better. This type of incident generally goes undetected.

On the other hand, asbestos-containing floor tiles have from 3 to 25 percent asbestos and are not friable. Exposures during removal of the tiles are considerably less than exposures during removal of sheet vinyl with asbestos-containing backing. An improbable release may occur where asbestos-containing floor tiles are overlaid with a secondary floor cover.

Asbestos-containing pipe insulation which has a damaged covering and is located in a busy hallway or above the suspended ceiling, in the return air plenum (i.e., the mixing space where conditioned air is returned to the air handler), poses a greater chance for fiber release than insulation which has its cover intact and is located in an inaccessible wall space or in a pipe chase. Methods for evaluating the relative chances for fiber release have been published by the EPA and are part of the AHERA Inspector/Management Planner's Training.

Fiber release potential changes when renovation and/or demolition is performed. Cutting, sawing, drilling, penetrating the wrapping, scraping, or any other form of damage may release fibers—even from asbestos cement (i.e., "transite") which is often used as a structural support (e.g., house eaves or free-standing buildings). Renovation and demolition may result in fiber release from any asbestos-containing material despite its apparent integrity and hardness.

Removal Procedures

Asbestos-containing materials which are directly affected by renovation are to be removed in accordance with OSHA 29 CFR 1910 and 1926 and the EPA National Emissions Standard for Hazardous Air Pollutants (NESHAPS), Subpart M. There is no time when the exposures are greater than during removal, and the costs may run into the millions. Thus, many building owners choose to "let sleeping dogs lie."

The buyer must be made aware of the acceptance of this liability and potential removal costs. All asbestos-containing materials will at some time have to be removed—subject to the fiber release potential. It is only a matter of time. A buyer must be apprised of this possibility, and the investigator may recommend an in-depth sampling of the building materials where the size of the building and potential for asbestos content may significantly influence the value of the structure.

Demolition Requirements

In the past, all ACM had to be removed prior to demolition of a building. Since 1990, however, ACM does not need to be removed before demolition if it meets one of the following criteria:[3]

1) Is a Category I non-friable ACM that has not become friable and is in good condition.

2) Is encased in concrete or other similarly hard material and is adequately wetted whenever exposed during demolition.
3) Was not accessible during testing and therefore was not discovered until after demolition began and, as a result of the demolition, cannot be safely removed. If not removed for safety reasons, the exposed ACM and any asbestos-containing debris must be treated as asbestos-containing waste material and kept adequately wet at all times until disposed of.
4) Is a Category II non-friable ACM and the probability is low that the material will become crumbled, pulverized, or reduced to powder during demolition.

Category I non-friable ACM is asbestos-containing packing, gaskets, resilient floor coverings, and asphalt roofing products. Category II non-friable ACM is all other asbestos-containing material which cannot be crumbled by manual effort. An attempt should be made in all cases to minimize possible fiber release into the ambient air during demolition. This generally requires wetting the material while it is undergoing demolition.

In brief, the cost for removing ACM in accordance with accepted removal practices is considerably higher than the cost for minimizing fiber release during demolition. Thus, the investigator may be able to more readily speculate as to the possible costs involved in a removal project.[3]

Basic Sampling Methodology

Although the investigator may not plan to perform a full-blown asbestos survey, limited sampling may be indicated. This may involve bulk sample collection of all friable building materials which may contain asbestos and should not be considered anything more than what it is—speculative sampling. A positive may confirm suspicions, but a negative does not confirm no asbestos content. Those materials that may be considered in a limited sampling include ceiling surfacing material, sprayed on beam fireproofing, and pipe lagging.

Without a comprehensive asbestos inspection, such as that which is required by AHERA, it is not recommended that a material be excluded as having a potential for containing asbestos; the scope of this chapter does not include the AHERA methodology. Training is available at many of the major university extension services.

Positives are noted, and the negatives remain potential positives—until further confirmed negative by a statistically acceptable number of bulk samples.   Many friable materials were batch mixed/formulated, and different amounts of asbestos may have been used in different areas, or the material may appear to be the same but was added at a later date.   The presence of one negative reduces the chances but does not eliminate them entirely.

Should samples be indicated, problems associated with bulk sample collection must be acknowledged.   Problems include: 1) not collecting enough samples of similar material, as mentioned above; 2) contamination of samples, due to not decontaminating equipment; and 3) the existence of multi-layers of different material.   These mistakes are easily made by beginners; and sample collectors may dislodge fibers, exposing themselves and others around the area where the sample(s) is (are) being taken.

Paramount to sample collection, one must keep clear, concise records of samples taken and sample locations.   Be specific as to the exact sample location, identifying more than material type and room numbers.   It is recommended that the inspector take notes as to the: 1) condition of each suspect material, sampled or not; 2) potential for damage; 3) physical description (e.g., soft, white, fibrous); and 4) volume of the suspected material, sampled or not.

Asbestos bulk sampling supplies include: 1) a HEPA air-purifying respirator and possibly disposable coveralls with a hood; 2) a plastic drop cloth to cover enough floor space to catch any visible debris generated; 3) the use of a surfactant-water spray bottle (any detergent will do the job or a non-foaming surfactant may be purchased from a safety supply house); 4) sample zip-lock bags, bottles, or other uncontaminated small containers; 5) a wet rag or HEPA vacuum to pick up debris; 6) a cutting/boring devise; and 7) a ladder.

The method of sample collection involves the following steps:

1) Clear the area of traffic and onlookers.   Some opt to perform sampling in the evenings when there are reduced numbers of people in the building.   Others close off the area, post "Warning: Do Not Enter" signs outside the entrance to the area, and/or lock the door(s).
2) If there is a potential for dropping, put down a plastic drop cloth to catch falling debris.
3) Don a HEPA air-purifying respirator and disposable coveralls.
4) Thoroughly wet the material to be sampled.
5) Dislodge a sample the size of a quarter, place it in the sample container, and seal the container.   A utility knife, boring tool, and specialty sampling device can be used; tweezers could be helpful.

6) Assure proper labeling of the container with a sample number, and properly record the information. Labeling the sample site or marking it with an indelible marker is suggested where marking/labeling is not going to damage the aesthetics of an area. Further, the sample location should be specified in writing and on a floor plan or blueprint.

7) Clean the sampling device with a wet cloth that can be properly discarded.

8) Clean fallen debris from around the area with a wet rag or HEPA vacuum. The latter should also be inspected before departing the area.

9) Clean off all visible debris. Doff the respirator and disposable coveralls.

Maintenance of a low profile and creation of minimal damage are advised. A low profile may be maintained by securing an area or working during off hours. Minimal damage to a building may be accomplished by taking samples in corners, behind fixtures, and behind furnishing.

Once again, sampling should be reserved for a Phase II ESA. Yet, some other scopes of work, as previously discussed, do require sampling. Prior to a Phase II being performed, the inspector should complete the AHERA Inspector/Management Planner's Course. The methodology is considered state of the art.

Ideally, the evaluation should only consider a worst case speculation as to asbestos-containing building materials. From the speculation can come a worst case cost estimate for removal; the client may make a decision to go to a Phase II, based on the findings.

Lead-Containing Material

As lead removal procedures are elaborate and expensive (not unlike that of asbestos), lead-containing material in and/or around a building may impact the value of the building and should be considered by the inspector. Lead-containing material is particularly important on residential property and in homes.

Lead has been used in paints, gasoline, and distribution pipes for drinking water. These sources result in air, dust, and soil lead contamination. The contaminated sources, in turn, may result in lead exposures through ingestion and/or inhalation.

Lead-Based Paint

Lead-containing paint is the most common source of lead exposure to preschool children. Containing up to 50 percent lead, the paint was in widespread use until the 1950s when it became common knowledge that exposures to lead posed a health hazard. Thereafter, exterior lead-based paint and decreased usage of interior lead-based paint continued until 1978.[6]

About 74 percent of privately owned, occupied housing units in the United States built prior to 1980, were coated with lead-based paints. Exposures to preschool children result when they ingest paint chips or paint-contaminated dust and soil. Many exposures also result when homes are remodeled or renovated without the proper precautions being taken. Lead-containing paint is typically found on kitchen and bathroom walls, doors, and wood trim of houses. It was used on children's playground equipment where small children may chew the surfaces and in house paints for interior/exterior windows.   The latter poses a particular problem, because the surfaces are abraded and worn by opening and closing the windows.[6]

In 1978, the manufacture and use of paints containing more than 0.06 percent lead by weight on the interiors and exteriors of residential surfaces, toys, and furniture were banned.[6] With proper labeling (i.e., "Warning: Contains Lead. Dried Film of This Paint May be Harmful if Eaten or Chewed."), the following products are exempt from the ban:[7]

1) Agriculture and industrial equipment paints
2) Industrial/commercial buildings, maintenance equipment, and traffic/safety line paints
3) Graphic art paints (i.e., paints marketed solely for billboards, road signs, identification markings in industrial buildings, and other similar uses)
4) Touch-up paints for agricultural equipment, lawn/garden equipment, and appliances
5) Catalyzed coatings marketed solely for use on radio-controlled model powered aircraft

The following products are exempt without proper labeling:

1) Mirrors with lead-containing backing paint
2) Artists' paints and related materials

3) Metal furniture articles, not for use as children's furniture and bearing factory-applied lead paint

Be forewarned! Exempted paints have been used in homes on occasion. Although a residence may have been built after the ban, this information alone is not sufficient to state with a high degree of certainty that there is no lead-containing paint in a residence. Only the probability can be discussed.

Lead in the Soil[6]

Leaded gasoline has resulted in an estimated 4 to 5 million metric tons of lead in the soil. The level of lead in soils located within 25 meters of a roadway has typically been 30 to 2,000 parts per million (ppm), ranging as high as 10,000 ppm. Soils contaminated by industrial activities have been as high as 60,000 ppm.

Even where the source of the lead contamination has been eliminated (e.g., leaded gasoline), lead may remain in the soil for extended periods of time. It is not normally eliminated from the environment without removal of the soil or paint. Thus, residences in and/or around contaminated areas may be subject to excessive airborne exposures. Blood lead levels generally rise 3 to 7 µg/dl for every 1,000 ppm increase in soil or dust lead concentrations. Exposures are affected by the availability of the lead in the soil/dust, access to the soil, behavior patterns, presence of ground cover (e.g., grass), and a variety of other factors.[6]

Lead in Drinking Water

Lead has been used in water distribution lines. Contaminated drinking water sources include: 1) lead connectors; 2) lead service lines or pipes; 3) lead-soldered joints in copper plumbing; 4) lead-containing solder in water coolers and drinking fountains; and 5) lead-containing brass faucets and other fixtures. Building codes for many of the older cities used to specify lead pipe. Chicago is one such city.[8]

Historically, lead pipes are found in buildings built before the 1920s. Copper pipes and lead solder (50 percent tin, 50 percent lead) came into general use in the 1950s. Lead solder has also been used in the construction or repair of cisterns (water storage vessels), and some cisterns were built with lead liners.[7]

In 1986, the use of lead in public drinking water distribution systems was banned, and lead content in brass was reduced to 8 percent. The most common source of water contamination is that of lead leaching from copper pipes with lead-soldered joints.[6]

Health Hazards Associated with Lead Exposures

The effects of lead poisoning in children are not clinically immediately noticeable. Secondary effects, or the symptomatic stage, include loss of appetite, vomiting, apathy, drowsiness, and inability to coordinate activities. The after effects include various behavioral and functional disorders, or brain dysfunction. Some studies suggest that the latter results in hyperactivity, impulsive behavior, slowed learning ability, withdrawal, and perceptual disorders. The third stage may be permanent and includes blindness, mental retardation, further behavior disorders, and death.[7]

Lead accumulates in the body and effects may be long lasting. Onset symptoms in adults are similar to flu symptoms. The more advanced symptoms may include periodic abdominal cramping, associated with severe constipation, nausea, and vomiting. Other signs include anemia, pallor, a purple "lead line" of the gums, and decreased handgrip strength. More advanced symptoms result in severe headaches, convulsions, coma, and collapse.

Exposure Potentials to Lead-Containing/ Contaminated Material[6]

The EPA estimated in 1992 that 15 percent of the children in the U.S. have elevated blood lead levels. A small town in Wisconsin had 85 percent of its children with elevated blood lead levels. The sources of exposure include lead in the drinking water and high estimated soil and dust concentrations, associated with older houses.[9]

Lead is a health hazard when inhaled or ingested. Dust and soil surfaces which contain lead may become airborne, therefore, ingested. Mechanical disturbance and winds cause the material to become airborne. In urban environments, lead is generally retained in the upper 2 to 5 centimeters of soil and is found at greater depths in rural areas where the ground may be subject to tilling and other farm activities.

Exposures are affected by the availability of the lead in the soil/dust, access to the soil, behavior patterns, presence of ground cover (e.g., grass), and a variety of other factors.

Lead is absorbed by the body more completely from drinking water than food, dust, or soil. Adults absorb 35 to 50 percent of the lead they drink, and children absorb more than 50 percent. Although lead in drinking water is not generally the primary source of exposure for children, infants have been poisoned by hot tap water, containing lead, used in preparing the baby formula.

Exposure levels to lead-contaminated water systems are affected by corrosiveness of the water, age of the lead component (newer ones pose a higher risk), quantity and surface area of the lead-containing materials, standing time, and temperature of the water.

Sampling Methodology for Paint[10]

In 1990, the Department of Housing and Urban Development (HUD) published guidelines for sampling and evaluating paint for lead content. These guidelines describe technical protocols, practices, and procedures as well as abatement practices. They also mandate that all HUD dwellings, constructed prior to 1978, be inspected for lead content in the paint with a completion date of 1994; and lead paint must be abated if amounts exceed published action levels of 0.5 percent lead by weight or 1 mg/cm^2 lead content.

HUD Limit for Lead in Paint: 0.5% Lead by Weight

The protocol involves collection of a surface sample of two square inches or larger when analysis is to be performed by atomic spectroscopic techniques (e.g., atomic absorption by inductively coupled plasma or graphite furnace). Should the samples be analyzed by the less sensitive X-ray fluorescence method, the minimum sample size should be nine square inches. Samples are taken by a heat gun with putty knives or a sharp cutting knife, then they are placed into zip-lock bags, labeled, and sent to a laboratory for analysis.

Two blanks must accompany each set of samples for each day sampling is performed. The blanks should be taken from known non-lead-containing paint. A preparation blank should be handled and stored along with all the other samples. The field blank should be analyzed upon receipt by the laboratory. Additionally, a random duplicate sample should be taken at a frequency of 1 per 20 samples.

Detailed procedures have been published in the HUD guidelines. Although only applicable to HUD residences and to American Indian dwellings, this method offer is a good, legally admissible approach to sampling for lead in paint. Some degree of testing is recommended when assessing residential buildings (i.e., single and multiple family housing).

Sampling Methodology for Soil[10]

EPA has a published method for soil sampling of surface materials. Using a 10- by 10-cm template, the area to be sampled should be marked. The surface should then be scraped to a depth of 1 cm with a stainless steel trowel or similar implement. The yield should be at least 100 grams of soil. Samples should be placed into a clean glass jar, labeled, and sent to a laboratory for analysis.

Basic Sampling Methodology for Water

There are various methods of sampling and evaluating results of lead in water. They are dependent upon the source (e.g., service mains and water fountain lines). The method described in this book is applicable only for samples taken from the end of a water line, not from intermediate fixtures and loops. The latter are sampled when making a determination as to the source of the lead contamination of the drinking water. This method is for a general diagnosis as to its presence and level of contamination of the end product.

Where lead is in the building supply lines which stem from the utility main, the highest lead levels in water occur after the water has been settling for an extended period of time and expelled directly into a drinking glass, without allowing the water to run prior to the first draw. In an occupied building, this time is generally in the morning.

Choose a faucet which does not have filters, softeners, or heaters. Remove any associated aerators, and collect the first draw after a period of settling. In industry, this may be prior to work, first thing on Monday morning. The sample should be collected in a 250-ml container which contains a couple of drops of nitric acid. Seal and label the container. Send the sample to a laboratory.[8]

The acceptable level of lead in drinking water is 15 ppb (parts per billion). Ideally, the lead content should be below the level reported, by the utility company, in the main water supply system is sometimes considered to be the limit which should promote concern and routing sampling to assure continued compliance.

Should the 15 ppb level be exceeded in the first draw, a follow-up sample is recommended after the water has been allowed to run for 30 seconds in the morning.[8] The first draw represents a worst case scenario. A significant first draw with an acceptable second is a symptom of that which may pose a problem in the future. This should be viewed with suspicion.

EPA Guidance Limit for Lead in Water: 15 ppb

Most cities will have records of lead levels in the water after treatment. Lead contamination may result anywhere in the system from the treatment plant to intermediate lines to lines in a water fountain Many cities will provide free sample bottles and analysis of residential drinking water, and all will supply information as to the lead levels sampled in their delivery system.

HAZARDOUS SUBSTANCES ASSOCIATED WITH BUILDINGS

Building materials are not the only source of hazardous substances in the construction of a building. Other associated fixtures, designs, and treatments may result in exposures to toxic substances that have few warning properties. The substances which may pose a concern are polychlorinated biphenyls, radon, pesticides, and electromagnetic radiation.

Polychlorinated Biphenyls

Polychlorinated biphenyls (PCBs) are a group of chlorinated, aromatic hydrocarbons with 209 possible structures.[11] These synthetic compounds range from heavy oily liquids to waxy solids. They have a high boiling point, chemical stability, low solubility in water, high solubility in fat, low electrical conductivity, and are non-flammable. By law, a substance is considered a PCB if it contains PCBs in excess of 50 ppm.

Uses

PCBs were manufactured in the U.S. from 1929 to 1979 for use in electrical products.   Principal uses were oil-insulated transformers, capacitors, and fluorescent light ballasts.   They were used in electromagnetic, heat transfer/hydraulic systems, natural gas pipeline compressors, air compressors, and industrial lubricants.   Some more obscure products they have been used in are paints, plasticizers, pesticide extenders, ceiling tiles, flame retardants, and fillers.   They are also found as a by-product in the production of organic chemicals.[12]

A transformer may have as much as 800 gallons of oil, and a ballast has about 1 to 1-1/2 ounces of oil.   The life expectancy for capacitors and transformers is 10 to 30 years, although some may not last more than a month while others may last in excess of 50 years.   The use of PCBs in transformers and ballasts has been banned, but it is not always clear as to the production date and/or content of the oil in those products which have not been withdrawn from use.   In 1979, the EPA issued regulations prohibiting the manufacture of PCBs after July 1 of the same year, unless specifically exempted by the EPA.

Health Hazards

PCBs are toxic to the liver and cause chloracne, an acne-like dermatitis.   As the fat soluble, chemically stable compounds are stored in body fat for extended periods of time, exposures are cumulative.   Laboratory animal studies link PCBs to reproductive failures, birth defects, gastric disorders, skin lesions, swollen limbs, and liver cancer.

Exposure Potentials

Improperly disposed of PCB-contaminated materials and leaking transformers have led to surface water contamination in the nation's water system.   Measurable amounts of PCBs can be found in soils, water, fish, milk, and human tissue.   Some fish in the Hudson River, Great Lakes, and other bodies of water are too contaminated for human consumption.

Problems with PCBs are minor compared to products of burned PCBs. Transformers and ballasts can catch on fire and occasionally blow up. When PCBs burn there is a chemical change.   Components of the heat decomposition include dibenzofurans and dibenzo-p-dioxins.   Suspected carcinogens, some of the dioxins (e.g., 2,3,7,8-tetrachlorodibenzo-p-dioxin) are among the most toxic substances known to man. Cases involving burning PCBs, resulting in dioxin contamination of people and areas, occur more frequently than are reported.

One such unreported incident involves a grocery store. One of the light ballasts caught fire and blew up. The by-products, with probable dioxin contaminants, were sprayed over the refrigerated meat. The store owner chose to clean it up and sell the meat.

There have also been reported cases of electrical workers working on a transformer and the transformer blowing up. The worker is subject to burns as well as furans.

Although PCBs do not have an odor, burned or burning ballast capacitor fluids may give off a noxious odor as well as soot and an oily liquid. This is thought to be associated with the volatilization of asphalt.

Evaluation Methodology

Recently, manufacturers have been labeling their products "No PCB." If a transformer or ballast is not so labeled and there are no records dating and/or clarifying the content, assume it does have PCBs—until proven otherwise.

EPA Acceptable PCB-Content: <50 ppm

With transformers belonging to a municipal utility company, the PCB content may or may not be a matter of record. Some keep very thorough records. Others only sample transformer fluid when the unit is serviced. If they don't have adequate records, a request may be made for sampling and subsequent analysis. Many will charge a fee, and some won't charge at all—depending on the volume of requests.

When a request is made for information concerning a specific transformer, the investigator should supply a map of the area with the relative location(s) clearly marked and their identifying numbers—if present. Also, the investigator should request information concerning ground-mounted vaults and provide identifying information on the area of concern. Not all identifying numbers are obvious (.e.g, there may be several numbers on a pole-mounted transformer). Some numbers also are so small and remote that not even high-powered binoculars will be adequate. The intent is to identify potential leak locations and places where leaks are apparent but content is unverified.

The most common, easily accessed transformers that get evaluated are the pole-mounted type. However, there are the less obvious, small, ground-mounted units, the large, compartmentalized in-ground units; and temporary portable transformers. If they are leaking or have leaked, the area around the transformer(s) will have visible signs of oil contamination. These should definitely be subject to suspicion. With a positive confirmation that the transformer does have PCB oil and with visible signs of leaking, the consultant can state with a high degree of probability that there is PCB contamination in and/or around a given area.

Radon and Its Decay Products[13]

Radon is an invisible, odorless, water soluble, inert gas which emits alpha particles. Alpha particles have poor penetrating abilities. Thus, they can only impact that with which they come into direct contact.

Radon and its decay, or daughter, products are the progeny of uranium-238, uranium-235, and thorium-232 as depicted in Figure 9-1. These elements occur naturally within the earth's crust, more in some parts than in others.

Sources of Radon

Minerals rich in uranium ores include various types of granite, shales, and phosphatic rocks. Granite has uranium concentrations averaging around 3 or 4 parts of contaminant per million parts of soil (ppm) and as high as 10 ppm (EPA 1987). Black shales may have concentrations as high as 20 ppm, and phosphate rocks may have up to 100 ppm uranium. The estimated average concentration in the earth's crust is only 1.0 to 1.6 ppm. The U.S. Environmental Protection Agency released a map of areas which are potential hot spots for high radon content in the soils which is provided in Figure 9-2. However, small isolated areas may pose a concern. Additional source information varies by state, usually the state agency which addresses radiation hazards.

URANIUM-238 AND -234 DECAY SERIES

U-238 (4.5 x 10⁹ y) ⟹Th-234 (24) ⇨Pa-234 (1.2 m) ⇨U-234 (2.5 x 10⁵ y) ⟹Th-230 (7.7 x 10⁴ y)

⟹Ra-226 (1.6 x 103 y) ⟹Rn-222 (3.82 d) ⟹Po-218 (3.05 m) ⟹Pb-214 (3.82 d) ⇨Bi-214

(19.7 m) ⇨Po-214 (164 Us) ⟹Pb-210 (21 y) ⇨Bi-210 (5.0 d) ⇨Po-210 (138 d)

⟹ Pb-206

URANIUM-235 DECAY SERIES

U-235 (7.1 x 10⁸ y) ⟹Th-231 (26 h) ⇨Pa-231 (3.5 x 10⁴ y) ⟹Ac-227 (22 y) ⇨Th-227 (18 d)

Ra-223 (11.2 d) ⟹Rn-219 (4.0 s) ⟹Po-215 (4.0 s) ⟹Pb-211 (36.1 m) ⇨Bi-211

(2.15 m) ⟹Tl-207 (4.79 m) ⇨Pb-207 (stable)

⟹   alpha decay
⇨   beta decay
( )   half-life

y   year   m   minute
d   day   s   second
h   hour   us 1.0 x 10⁻⁶ seconds

Figure 9-1. Uranium decay series with radon daughters.

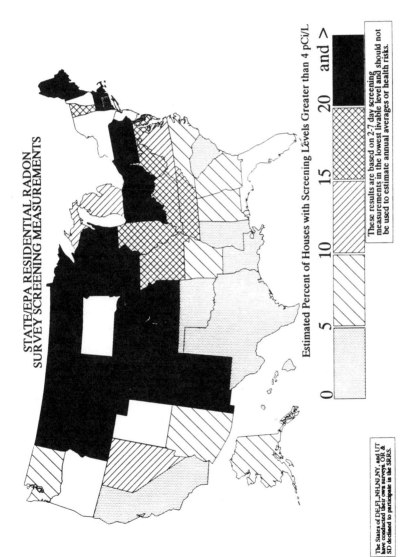

Figure 9-2.   State/EPA residential radon survey measurements.   Source: EPA.

Health Hazards

The alpha particles emitted from radon and its daughters have very little ability to penetrate the skin tissues. These radioactive particles do, however, enter the lungs and digestive tract. In the lungs, the emitted alpha particles can cause cellular damage. The result is lung cancer. Digestive tract exposures to radon are believed not to be a high risk, because a layer of food as thin as two thousandths of an inch can stop radon from affecting the cellular lining of the digestive system. See Table 9-5.

Exposure Potentials for Radon Gas

Radon gas and its daughters become trapped in homes and in ground-water. The most common radon nucleotide/gas has a half-life of 3.8 days and will eventually deplete itself if not continuously replenished. The probability for airborne radon in a house is based on the building structure, materials of construction, geographic location, and geologic makeup of the soil. The pathways which radon may enter a home are depicted in Figure 9-3.

Radon levels are highest when the living space is closest to the soil and when a building is airtight. An airtight basement which has cracks in the foundation has a greater likelihood for high levels of radon gas than a well-ventilated ground level structure.

Uranium-containing rock is mined for building materials and construction of solar cells. Building materials most likely to emit radon are uranium-rich granites, pegmatites, phosphate slag, and alum shale. The contribution of building materials to the overall radon levels in a house is of less concern.

Uranium-rich ores are found in western Colorado and adjacent parts of Utah, Arizona, Wyoming, and New Mexico. These areas have a higher potential for radon gas than states which do not have uranium-rich ores (e.g., Louisiana, Alaska, and Arkansas).

Radon becomes trapped in homes where it has risen from the ground or been emitted from building materials. In porous soils or soils which have fractures, cracks, and faults, the gas escapes and rises to the surface.

The EPA has published an "achievable," recommended limit for airborne levels of radon in a home. It is 4 picoCuries per liter of air (pCi/l). There is a record of one dwelling in Pennsylvania with a reading as high as 3,125 pCi/l. Radon measurements by state are depicted in Table 9-6.

Table 9-5.   Radon Risk Evaluation

pCi/l	WL	Estimated Number of Lung Cancer Deaths Owing to Radon Exposure (out of 1,000)	Comparable Exposure Levels	Comparable Risk
200	1	440–770	1,000 times average outdoor level	>60 times non-smoker risk 4-pack-a-day smoker
100	0.5	270–630	100 times average indoor level	20,000 chest x-rays per year
40	0.2	120–380	100 times average outdoor level	2 pack-a-day smoker
20	0.1	60–210		1 pack-a-day smoker
10	0.05	30–120	10 times average indoor level	5 times non-smoker risk
4	0.02	13–50	10 times average outdoor level	200 chest x-rays per year
2	0.01	7–30		non-smoker risk of dying from lung cancer
1	0.005	3–13	average indoor level	non-smoker risk of dying from lung cancer
0.2	0.001	1–3	average outdoor level	20 chest x-rays per year

EPA.

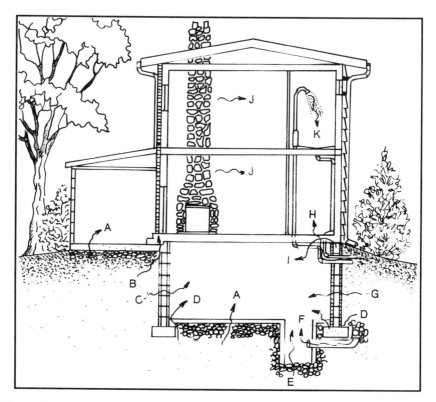

Figure 9-3.   Major routes of entry for indoor radon. Source: EPA
Legend: A. cracks in concrete slabs; B. spaces behind brick
veneer walls that rest on uncapped hollow--block foundation;
C. pores and cracks in concrete blocks; D. floor-wall joints; E.
exposed soils, as in a sump; F. weeping (drain) tile, if drained
to open sump; G. mortar joints; H. loose-fitting pipe penetration; I. open tops of block walls; J. building materials such as
some rock; K. water (from some wells).

Soluble in water, radon readily dissolves in associated groundwater.
In public water systems, this water is treated and stored for periods of time
which allows most of the dissolved radon to decay or escape. However,
private water wells may have high levels of radon gas, typically greater
than 10 times that found in public supplies. Depending on location, private
wells used as a water source on the property should be considered for radon
testing of the water.

Table 9-6.   Indoor Radon Measurements in the United States.

pCi per liter				pCi per liter			
State	Geom. Mean	Arith. Mean	Max.* Read	State	Geom. Mean	Arith. Mean	Max.* Read
AL	1.59	2.93	49.9	NV	1.81	4.40	67.5
AK	1.02	2.86	72.7	NH	2.63	5.49	72.7
AR	1.36	1.95	7.2	NJ	2.27	2.37	1,234.6
AZ	1.35	2.94	23.4	NM	2.37	4.24	213.8
CA	1.14	2.17	67.9	NY	1.22	2.72	394.7
CO	3.22	7.81	691.3	NC	1.49	2.59	30.1
CT	1.75	3.32	152.9	ND	2.83	4.00	33.1
DC	1.39	3.19	152.9	NW	1.19	2.37	70.5
DE	1.17	1.80	10.6	OH	3.00	5.22	127.1
FL	1.49	3.62	90.5	OK	1.29	2.29	27.3
GA	1.69	3.11	40.8	OR	0.91	1.50	187.7
HI	0.36	0.36	0.4	PA	5.04	12.39	3,125.4
ID	3.31	6.46	126.3	RI	1.90	4.95	153.2
IL	2.28	4.79	396.9	SC	1.07	1.59	153.2
IN	3.07	5.90	167.4	SD	2.62	6.70	128.7
IA	1.91	3.04	25.4	TN	2.38	4.15	164.8
MD	2.39	4.81	171.5	WA	0.67	1.39	144.3
MA	1.63	2.93	95.0	WV	2.06	5.61	65.3
MI	1.54	2.76	63.8	WI	2.11	3.60	56.3
MN	2.84	4.13	51.8	WY	3.51	9.72	111.5
MS	1.01	1.49	9.8	All USA	2.12	6.38	3,125.4
MO	1.68	2.54	50.5				
MT	2.97	4.78	63.2				
NB	2.95	4.55	17.1				

*Numbers rounded to the nearest tenth.

Lao, Kenneth Q.: Controlling Indoor Radon. Van Nostrand Reinhold, New York, 1990. pp. 44-46.

In the U.S., waterborne levels of radon average 200 to 600 pCi/l, in both public supplies and private wells. The highest recorded level is 1,130,000 pCi/l which was water sampled from a private well. Due to evaporation and holding time, surface waters normally contain low levels of radon, averaging 10 pCi/l.

Typically, only 1/10,000th of the radon in water becomes airborne. It is important to note that the gas is not as readily absorbed in the stomach as it is in the lungs. Airborne levels are caused when household water is agitated and aerosolized. For instance, a shower can become a source of aerosolized, airborne radon-containing water droplets. Heating also increases the release rate of radon from water into the air. Thus, if the water burden of radon is 20,000 pCi/l, the probable airborne levels are 2 pCi/l. The recommended action level for waterborne radon is 20,000 pCi/l.

Basic Sampling Methodology for Airborne Radon

State health departments, radiation protection offices, or public water works continuously perform sampling, maintaining documents which are available for public review. Some states provide home monitoring for radon gas as a service to the public, at a nominal fee.

Radon testing is designed to detect radon or its decay products (^{218}Po, ^{214}Pb, and ^{214}Bi) by measuring alpha particles from the radon decay. The most common method of sampling for radon in homes is the use of charcoal canisters which should be set out for a minimum of two days, the time recommended by the EPA. This is considered short-term testing, indicating levels for a limited time. Long-term testing of up to a year is desirable to obtain a realistic average. Otherwise, a worst case scenario can be very informative if performed under the proper conditions.

EPA Recommended Limit for Radon in Homes: 4 pCi/l

In preparation for sampling, the testing area should be sealed airtight for at least 12 hours prior to and during the test period. This should be accomplished by closing all windows and doors. Fans and ventilation systems which supply outside air (e.g., attic fans) should not be operated. The canister should be placed where it represents the building occupants' breathing zone, not in an air pocket (e.g., inside a closet or drawer). Record the start date, time, and location of placement. After exposure for the time designated by the given canister, record the stop date and time. Seal the canister, and send it to a laboratory for analysis.

Pesticides

The use of pesticides has not always been adequately controlled. Runoff from farms and construction sites into surface waters led to the ranking of pesticides as second only to metal and industrial pollutants of the toxic substances most widely reported to be contaminating rivers.

Chlordane

Chlordane used to be sprayed, before its ban, in and around homes for termite control. It is a viscous amber liquid and is retained in the environment for extended periods of time and becomes airborne, particularly in heated homes. There has been extensive sampling for chlordane in homes by government agencies over the past ten years, because they have found excessive airborne levels in many of the older homes which had been treated with chlordane. Not only is chlordane absorbed through the lungs, but it is rapidly absorbed through the skin and can be ingested.

DDT

DDT was banned in 1963. It too was used extensively for pest control and is retained in the environment for extended periods of time.

Dioxins[15]

The most toxic dioxin, 2,3,7,8-tetrachlorodibenzo-p-dioxin occurs in trace amounts as an impurity in 2,4,5-T. This herbicide was used in Vietnam, under the heading of Agent Orange, to clear excessive foliage. They have also been used domestically in much lower concentrations in the United States to clear pastures and other areas of unwanted vegetation or mixed with waste oil for dust control. Some of the dioxins are the most deadly substances known to man.

The compounds have been discovered at inactive industrial sites, municipal incinerators (where dioxin has been produced as a by-product of the burning of other organic compounds), toxic waste dumps, roads, and pastures.

Most commercial pesticides are now being controlled, but before they became controlled the only reason for an applicator to restrict their use was the cost of using more than what was necessary. It is extremely difficult, if not impossible, to track prior usage of pesticides. The only way to confirm its presence is through air sampling and soil or swipe samples. This can be expensive.

Electromagnetic Fields

There is presently unsettled controversy involving electromagnetic fields (EMF) and associated health hazards. In 1974, an epidemiological study implicated electrical transmission lines as the cause of childhood leukemia. There have since been numerous studies, none of which are conclusive and irrefutable. Some of the more recent studies are implicating high exposure levels to EMF on the job may lead to breast cancer in men. The increased incidence is estimated to be six times that of non-occupationally exposed workers. This topic is controversial and has yet to be widely addressed in site assessments. Yet, an awareness of this topic may be pertinent in some situations.

SUMMARY

Where an assessment involves buildings, some manner of investigation should be performed of the building materials. After reviewing building records and gathering pertinent building schematics, the investigator may include in an assessment an investigation of any of the following topics:

- Asbestos
- Lead-containing paint
- Lead-contaminated soil
- Lead in the water supply system
- Radon
- PCBs in transformers and light ballasts
- Pesticides
- Electromagnetic fields

An assessment should always include an investigation into asbestos. In residences, an evaluation of the lead content of paint is a requirement for HUD structures and recommended for others. Topics which may require attention include lead content of the water, lead content of the soil, PCVs, and radon. Other areas of concern may also include pesticides and electromagnetic fields.

REFERENCES

1. U.S. EPA: *Asbestos/NESHAP Regulated Asbestos Containing Materials Guidance.* [Bulletin]. Office of Toxic Substances, Washington, DC, EPA 340/1-90-018. p. 12.
2. U.S. EPA: *Asbestos/NESHAP Adequately Wet Guidance.* [Bulletin]. Office of Toxic Substances, Washington, DC, EPA 340/1-90-019. p. 8.
3. U.S. EPA: *Asbestos/NESHAP Regulated Asbestos Containing Materials Guidance.* [Bulletin]. Office of Toxic Substances, Washington, DC, EPA 340/1-90-018. p. 12.
4. Natale, Anthony and Hoag Levins: *Asbestos Removal and Control: An Insider's Guide to the Business.* Source Finders Information Corporation, Voorhees Township, New Jersey, 1984.
5. U.S. EPA: *Asbestos/NESHAP Adequately Wet Guidance.* [Bulletin]. Office of Toxic Substances, Washington, DC, EPA 340/1-90-019. p. 18.
6. Houk, Vernon: *Preventing Lead Poisoning in Young Children.* U.S. Department of Health And Human Services, Washington, DC, October 1991. pp. 18-19.
7. "Lead-Based Paint," *Code of Federal Regulations* 16:1303, January 1986.
8. Ness, Shirley A.: *Air Monitoring for Toxic Exposures.* Van Nostrand Reinhold, New York, 1991. pp. 419-420.
9. U.S. EPA: "Lead Cleanup in the Midwest." *EPA Journal,* (March/April 1992).
10. HUD: *Guidelines for Lead-Based Paint.*
11. *PCB Manual Introduction.* [Product Bulletin]. Texas Department of Health.
12. U.S. EPA: *Toxics Information Series.* Environmental Protection Agency, Washington, DC, OPA 59/0.
13. Lao, Kenneth Q.: *Controlling Indoor Radon.* Van Nostrand Reinhold, New York, 1990.

14. Ibid. 182.
15. Collins, Carol C.: *Our Food, Air, and Water: How Safe are They?* Facts on File Publications, New York, NY, 1984. p. 208.

Chapter 10

Industrial/Commercial Activities

INTRODUCTION

The major generators of hazardous wastes are industrial activities and commercial operations. These activities contribute to over 90 percent of all hazardous waste. Thus, an understanding of the various industrial/commercial activities, their processes, and the types of wastes typically generated is vital for an investigator to be able to project possible contamination of the property.

East topic covered in a Phase I assessment is leading up to the "types of activities conducted on and/or around the property." All this information culminates with, "What hazardous wastes might have been, or are presently being generated by, a given identified activity?" The answer to this question provides one of the more important pieces to the puzzle assembled by the investigator's speculation as to the potential for hazardous waste impact on the property.

The speculative process may require additional expertise, particularly for projecting potential impact of a specific industrial activity. Typically, those with a broad base of expertise in the industrial processes and the chemical hazards are the industrial hygienists, and those knowledgeable in the generation of hazardous wastes by industry type are environmental engineers. Other professionals with some understanding of the processes, but not necessarily the chemical hazards, include chemical engineers, industrial engineers, and some mechanical engineers. Many of the latter may have considerable expertise in a specific area. For instance, a chemical process engineer in a paint manufacturing facility will be an excellent source of information on paint manufacturing.

If there are no present or were no past industrial/commercial activities, the contents of this chapter are mute. If there are any industrial activities associated with the property, the contents herein may be useful to a well researched investigator.   Otherwise, all industrial activities should be evaluated by someone experienced in this area.

The intent is to provide an investigator with a basic understanding as to the typical, more common hazardous waste generator activities.   More in-depth knowledge in these areas will require further reading and interviewing people who work with the processes routinely.   However, any efforts to evaluate an activity based on interviews alone could lead to misguided information.

INDUSTRIAL PROCESSES

Process descriptions and industrial activities within a specific industry type are generally consistent.   Facilities may vary.   Chemicals may vary. Management practices may vary.   Yet, the general process descriptions and many of the chemicals used and generated are similar.

Many of the industries mentioned herein typically generate large amounts of waste.   Yet, to make a point, a few of the succeeding industry types are not generally thought to be associated with hazardous chemicals.

Petroleum Processing and Refining

The petroleum and allied industries are the largest generators of hazardous waste of any of the industries.   They have pipelines, tanks, and storage vessels which may leak into the ground, and they generate airborne wastes as well.   In 1980, an EPA survey indicated that 20 percent of the petroleum refineries which were evaluated for air pollution were not in compliance with federal environmental regulations.[2]   Compliance is often expensive and affects production.

Petroleum products are extracted from natural gas and crude oil. Crude oil is a liquid, containing gaseous and solid materials.   There are over 3,000 chemicals which may be refined from various grades of crude petroleum, ranging from natural gas to asphalt.   Only a few of these are considered toxic.   Table 10-1 has a breakdown of typical gasoline components which are considered "toxic."   Most of those which remain unmentioned do, however, pose a flammability hazard.

After crude is extracted from the ground, it is either shipped or piped to a refinery.   At the refinery, the raw material is fractionated into its components. Over 50 percent of the total crude is gasoline. The remaining constituents include kerosene, alcohols, solvents, precursors to plastics,

Table 10-1.   Toxic Components of Gasoline

Chemical Component	Percent by Volume
Benzene	<4.9
Ethylbenzene	<1.4
Xylene	<7.7
Toluene	<6.5
Hexane	<3.0
Cyclohexane	<2.4
May Also Contain	
Methyl tertiary butyl ether	<15.0
Ethyl alcohol	<10.0

Chevron Environmental Health Center: MSDS for Chevron Unleaded Gasoline. [Bulletin]. Chevron, Richmond, CA. June 1989. pp 5-7.

synthetic rubber, paints and varnishes, various oils, waxes, corrosives, and asphalt.

Processing starts with fractional distillation.   The components are converted to other compounds by cracking (e.g., breaking), combining (e.g., polymerization), and rearranging (e.g., catalytic reforming).   Impurities are removed (e.g., hydrogen sulfide is separated and converted to sulfur). Many of the products are blended (e.g., gasoline blends), and waste is recycled or used in another process.

All crude oil, intermediate processes, and end products are container-ized in large storage vessels.   These vessels may leak or may have leaked in the past.   Although most of the constituents are sold or recycled, some of the waste used to go to settling ponds which may or may not have had liners.[1]   Settling ponds should no longer be used.   See a sample process flow chart in Figure 10-1.

Special Considerations

Petroleum refineries are hard to miss.   Acres of property abound with aboveground storage tanks, cracking towers, and process equipment. However, some locations have been abandoned and may have been replaced by residential homes.   Waste discarded into old settling ponds may still be present in some of the abandoned locations.

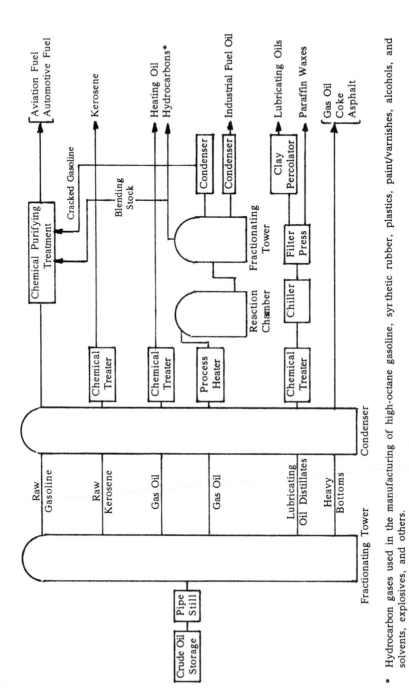

Figure 10-1. Process flow chart for petroleum refinery. The process description is general, simplified, and waste products are not included (Information Source: Collier's Encyclopedia, 1992.)

* Hydrocarbon gases used in the manufacturing of high-octane gasoline, synthetic rubber, plastics, paint/varnishes, alcohols, and solvents, explosives, and others.

Paint Formulators

Paints, varnishes, and lacquers are all surface coatings. Manufacturers divide their products into trade-sale products and industrial finishes. Ingredients include binders (i.e., vehicles), solvents (i.e., thinners), pigments, and additives.

The binders help the paint adhere to the surface and remain adhered to the surface when the solvents have evaporated. Binders may oxidize, polymerize, or be baked to a hard finish. Constituents may include, but not be limited to, disocyanates, acrylonitrile, vinyl acetate, and vinyl chloride.

The solvents are what thin the binder/pigment mix so the paint can be spread over a surface. They are the component which evaporates, allowing the coating to harden. Some solvents include alcohols, esters, ketones, esters, mineral spirits, and water. Benzene, tetrachloroethane, and carbon tetrachloride had been solvents of the past, but trichloroethylene is still used in industrial paints.[4]

The pigments are generally in powder form and provide color. Earlier powders contained lead and lead-zinc pigments. Other colorants include cadmium sulfide (yellow), chromium oxide (green), cobalt (blue), iron oxide or cadmium selenide (red), and manganese silicate (transparent, providing bulk). Metal primers may contain red lead oxide, and industrial paints may contain lead chromate.[4]

Additives include anti-foaming agents, plasticizers, freeze-thaw stabilizers, buffers, preservatives, and anticorrosive. These may contain ethylene glycol or organic mercurial fungicides.[4]

Dry pigments are weighed, mixed, and fed through hoppers or chutes into mills where they are dispersed in the appropriate resin vehicle. The milled pigments are transferred to a large mixing vat where all remaining components are added. The components are generally fed by an enclosed system of pipes from remote containers. Pipes may be aboveground or underground. The storage vessels are generally quite large and may or may not be on a diked concrete pad. All paint components are potential environmental contaminants.

Special Considerations

Paint manufacturing is generally performed in a large manufacturing facility, but formulators of the past have mixed and developed paints in a garage, the backyard, or a small building which has since been converted to a retail store.

Printing Operations

The four fundamental printing methods are letterpress, lithography, gravure, and flexography. Letterpress is the oldest process. It involves printing from a raised/relief surface which receives ink, transferring it under pressure to paper. The plate is cast from molten lead which is poured into the mold at the print shop. Photoengraving of metal blocks may involve dichromates, alcohol, nitric acid, cyanide chloride, and mercuric chloride.[5]

Lithographic printing is the chemical treatment of a photosensitive printing plate to make it selectively pick up ink. Chemicals which may be involved in this process include hydrofluoric or nitric acid, gum arabic, blanket wash (e.g., xylene, methylene chloride, or 1,1,1-trichloroethane), alcohol, and acrylates.[5]

Gravure printing is similar to lithographic printing. Many of the same chemicals are involved with a few more added to the list. Before etching a varnish is applied to the surface of the cylinder, and etching may be done with ferric chloride.[5]

Flexography is a more recent process. It is widely used for printing on plastics. Rubber printing plates are prepared, some of which had asbestos in the matrix in the past.[5]

Other methods of printing are variations of those mentioned or may involve silk screening which requires larger quantities of solvent for cleaning. The inks are similar.[5]

After a plate has been prepared, it is installed onto a roller or a surface of the press. Ink is applied to the surface of the plate and adheres to the raised or specially treated areas. Paper is rolled over the surface of the ink-treated plate, dried, cut, and stacked. The rollers are then cleaned with a blanket wash solvent.

Wastes may include various flammable solvents, corrosives, sensitizing resins, and petroleum distillates. Ink sludges may also have solvents, heavy metals, and carcinogenic dyes. Heavy metals are used in some drying compounds, and solvents are used in extenders. The waste is generally retained and later disposed of in 55-gallon drums.[6]

In brief, the major concern in present day printing activities is the flammable cleaning solvents (e.g., isopropanol) and occasionally lead. The older printing operations used plates poured from molten lead.

Special Considerations

Although many of today's printing operations are housed in a print shop, they used to be located in office buildings, shops which are now used as retail stores, or in a building located behind the printers home.

Paper Manufacturing

Wood is reduced to chips, then pulped (i.e., reduced to a fiberous compost) and bleached. This composition is then chemically treated with sodium sulfite or soda ash, caustics, various salts, and/or peroxides, depending upon the type of process required for a given paper. A process flow chart is presented in Figure 10-2 for Kraft paper manufacturing.

The pulping process may be one of several chemical treatments, the most frequently used being the Kraft process. The latter involves caustic, sodium sulfide, calcium carbonate, and lime. These are recycled during processing. All other processes may involve one or a combination of the following: caustics, oxidizers, solvents, hydrogen sulfide, and petroleum distillates. Various additives (e.g., alum, rosin, and wax emulsions) are mixed with the pulp.[7] Then, the pulp is flowed onto a large paper roller, rolled to form large sheets of paper, dried, and cut. Mixing occurs in large vats which are fed by an enclosed system of pipes. Storage containers for the chemical constituents are generally aboveground.

By-products of the Kraft process can be sold, so the waste is minimal. These by-products include resins, methyl alcohol, turpentine, and oils.[7,8]

One of the major concerns associated with pulp mills, which are part of paper manufacturing, is dioxin in the bleach effluent which was in the past generally discharged into the water source (e.g., stream or river) adjacent to the property, used for processing. This discharge is being controlled today but was a big pollution problem of the past.[9]

Metal Manufacturing

Metal manufacturing involves fabrication by rolling, drawing, forging, extruding, and casting the metal alloys. After the product has been formed it may be welded, electroplated, etched, pickled, degreased, and painted. Fabrication may involve minimal coating of the metal, and after-treatments involve various component wastes which depend on the type of activity and materials being used.

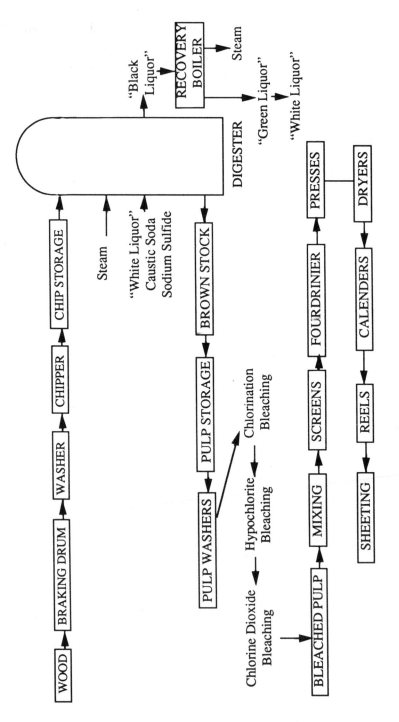

Figure 10-2. Process flow chart for paper manufacturing.

Electroplating generates the greatest volume of toxic wastes and some of the most hazardous chemicals (e.g., cyanide salts and heavy metals). Hazardous substances associated with other metal treatments include solvents, caustics, heavy metal sludges (e.g., chromium and copper), paints, and oxidizers.[10,11] In brief, metal manufacturing generates considerable toxic wastes.

Special Considerations

Metal operations vary from in-house metal artwork to large manufacturing facilities. Past activities concerning the former may be difficult to detect by a historic usage search. Yet, a small operator may generate many of the same wastes.

Wood Preserving

Wood preservatives are extremely toxic and used in large quantities. These preservatives include creosote, pentachlorophenol, and inorganic arsenical compounds (e.g., chromium arsonate). The wood may be conveyed through a large vat containing the preservatives and sometimes sprayed, or it may enter into an enclosed pressure treatment container preconditioned with solvents. Wood is pressure treated to force the chemicals into the pores, or it is soaked in the chemical.

Due to the large quantities of chemicals used in this process, the toxic material not only has an opportunity to become airborne, but the saturated wood may be conveyed over or onto uncovered, porous soil. Considerable contamination should be anticipated where there has been no ground covering or where runoff is possible (e.g., cracks in the concrete).

Special Considerations

Wood preserving activities may be included as part of a sawmill's activities after the wood has been cut, or it may be performed on a small scale where the treatment area is no larger than a shack.

Pesticide Formulators/End-Users

A pesticide is a chemical used for the destruction of unwanted varmints, and it may range from slightly toxic to extremely hazardous. Pesticides are chemically extracted, synthesized, and mixed to meet various requirements. Many are diluted with a solvent or water. Others are combined with another substance for enhancement of the effects. They may be formulated, stored, and transported in concentrated form.

Upon receipt of the concentrate, the end-user dilutes the chemical and applies it in accordance with the manufacturer's instructions. Typical locations where pesticides are applied are homes, restaurants, commercial buildings, farmlands, and golf courses. Those pesticides which have a long environmental life expectancy should be subject to suspicion more than the highly toxic substances which biodegrade to non-toxic substances within days of their application. Some examples of long-term pesticides include DDT, Kepone, and chlordane. Waste is in the form of rinse water, empty containers, and unused pesticides, or chemicals may have been spilled or leaked from their containers.[13]

Special Considerations

Pesticides are generally formulated by a large chemical manufacturer. Yet, they may be repackaged at a separate location or mixed in an office building/garage where a small pesticide treatment operator is housed.

Electronics Industry

The electronics industry includes the production of computer circuit boards and computer chips. Circuit board manufacturing involves heated vats of lead wave-solder and manual soldering with the use of a corrosive flux. The final product is cleaned with a degreasing solvent.

The manufacture of computer chips is more involved than that of circuit boards. A chip is a miniaturized circuit board. Semi-metal ingots (e.g., silicon and gallium) are grown and sliced into wafers. These wafers are cleaned, lapped, and prepared for the photolithographic processing.[14]

In photolithography, the wafers are oxidized, treated/exposed, etched, doped, and metallized. Oxidation is the layering of the metal oxide (e.g., silicon dioxide) over the surface of the wafer. In photolithography, a thin layer of polymer coats the surface of the wafer. The treated wafer is then exposed to ultraviolet light, shining through the template of the circuit design desired. The exposed areas become soluble and stripped (e.g., sulfuric/chromic acids, phenols, or perchloroethylene) from the surface, leaving a mask behind. Then, the oxide coating in the unprotected area is etched away (e.g., wet etching: hydrofluoric acid or nitric acid; gas etching: gallium arsenide or carbon fluoride) and doped (e.g., phosphine or arsine) to make the remaining unprotected portion a semiconductor. Ion implantation may be used in place of doping. The final step is metallization (e.g., chromium, gold, copper, or platinum) or deposition of a layer of high conductivity metal, leaving a connecting layer of circuitry.[14]

Special Considerations

Many of manufacturing activities have a tendency to be housed in building which may later be converted to office space, and many of their buildings are used exclusively for office space. If an electronics firm predates an office complex, the structure may or may not have been used for manufacturing.

Furniture and Allied Wood Products

Allied wood products include plywood, particle board, cabinets, household furniture/upholstery, and wood office accessories. Wastes include sensitizers, solvents, ignitable materials, and heavy metals.[15]

Leather Products

Leather undergoes a preservative treatment/tanning process. The skin is then cut, molded, embossed, hammered, trimmed, bonded, stitched, dyed, and glued. Potential hazardous substances associated with the leather industry include solvents (e.g., toluene and carbon tetrachloride), heavy metal salts, acids, dyes, and lacquers.[16]

Other Industries

Industries which generate hazardous wastes and may be overlooked include the following: textiles (e.g., formaldehyde in permapress clothes and jeans), ceramic manufacturers (e.g., heavy metal pigments), pharmaceutical and cosmetics manufacturers (e.g., formaldehyde), plastics manufacturers (e.g., methacrylates and isocyanates), foundries (e.g., silica), glass products (e.g., hydrogen fluoride for etching), art supplies (e.g., solvents and heavy metal pigments), and airplane and auto manufacturing (e.g., degreasing solvents and paints).

COMMERCIAL ACTIVITIES

Commercial activities are the sale of goods/merchandise and services. Knowledge as to hazardous substances used and generated is necessary for a complete environmental evaluation. A few of the more common activities associated with the generation of hazardous substances are discussed in brief within this chapter. New commercial enterprises arise daily, and additional queries may be necessary.

Many of the activities mentioned are commonly understood to manage hazardous substances which could contaminate the environment; and a few are not generally given a second thought, although the potential exposures should be noted. Commercial operations range from the gasoline service stations to dry cleaners to dental offices.

Service Stations

Service stations store gasoline in underground storage tanks. Many of the older, unprotected tanks have been found to leak, particularly around the pipe connections. Even where newer tanks have been installed, there may be contaminated soil from prior experiences. There are also reported cases of newly installed, protected tanks which were not properly installed and developed a hole upon insertion into the ground (e.g., placement of the tank on a sharp rock). A diagram of a typical service station is found in Figure 10-3.

Many service stations also perform vehicle maintenance. Potential environmental exposures associated with this are mentioned in the next section.

Special Considerations

Many of the older service stations have been abandoned and all evidence of their prior use covered with cement. These sites have since been converted to convenience stores, courthouses, dry cleaners, and fruit stands to name a few.

Vehicle Maintenance

Vehicle maintenance may involve mechanical and/or body repairs. Although these operations appear to be minor contributors to the overall pollution of the environment, there are so many shops that these small operations can become part and parcel of a large environmental problem.

Auto body repair shops used to use lead to repair auto bodies. Lead-containing batteries become refuse, and leaking batteries are often left on the premises when the site is abandoned. Many of the shops use caustic rust removers, resins, degreasers, paint thinners, and heavy metal-containing paints. Some of the other wastes which may be generated include the following:

- Tires
- Anti-freeze
- Brake fluid
- Asbestos brake pads/exhaust gaskets
- Transmission fluid
- Power steering fluid

Also in the past, prior to "bondo," auto body repair work was done with a lead paste, and lead-containing batteries were not recycled. Many old batteries were deposited on the property.

The mechanical repair shops use and dispose of motor oil. They also use degreasing solvents and glues. Waste motor oil is one of the most commonly mismanaged substances used by small commercial activities and do-it-yourselfers. Motor oil presently is being recycled by most shops. Yet, in the past, it was common to dump the spent motor oil on their own premises or in an abandoned field, remote to their shop.

Special Considerations

Vehicle maintenance may be performed anywhere from in a residential garage or out in a field to a full service gasoline station or large tin building.

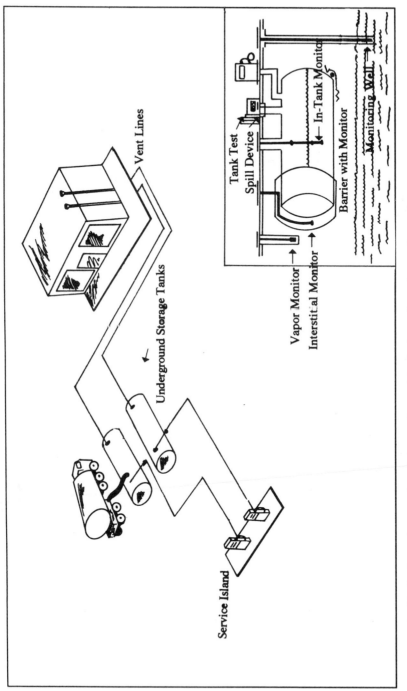

Figure 10-3. Typical service station schematic and leak detection alternatives diagram.

Dry Cleaning

Dry cleaning operations involve the use of non-aqueous solvents to clean garments which cannot be treated with water. Formerly, high toxicity, low flammability solvents (e.g., carbon tetrachloride) were used. More recently, however, low toxicity, high flammability solvents (e.g., petroleum naphtha) are being used. These latter solvents are recovered and recycled, or they are disposed of in accordance with strict EPA regulations.

Past usage of highly toxic chemicals in the dry cleaning industry may have resulted in backyard dumping of the waste. Present day usage of low toxicity chemicals poses a minimal threat to the environment.

Laboratories

All laboratories store various quantities of hazardous chemicals, dependent upon the type of laboratory. Although some may house a couple of 55-gallon drums of a given chemical, most maintain quantities below a gallon in volume. Because a laboratory is generally associated with chemists, don't assume that the chemicals are, or have been, properly managed. Wastes generated include solvents, highly poisonous chemicals, caustics, oxidizers, and flammable liquids. These may also be emitted into the environment by way of the local exhaust systems.

Other Commercial Operations

Commercial operations which generate waste and may be overlooked include furniture sales (e.g., repair paints and glues), dental offices (e.g., mercury from the amalgam used in the fillings), hospitals (e.g., ethylene oxide used in the sterilizers), and machine shops (e.g., solvents).

SUMMARY

Knowledge regarding manufacturing processes and certain commercial activities is pertinent in regard to identifying possible hazardous substance contamination of property(ies) once the potential for a given activity has been determined through the historic usage search and interviews. When assessing industrial/commercial properties of properties which are thought to have been used for these purposes, it is vital that the investigator have access to information regarding the following:

- Processes
- Wastes generated
- Means for contaminating the environment
- Typical control measures

If not familiar with these items, the investigator is well advised to seek assistance from someone who does know.

REFERENCES

1.   Statistical Policy Division: *Standard Industrial Classification Manual.* Office of Management and Budget, Washington, DC, 1991. p. 57.
2.   McNeil, Mary: *Environment and Health.* Congressional Quarterly, Inc., Washington, DC, 1981. p. 9.
3.   Parmeggiani, Dr. Luigi: *Encyclopaedia of Occupational Health and Safety.* ILO Publications, Geneva, Switzerland, 3rd ed., 1983. pp. 1659-1665.
4.   Ibid. pp. 1586-1587.
5.   Ibid. pp. 1790-1795.
6.   U.S. EPA: *Printing and Allied Industries.* [Bulletin]. U.S. EPA, Washington, DC, EPA/530-SW-90-027g.
7.   Parmeggiani, Dr. Luigi: *Encyclopaedia of Occupational Health and Safety.* ILO Publications, Geneva, Switzerland, 3rd ed., 1983. pp. 1588-1591.
8.   U.S. EPA: *Paper Industry.* [Bulletin]. U.S. EPA, Washington, DC, EPA/530-SW-90-027o.
9.   U.S. EPA: *Estimating Exposures to 2,3,7,8-TCDD.* [Draft Report]. Office of Health and Environmental Associations, Washington, DC, EPA PB88231196.
10. Parmeggiani, Dr. Luigi: *Encyclopaedia of Occupational Health and Safety.* ILO Publications, Geneva, Switzerland, 3rd ed., 1983. pp. 1349-1350.
11. U.S. EPA: *Metal Manufacturing.* [Bulletin]. U.S. EPA, Washington, DC, EPA/530-SW-90-027n.
12. U.S. EPA: *Pesticide End-Users/Application Services.* [Bulletin]. U.S. EPA, Washington, DC, EPA/530-SW-90-027i.

13. Wade, Richard, Ph.D., M.P.H., Michael Williams, et. al.: *Semi-conductor Industry Study.* [Document].   California Department of Industrial Relations, Division of Occupational Safety and Health, 1981.
14. U.S. EPA: *Furniture/Wood Finishing.*   [Bulletin].   U.S. EPA, Washington, DC, EPA/530-SW-90-027c.
15. U.S. EPA: *Leather/Leather Production.*   [Bulletin].   U.S. EPA, Washington, DC, EPA/530-SW-90-027r.

Chapter 11

Special Resources

INTRODUCTION

Special resources refer to a broad category of items which make the property and/or buildings unique. The property may be the habitat for an endangered reptile, or a building may have been the childhood home of a former president. It may be a special habitat for migrating birds, or it may have unique aesthetic qualities. Many of these resources are protected. Therefore, development of the land is restricted by law. These restrictions could impact the plans for property development and defuse the developer's intended use for the land.

A special resources query is not typically required for a Phase I environmental site assessment. Many of the components are often included in a separate assessment, commonly referred to as an environmental impact statement (e.g., endangered species). Yet, an abbreviated review of special resources and the probability for impact is required by some clients, especially where the property is going to be developed. This *generally* applies to undeveloped land only.

Although the impact special resources may have on a site is not as potentially costly, plans can be affected and criminal/civil suits are a possibility. An awareness of the components and their potential impact will allow the investigator to assist the client's decision-making process when discussing the scope of work—where the client plans to develop the property.

With the aid of local agencies, the investigator can generally identify potential problem areas of concern. These agencies may be the local planning department, U.S. Army Corps of Engineers, U.S. EPA, or any of the state or local regulatory arms for the EPA.

Yet, a more in-depth review of special resources will frequently require a specialist. For example, the identification/quantification of an actual impact on the northern spotted owl will require the services of a

221

biologist or an ornithologist. The investigator discovers probability for impact. The specialist clarifies and defines.

Topics discussed in this chapter are some of the more prevalent issues speculated on in Phase I site assessments. The intent is to introduce them to the reader, not to detail particulars.

THREATENED AND ENDANGERED SPECIES[1,2,3]

As of 1991, there were more than 600 mammals, birds, reptiles, fish, mollusks, plants, and other life forms native to the United States which were officially protected as endangered or threatened. An "endangered" species is one that is in danger of extinction throughout all or a significant portion of its range. A "threatened" species is one which is likely to become endangered within the foreseeable future. Both are protected.

The Federal Endangered Species Act was passed into law in 1973. The purpose of this act was to protect certain species of plants, fish, and wildlife which are in danger of becoming extinct and to conserve the ecosystems upon which these species depend. The Act specifically prohibits the "taking" of any species, listed by the federal government. The term "taking," originally defined as harm or harassment of individuals of a protected species, has been broadened to include the prohibition of acts or activities which may harm the species indirectly by adversely affecting its habitat, as well as those which directly harm the species. The U.S. Fish and Wildlife Service, a division of the Department of the Interior, is charged with its enforcement.

The initial step to comply with the Endangered Species Act is to determine whether or not habitat for the species exists on the property. The Fish and Wildlife Service publishes habitat descriptions; if after reading them one is reasonably certain they do not have the described habitat, plans may proceed without further delay. If, on the other hand, the investigator is uncertain, the Fish and Wildlife Service or a qualified biologist may be consulted. See Figures 11-1 and 11-2.

The U.S. Fish and Wildlife Service can determine whether or not habitat for an endangered species does or does not exist on the property. The agency requires the following information in writing:

- A map showing the location of the property
- Size of the property
- Description of the area's vegetation
- A recent aerial photograph, if available

Scientific Name / Common Name	Status *				Family	Distribution **
Abronia macrocarpa / large-fruited sand verbena	G1	S1	LE	E	NYCTAGINACEAE Four o'clock Family	Freestone, Leon, and Robertson Counties
Acleisanthes crassifolia / Texas trumpets	G2	S2	C2		NYCTAGINACEAE Four o'clock Family	Kinney, Maverick, and Val Verde Counties; Coahuila, Mexico
Acleisanthes wrightii / Wright's trumpets	G2	S2			NYCTAGINACEAE Four o'clock Family	Pecos, Reeves, Terrell, and Val Verde Counties
Adelia vaseyi / Vasey's adelia	G2	S2			EUPHORBIACEAE Spurge Family	Cameron and Hidalgo Counties; Tamaulipas, Mexico
Agalinis auriculata / auriculate false foxglove	G2	SX	C2		SCROPHULARIACEAE Snapdragon Family	Tarrant County; AR, IA, IL, IN (H), KS, MD (H), MI, MN (H), MO, MS, NJ (H), OH, OK (?), PA, SC, TN, VA (H), WI (H), and WV
Agave chisosensis (see **Agave glomeruliflora**)						
Agave glomeruliflora / Chisos agave	G2Q	S2	C2		AGAVACEAE Agave Family	Brewster and Culberson Counties; Coahuila, Mexico
Agrimonia incisa / incised groovebur	G3	S1	C2		ROSACEAE Rose Family	Jasper County; AL, FL, GA, MS, and SC
Allium elmendorfii / Elmendorf onion	G2	S2			LILIACEAE Lily Family	Atascosa, Bexar, Kenedy, Llano, San Patricio, and Wilson Counties
Ambrosia cheiranthifolia / South Texas ragweed	G1	S1	C1		ASTERACEAE Sunflower Family	Cameron (H), Jim Wells, Kleberg, and Nueces Counties; Tamaulipas, Mexico
Amsonia tharpii / Tharp's blue-star	G1	S1	C2		APOCYNACEAE Dogbane Family	Pecos County; NM

Figure 11-1. Threatened/Endangered Plant List for Texas.   Source: Texas Parks and Wildlife, January 31, 1992.

SCIENTIFIC NAME	COMMON NAME	GLOBAL RANK	STATE RANK	FEDERAL STATUS	STATE STATUS
*** AMPHIBIANS					
BUFO HOUSTONENSIS	HOUSTON TOAD	G1	S1	LE	E
EURYCEA NANA	SAN MARCOS SALAMANDER	G1	S1	LT	T
EURYCEA NEOTENES	TEXAS SALAMANDER	G3	S3	C2	
EURYCEA SP 1	JOLLYVILLE PLATEAU SALAMANDER	G1	S1		
EURYCEA SP 2	SALADO SPRINGS SALAMANDER	G1	S1		
EURYCEA SP 3	BARTON SPRINGS SALAMANDER	G1	S1	C2	
EURYCEA TRIDENTIFERA	COMAL BLIND SALAMANDER	G1	S1	C2	T
HYPOPACHUS VARIOLOSUS	SHEEP FROG	G5	S2		T
LEPTODACTYLUS FRAGILIS	WHITE-LIPPED FROG	G5	S1		E
NOTOPHTHALMUS MERIDIONALIS	BLACK-SPOTTED NEWT	G1	S1	C2	E
PLETHODON SERRATUS	SOUTHERN REDBACK SALAMANDER	G5	S1		
RANA GRYLIO	PIG FROG	G5	S2		
RANA PIPIENS	NORTHERN LEOPARD FROG	G5	S1		
RHINOPHRYNUS DORSALIS	MEXICAN BURROWING TOAD	G5	S2		T
SIREN INTERMEDIA TEXANA	RIO GRANDE LESSER SIREN	G5T2	S2	C2	E
SMILISCA BAUDINII	MEXICAN TREEFROG	G5	S3		T
TYPHLOMOLGE RATHBUNI	TEXAS BLIND SALAMANDER	G1	S1	LE	E
TYPHLOMOLGE ROBUSTA	BLANCO BLIND SALAMANDER	G1	S1	C2	E
*** ARACHNIDS					
ARCHEOLARCA GUADALUPENSIS	GUADALUPE CAVE PSEUDOSCORPION	G1	S1	C2	
MICROCREAGRIS TEXANA	TOOTH CAVE PSEUDOSCORPION	G1	S1	LE	
NEOLEPTONETA MYOPICA	TOOTH CAVE SPIDER	G1	S1	LE	
TEXELLA REDDELLI	BEE CREEK CAVE HARVESTMAN	G1	S1	LE	
*** BIRDS					
AIMOPHILA AESTIVALIS	BACHMAN'S SPARROW	G3	S2	C2	T
AIMOPHILA BOTTERII TEXANA	TEXAS BOTTERII'S SPARROW	G4TU	S3	C2	T
AMMODRAMUS BAIRDII	BAIRD'S SPARROW	G3	S?	C2	
AMMODRAMUS HENSLOWII	HENSLOW'S SPARROW	G4	S?	C2	
ARREMONOPS RUFIVIRGATUS	OLIVE SPARROW	G5?	S?	C2	
BUTEO ALBICAUDATUS	WHITE-TAILED HAWK	G5	S2		T
BUTEO ALBONOTATUS	ZONE-TAILED HAWK	G5	S3		T
BUTEO NITIDUS MAXIMUS	NORTHERN GRAY HAWK	G5T5	S1	C2	T
BUTEO REGALIS	FERRUGINOUS HAWK	G4	S3	C2	
BUTEOGALLUS ANTHRACINUS	COMMON BLACK-HAWK	G5	S2		T
CAMPEPHILUS PRINCIPALIS	IVORY-BILLED WOODPECKER	G1	SX	LE	E
CAMPTOSTOMA IMBERBE	NORTHERN BEARDLESS-TYRANNULET	G5	S3		T
CHARADRIUS ALEXANDRINUS NIVOSUS	WESTERN SNOWY PLOVER	G4T3	S2	C2	
CHARADRIUS ALEXANDRINUS TENUIROSTRIS	SOUTHEASTERN SNOWY PLOVER	G4TU	S2	C2	
CHARADRIUS MELODUS	PIPING PLOVER	G2	S2	LT	T
CHARADRIUS MONTANUS	MOUNTAIN PLOVER	G3	S2	C2	
CHONDROHIERAX UNCINATUS	HOOK-BILLED KITE	G5	S1		
DENDROCYGNA BICOLOR	FULVOUS WHISTLING-DUCK	G5	S4	C2	
DENDROICA CERULEA	CERULEAN WARBLER	G5	S?	C2	
DENDROICA CHRYSOPARIA	GOLDEN-CHEEKED WARBLER	G2	S2	LE	E
EGRETTA RUFESCENS	REDDISH EGRET	G4	S2	C2	T
ELANOIDES FORFICATUS	AMERICAN SWALLOW-TAILED KITE	G5	S2	3C	T
FALCO FEMORALIS SEPTENTRIONALIS	NORTHERN APLOMADO FALCON	G4T2	S1C	LE	E
FALCO PEREGRINUS ANATUM	AMERICAN PEREGRINE FALCON	G3T2	S1	LE	E
FALCO PEREGRINUS TUNDRIUS	ARCTIC PEREGRINE FALCON	G3T1	S1	LT	T
GEOTHLYPIS TRICHAS INSPERATA	BROWNSVILLE COMMON YELLOWTHROAT	G5TU	S?	C2	
GLAUCIDIUM BRASILIANUM	FERRUGINOUS PYGMY-OWL	G5	S3	C2	T
GRUS AMERICANA	WHOOPING CRANE	G1	S1	LE	E
HALIAEETUS LEUCOCEPHALUS	BALD EAGLE	G3	S2	LE	E
HISTRIONICUS HISTRIONICUS	HARLEQUIN DUCK	G5	S?	C2	
ICTERUS CUCULLATUS CUCULLATUS	MEXICAN HOODED ORIOLE	G5TU	S?	C2	
ICTERUS CUCULLATUS SENNETTI	SENNETT'S HOODED ORIOLE	G5TU	S?	C2	
ICTERUS GRADUACAUDA AUDUBONII	AUDUBON'S ORIOLE	G5T?	S?	C2	
LANIUS LUDOVICIANUS MIGRANS	MIGRANT LOGGERHEAD SHRIKE	G4T2	S?	C2	
LATERALLUS JAMAICENSIS	BLACK RAIL	G5	S2	C2	
MYCTERIA AMERICANA	WOOD STORK	G5	S2		T
NUMENIUS AMERICANUS	LONG-BILLED CURLEW	G5	S5	C2	
NUMENIUS BOREALIS	ESKIMO CURLEW	G1	S1	LE	E
PACHYRAMPHUS AGLAIAE	ROSE-THROATED BECARD	G4G5	S2		T
PARULA PITIAYUMI NIGRILORA	TROPICAL PARULA	G5TU	S3	C2	T
PELECANUS OCCIDENTALIS	BROWN PELICAN	G5	S1	LE	E
PICOIDES BOREALIS	RED-COCKADED WOODPECKER	G2	S2	LE	E
PLEGADIS CHIHI	WHITE-FACED IBIS	G5	S2	C2	T
STERNA ANTILLARUM	LEAST TERN	G4	S?	LE	
STERNA ANTILLARUM ATHALASSOS	INTERIOR LEAST TERN	G4T2	S1	LE	E
STERNA DOUGALLII	ROSEATE TERN	G3	S?	LT	
STERNA FUSCATA	SOOTY TERN	G5	S2		T
STRIX OCCIDENTALIS	SPOTTED OWL	G3	S1	C2	
TYMPANUCHUS CUPIDO ATTWATERI	ATTWATER'S PRAIRIE-CHICKEN	G4T1	S1	LE	E
TYMPANUCHUS PALLIDICINCTUS	LESSER PRAIRIE-CHICKEN	G3	S3		
VERMIVORA BACHMANII	BACHMAN'S WARBLER	GH	SX	LE	

Figure 11-2. Threatened/Endangered Animal List for Texas. List has global, state, and federal status for each entry. Source: Texas Parks and Wildlife, January 8, 1992. p 1.

- Ground photographs of the project area, if available
- A brief description of the planned activity
- Requesting party's address and telephone number

Some reviews may require a site visit, and a habitat review may take six to eight weeks. The requesting party will be notified if a site visit is necessary. Other wildlife will require an on-site survey by a U.S. Fish and Wildlife biologist or a private consultant versed in the subject.

If habitat is found on the property, the easiest direction is to prevent development or other use of the land. However, the Act does provide some flexibility in regulating the "incidental taking" of a listed species. An incidental take is a taking of the species that is the result of an otherwise lawful activity. The take must not be the intended purpose of the action. Hence, the U.S. Fish and Wildlife Service may issue permits to individual property owners or regional entities for the incidental taking of a federally listed species. A habitat conservation plan must be developed and approved before such a permit can be issued. The habitat conservation plan must specify:

- Impact likely to result from the proposed incidental take
- Steps that would be taken to monitor, minimize, and mitigate such impacts, and the funding available to implement such steps
- Alternative actions to the incidental taking that were considered and the reasons why such alternatives are not being utilized
- Any other measures the U.S. Fish and Wildlife Service may require as being necessary or appropriate

Although it is possible to prepare such a plan for an individual tract of land, the process can be expensive and time-consuming. Very few opt to go this route. The buyer with plans to develop the land may decide to look elsewhere.

There are civil and criminal penalties associated with violating the provisions of the Endangered Species Act. Individual violators may be fined up to $100,000 and/or sentenced to a year in jail, and organizations may be fined up to $200,000.

CRITICAL AND UNIQUE HABITAT[1]

The distinguishing difference between endangered species and critical/unique habitat is "coverage." Whereby endangered species includes import/export concerns and a consideration for the actual endangerment of the species, the critical/unique habitat is directed toward protecting the environmental setting which is conducive to the survival of a species.

Recovery of an endangered species requires stopping and reversing its decline and then ensuring its long-term survival in nature. This generally requires "habitat protection," research, captive breeding and reintroduction, or special wildlife and habitat management techniques.

For example, the American bald eagle population was estimated to be less than 400 nesting pairs in the 1960s. Protection of habitat, along with stricter law enforcement, reintroduction, public education, and ban on the use of DDT in the United States reversed the dwindling numbers. In 1991, 30 years later, over 3,000 nesting pairs were counted. Habitat protection included the ban on DDT.

Another example is the whooping crane, which in the late 1940s was reduced to fewer than 20 birds in the whole world. However, a captive breeding flock has been managed since 1967, and the total number of whooping cranes currently exceeds 200. The natural habitat for the crane is grassy marshlands and bogs. These had been replaced with croplands and cities. Although an attempt had been made to protect the whooping crane's wintering grounds along the gulf coast of Texas in the late 1960s, the nesting grounds also needed protection.

BUILDINGS/STRUCTURES OF HISTORIC VALUE[4,5,6,7]

The National Historic Preservation Act of 1966 established the legal and administrative context within which local historic preservation commissions relate to, and participate in, the nation's historic preservation program. The reason for enactment was to respond to public concern that many historic resources were not receiving adequate attention.

Section 106 of the National Historic Preservation Act requires that federal agencies consider what effects their actions—and actions they may assist, permit, or license—may have on historic properties, and that they give the Advisory Council on Historic Preservation a "reasonable opportunity to comment" on such actions. The Advisory Council is an independent federal agency. Its role in the review process is to encourage agencies to consider, and when feasible adopt measures that will preserve historic properties. They do not have the authority to require agencies to halt or abandon projects, but they work in association with local and state governments to identify and agree on ways to protect the properties of historic significance.[8]

The Tax Reform Act of 1986 permits owners and some lessees of historic buildings to take a 20 percent income tax credit on the cost of rehabilitating industrial, commercial, or residential properties. The intent was to preserve the most important vestiges of our national heritage.[9]

A nationally certified historic structure is one of the following:

- A structure individually listed in the National Register of Historic Places
- A structure certified by the National Parks Service as contributing to a registered district

The National Historic Preservation Act defines historic property as "any prehistoric or historic district, site, building, structure, or object, included in, or eligible for, inclusion in the National Register." Properties may be nominated for inclusion under any one of five categories: district, site, building, structure, or object. Archeological resources may fall under sites. See Figures 11-3 and 11-4.

A National Register designation does not require the owner to provide public access, obligate the owner to maintain the property, or impose restrictions regarding alterations or renovations to the property—unless either grant assistance or federal tax credits have been involved. It is up to the state and local governments to assess the properties.

State and local governments also register properties for their area of coverage. The state historic preservation agency provides further guidance for area nominations, and requirements for listing a property and the incentives vary.

The process of listing a property in the National Register of Historic Places is jointly conducted by the federal government, represented by the National Park Service of the Department of Interior; and the state, represented by the governor-appointed State Historic Preservation Officer.

The Regional National Park Service will have the pertinent information for the appropriate state. If a building is less than 50 years old, there is very little probability that it will have been listed; if listed, it may have received federal funding and/or a tax break.

In brief, the purchase of a locally, state, or federally designated historic structure (or building) may have some strings attached (e.g., restrictions, special maintenance requirements). An awareness of the possibilities may alert the consultant to spend a little extra time reviewing the lists—local, state, and federal.

Figure 11-3. National Historic Building. Miss Laura's, Ft. Smith, Arkansas, is the only bordello listed on the National Historic Registry.

ARCHEOLOGICAL RESOURCES[4]

Archeological resources are protected under the National Preservation Act of 1966. The basic treatise is that federal and state property must be subject to an archeological resources review prior to land development or any activities which may disturb artifacts of historic value. Federal and state land includes property which is receiving or will receive a federal grant and permits on, around, or about federal property. Included are HUD projects and properties managed by the Resolution Trust Company (RTC).

Figure 11-4. Archeological site (grounds around the old Dr. Pepper building were excavated for old artifacts. Traffic and construction activities were limited prior to and during the dug.

The investigator may obtain information from the state historic preservation office. Should they indicate no known problem, they will likely comment that should any artifacts be discovered during excavation, a work stoppage should be accomplished until further evaluation from the state historic preservation office.

WETLANDS[10,11]

"Wetlands" is a collective term for marshes, swamps, bogs, and similar areas that often develop between open water and dry land. According to the EPA, these wet areas are found in every county of every state in the United States. In the 1600s, it was estimated that over 200 million acres of wetlands existed in 48 states. By the mid 1970s, there were approximately 99 million acres of wetlands in 48 states, less than half of what was available in the 1600s. In the 1970s, there was an estimated 200 million acres in Alaska and less than 100,000 acres in Hawaii, but there is no estimate as to the losses since then. See Table 11-1.

In the past, wetlands were considered by many to be wastelands—a breeding ground for mosquitoes and flies or a source of foul odors. Wetlands were not only to be avoided, but eliminated. Thus, more than half of America's original wetlands have been destroyed. They have been drained and converted to farmland, filled for housing developments and industrial facilities, or used as dumping grounds for household and industrial wastes. Recently, however, scientists have discovered these unsightly wetlands are a valuable natural resource.

Wetlands provide important fish and wildlife habitats, help improve water quality, reduce flood and storm damages, control shoreline erosion, and provide a vehicle for recreation/aesthetics. They are critical to the survival of a wide variety of animals and plants, some of which are rare and endangered species. Wetlands are also croplands for blueberries, cranberries, and wild rice. Many fish and shellfish are harvested from wetlands, and furbearers (e.g., mink) depend upon wetlands.

Water quality is improved by wetlands by removing and retaining nutrients, processing chemical and organic wastes, and reducing sediment loads to receiving waters. Wetlands serve as retaining tubs, storing flood waters that overflow riverbanks or surface water that collects in isolated depressions.

The wetlands which are located between rivers and high ground provide a buffer zone against erosion. Some states even recommend planting wetland vegetation to control shoreline erosion in coastal areas.

Many of the wetlands are used by hunters and fishermen. They are a source of aesthetic beauty to the artist and provide popular sites for recreational activities (e.g., hiking, boating, and swimming).

Under the Clean Water Act Section 404, the EPA is charged with the responsibility for restoring and maintaining the chemical, physical, and biological integrity of the nation's water and protecting the wetland resources. In order to accomplish this, the EPA requires permitting to regulate dredged discharges or fill material into many of the nation's wetlands. Activities for which permits may be required include, but are not limited to the following:

Table 11-1. Major Causes of Wetland Loss and Degradation

Human Impacted Causes
Drainage
Dredging and stream channelization
Deposition of fill material
Diking and damming
Tilling for crop production
Grazing by domesticated animals
Discharge of pollutants
Mining
Alteration of hydrology

Natural Threats
Erosion
Subsidence
Sea level rise
Droughts
Hurricanes and other storms
Overgrazing by wildlife

U.S. EPA: *America's Wetlands—Our Link Between Land and Water.*
[Bulletin]. U.S. EPA/Fish and Wildlife Service. Washington, DC. p. 6.

- Placement of fill material
- Ditching activities, when the excavated material is sidecast
- Levee and dike construction
- Mechanized land clearing
- Land leveling
- Most road construction
- Dam construction

These "404 permits" are submitted to the U.S. Army Corps of Engineers. Some activities will be restricted, and many will be disallowed.

Section 404 defines wetlands as "semi-aquatic lands that are either inundated or saturated by water for varying periods of time during the year, and that under normal circumstances do support a prevalence of vegetation typically adapted for life in saturated soil conditions." The main categories are coastal and inland wetlands.

Coastal wetlands are those which are located along the United States coastal regions where estuaries pour into the ocean, creating an environment of varying salinities. Certain grasses and grasslike, salt-loving plants have adapted to this rather difficult environment, creating "coastal marshes." They are particularly abundant along the Atlantic and Gulf coasts; mangrove swamps, dominated by salt-loving shrubs or trees, are common in Hawaii and southern Florida.

Inland wetlands are those which occur in the nation's interior. The more common locations are in floodplains, along rivers and streams, in isolated depressions surrounded by dry land, and along the edge of lakes and ponds. Some may even exist as the upper edges of coastal marshes where saltwater influence terminates. Inland wetlands include marshes and wet meadows dominated by grasses and herbs, shrub swamps, and wooded swamps dominated by trees. See Figure 11-5 and Table 11-2.

There are some generalized characteristics which would indicate a strong probability that land will be considered a wetland by the U.S. Army Corps of Engineers. These characteristics are as follows:

- Area occurs in a floodplain or otherwise has low spots in which water stands at, or above, the soil surface during the growing season. Caution: Most wetlands lack both standing water and waterlogged soils during at least part of the growing season.
- Area has plant communities that commonly occur in areas having standing water for part of the growing season (e.g., cattail marshes).
- Area has soils that are called peats or mucks.
- Area is periodically flooded by tides, even if only by strong, wind-driven, or spring tides.

Many wetlands can be identified by these characteristics. Yet, there are a few situations which are unclear (e.g., boundary areas). In such instances, the Corps may be consulted.

To further complicate matters, many states have their own wetlands protection laws; in some cases, local governments may implement their own programs. State and local regulations are often stricter than the federal laws. Investigators should become familiar with their own state requirements.

Although property which is associated with wetlands may appear to be ideal for a development, its use may be restricted or prohibited entirely. If the proper channels are not followed, the EPA can impose fines and willful violations of the Act are felonies. Negligent violations are a misdemeanor.[12] A developer may have to not only pay a fine and have to deal with work stoppage but also may be subject to legal repercussions.

Figure 11-5. Wetland designated by the U.S. Army Corps of Engineers. This area is water bound less than two months a year.

WILD AND SCENIC RIVERS[13]

The Wild and Scenic Rivers Act, adopted in 1970, controls development in and around the nation's wild and scenic rivers system.   The minimum criteria for inclusion is "free-flowing streams which possess outstanding, remarkable scenic, recreational, geological, fish and wildlife, historic, cultural, and other similar values."

In order to qualify for inclusion in the national system, a state free-flowing river area must be designated as a wild, scenic, or recreational river by act of the state legislature and approved by the Secretary of the Interior. The Act designated 53 rivers which are included in the system and designated 90 rivers for potential addition. See Table 11-3.

Table 11-2. Well Known Wetlands in the United States

Pocosins of North Carolina
    Bogs and fens of the Northeastern and North Central states and
        Alaska
    Inland saline and alkaline marshes and riparian wetlands of the
        arid and semiarid West
Prairie potholes of Minnesota and the Dakotas
Vernal pools of California
Playa lakes of the Southwest
Cypress-gum swamps of the South
Wet tundra of Alaska
Tropical rain forests in Hawaii

The three classes of river areas as described in the Act are defined as follows:

- *Wild River Areas* - Those rivers or sections of rivers that are free of impoundments and generally inaccessible except by trail, with watersheds or shorelines, essentially primitive and unpolluted.
- *Scenic River Areas* - Those rivers or sections of rivers that are free of impoundments, with shorelines or watersheds still largely primitive and shorelines largely undeveloped, but accessible in places by roads.
- *Recreational River Areas* - Those rivers or sections of rivers that are readily accessible by road or railroad, that may have some development along their shorelines, and that may have undergone some impoundment or diversion in the past.

The emphasis of the Act is to protect the values which make a river outstanding or remarkable, while providing river-related outdoor recreation opportunities in a primitive setting. Thus, development is restricted in all cases and prohibited in others.

An awareness of where these rivers are and whether planned development is going to be impacted is an important consideration in some cases. The number of rivers which a consultant would require knowledge

Table 11-3.   Originally Designated Wild and Scenic Rivers[13]

Alaska	Alaska (cont'd)	Michigan	New York, Pennsylvania, and New
Alagnak	Birch Creek	Pere Marquette	Jersey
Alatna	Beaver Creek	Au Sable	Delaware/Upper
Aniakchak	Delta		Delaware
Charley	Fortymile	**Minnesota and**	
Chilikadrotna	Gulkana	**Wisconsin**	**North Carolina, South**
John	Unalakleet	Saint Croix	**Carolina, and Georgia**
Kobuk		Lower Saint Croix	Chattooga
Mulchantna	**Arizona**		
Noatak	Verde	**Missouri**	**Oregon**
North Fork of the		Eleven Point	Rogue
Koyukuk	**California**		Illinois
Salmon	Feather	**Montana**	Owyhee
Tinayguk	American	Flathead	
Tlikakila	Tuolumne	Missouri	**Tennessee**
Andreafsky			Obed
Ivishak	**Idaho**	**Nebraska and South**	
Nowitna	Clearwater	**Dakota**	**Texas**
Selawik	Segments of the Salmon	Missouri	Rio Grande
Sheenjek	Rapid River		
Wind	Saint Joe	**New Mexico**	**Washington**
Alagnak		Missouri	Skagit
	Idaho and Oregon		
	Snake		**Wisconsin**
			Wolf

U.S. Congress: Wild and Scenic Rivers Act. 16 U.S.C. 1271-1287, 1970. pp. 16-31.

about as to the location requires a one-time review of the federal listings. This information may be obtained through the Regional National Parks Services.

COASTAL DUNES AND BEACHES[15,16]

The sand dunes and beaches that lend beauty to the coastal landscapes also serve a practical purpose. They give resilience to the barrier shoreline, our frontline defense against tropical storms and hurricanes, and help reduce the impact of beach erosion. Dunes absorb the impact of storm surge and high waves, preventing or delaying intrusion of waters into inland areas. They hold sand that replaces eroded beaches after storms and buffer windblown sand and salt spray.

Subsequently, many coastal states have instituted laws to not only control, manage, and protect these areas, but also to preserve those already present and to promote dune building. The restrictions vary from state to state, and the responsible agency varies as well. Some states may prohibit construction of buildings or impose restrictions. Many will require permits. To identify the proper state controlling agency, the investigator must seek government assistance from a designated state agency.

SUMMARY

Special resources should be considered for inclusion in a Phase I assessment where there are plans to develop the property. Raw land is particularly subject to such plans. Even if there are no plans to develop the land, the purchaser will someday want to sell the property, and wary developers may identify the restrictions and choose to look elsewhere. This could leave an investor "holding the bag."

REFERENCES

1. U.S. Fish and Wildlife Service: *Endangered Species.* [Product Bulletin]. U.S. EPA/ Department of the Interior, Washington, DC.
2. Bureau of National Affairs, Inc.: *Endangered Species Act.* Washington, DC, S-829; 71:8201, March 10, 1989.

3.   Kingma, Hildy L.: *Endangered Species Information*   [Product Bulletin].   City of Georgetown, Division of Development Services, Georgetown, Texas, November 16, 1992.

4.   Advisory Council on Historic Preservation: *National Historic Preservation Act of 1966*.   16 U.S.C. 470, 2nd ed., 1984.

5.   Texas Historical Commission: *Nominating Properties to the National Register of Historic Places*.   [Product Bulletin].   National Register Programs, Austin, Texas, April 1992.

6.   Texas Historical Commission: *Protecting Historic & Prehistoric Properties Through Designation*.   [Product Bulletin].   National Register Programs, Austin, Texas, April 1992.

7.   National Park Service: Historic Preservations and Historic Properties. *Local Preservation News*.   Interagency Resources Division, Washington, DC, 1990.

8.   National Park Service: What is Section 106 Review? *Local Preservation News*.   Interagency Resources Division, Washington, DC, 1990.

9.   National Park Service: What Are the Historic Preservation Tax Incentives?   *Local Preservation News*.   Interagency Resources Division, Washington, DC, 1990.

10.   U.S. EPA: *America's Wetlands—Our Vital Link Between Land and Water*.   [Product Bulletin].   U.S. EPA, Washington, DC.

11.   U.S. Army Corps of Engineers: *Recognizing Wetlands*.   [Product Bulletin].   National Technical Information Service, Springfield, Virginia.

12.   Wilson, Albert R.: *Environmental Risk: Identification and Management*.   Lewis Publishers, Inc., Chelsea, Michigan, 1991.   p. 36.

13.   U.S. Congress: *Wild and Scenic Rivers Act*.   16 U.S.C. 1271-1287, 1970.   pp. 16-31.

Chapter 12

Putting it all Together

INTRODUCTION

Each topic is an integral part of a web of interrelated components. Exclude some of these components, and the end result may be disjointed, incomplete. Additions provide strength, and deletions weaken.

The investigator has been given the tools and must now put them to use. As the research culminates with an extensive amount of data, the investigator should have a well studied impression as to the potential for hazardous substance contamination of the property. Then, the investigator must design a method for consolidating, summarizing, projecting risks, making recommendations, and projecting costs.

SUMMARY OF THE COMPONENTS

Up to this point, all information has been collected part-and-parcel by topic. Now, each topic must be consolidated and integrated to address the "potential impact, or risk, of hazardous substance contamination on and/or around the property."

The environmental setting disclosed the potential for migration of identified contaminants to the groundwater, and to or from, the surrounding areas. If there are no potential contaminants, the issue is mute. Yet, property usage allows for speculation as to the possible presence of hazardous substances in the environment.

The historic usage provides information so projections can be made as to the potential for hazardous substance contamination of the property, originating from the property. This is based on identified prior owners, listed users, aerial photographs, and fire insurance maps.

The regulatory agency listings disclose uses of the surrounding properties as well as the property being assessed. From this information, the investigator may determine hazardous substances generated in and/or around surrounding properties. The listings of sites where hazardous substance use and/or misuse is of "known" sites only.

The property and area reconnaissance is a means for assessing existing conditions which may disclose prior uses and/or misuses of property. Signs and symptoms of misuse may be the only clue available to the investigator.

Interviews are the last chance the investigator has to properly assess the possibilities. They are a means whereby the investigator may obtain "unrecorded" information, not generated by any records search.

Knowledge of industrial/commercial activities, their processes, and wastes generated is vital in projecting the hazardous substance usage and waste generation. This information disclosed possibilities.

In brief, the usage information is generated through a records review (i.e., historic usage of the property and the regulatory agency listings). Usage may also be disclosed through intangibles (i.e., property and area reconnaissance and interviews). If a hazardous substance contamination potential exists, migratory possibilities (i.e., environmental setting) may be assigned a risk factor.

Upon completion of a Phase I site assessment, potential risk is only speculative. Once it has been determined that the possibility exists for impact of hazardous substances on the property, a Phase II may be initiated to confirm or deny.

Other components may impact the value and/or intended use of property. Hazardous building materials may devalue a building, therefore, the property. Special resources may limit property usage, thus, limiting its value. The impact of these components is generally not as expensive as that of environmental contaminants, but their impact can still be debilitating.

REPORT FORMAT

The ultimate challenge lies in taking all the documents, data, diagrams, drawings, and notes, then reducing the voluminous information packages to a simple, easy-to-follow report. Although some clients request all the substantiating data, the body of the report may be reduced considerably.

A practical approach is to use an outline. One such outline follows:

- Background information
- Purpose and scope of work

- Environmental setting
- Historic usage of the site
- Regulatory agency reviews
- Site and area reconnaissance
- Interviews
- Building materials
- Special resources
- Summary of projected risks
- Recommendations
- Cost projection for recommended actions

There are as many different means for consolidating the information as there are consulting firms. Another approach is that which is published in the widely read *Environmental Evaluations for Real Estate Transactions: A Technical and Business Guide.*[1] The chapters of the latter book follow the above outline with only a few adaptations. A means for assigning a numeric risk is also discussed.

Whatever outline is chosen, some of the subjects discussed within each chapter may be irrelevant. Thus, they may be stricken from the list on a case-by-case situation, unless the client has a well-defined outline and requires all topics to be discussed. The topics which are irrelevant may warrant a comment, "Not relevant" or "Not applicable."

PROJECTED RISK(S)

As mentioned earlier, "zero" risk does not exist. Yet, possibilities, based on all the information collected, allow the consultant to project.

The primary concern is for hazardous substance contamination of the environment—its potential for impacting the health of those people located within the surrounding areas and for impacting the groundwater, particularly those sources which supply drinking water to large communities.

Many consultants identify "risk sources," then assign a level of risk to each. Some assign a numeric value. Many classify each risk qualitatively.[1] If most topics and subtopics pose a low risk, then a general statement may be in order. A few moderate and high risks may be mentioned separately. Some consultants list the topics in a table and assign a risk factor to each one. In Table 12-1 the numeric risk values range from 1 to 3. Qualitatively this translates to low, moderate, and high potential for impact on the property.

Table 12-1. Example of a Potential Risks Listing of Sources—Property Type is Newly Constructed Residence

Topic	Numeric Risk	Qualitative Risk
Building Materials		
Asbestos	1	Low
Lead-based paint	1	Low
Lead-content in water	1	Low
Lead-contaminated soil	1	Low
Radon	1	Low
PCBs in transformers	1	Low
Pesticides	2	Moderate

On the other hand, the sources may be consolidated. The issues of ultimate concern are not whether there is a source, but "What is the potential impact?" Instead of addressing each component separately, the main issues may be discussed. The sources contribute, but the main issues are the purpose of the assessment. There is a potential risk for any or all of the following occurrences:

- Hazardous Material Contamination of the Soil
- Hazardous Material Contamination of the Surface Water
- Hazardous Material Contamination of the Groundwater
- Hazardous Materials in the Building(s)
- Hazardous Materials Migration
- Special Resource Impact on Development Plans

A discussion of probable risk for each of the above items is direct and simple, whereas an evaluation of the components sources can confuse the issue. The point is simplicity.

Some consultants have developed an algorithm, a mathematical model, to assign a level of risk numerically. One such approach is published as a "comprehensive risk score," scores ranging from zero to over 90, with an assigned risk level, Levels 1 through 4, which is related to the score. Level 1 represents "background" risks which are associated with all properties, and Level 4 is the worst case scenario where there is a high degree of certainty for an occurrence. The publication discusses the method but does not provide details.[2]

Most consultants classify a risk qualitatively—"low," "moderate," or "high." A "low" risk says, "It is unlikely." It covers all negative findings and improbable exposures. For instance, a building is constructed of tin and gypsum board with a concrete foundation. Most gypsum board was not formulated with asbestos; however, some was. The odds are against it. Thus, there is a low probability that asbestos products were used in the building. A residence in an area where the recorded levels of radon in homes is low and where the structural conditions are not conducive to trapping radon gas has the probability of elevated levels of radon is being low.

A "moderate" risk says, "There is a chance!" It can go either way. Additional information or some sampling is generally recommended. The client may decide the potential impact is minimal, and the cost for a Phase II is not justified. Yet, the client must be informed of all the possibilities. For instance, a site has several 55-gallon drums of unconfirmed waste motor oil on the premises. The property is presently used for cattle grazing. The contents of the drums have contaminated a nearby pond, and the fish are thriving. The possibility that the contents are hazardous (e.g., toxic or flammable) is moderate. The soil is noticeably contaminated. Thus, the consultant may recommend confirmation analysis of the contents of the drums, proper disposal, and some soil analysis where contamination may have occurred. This is a Phase II recommendation.

A "high" risk says, "There is a strong possibility that a condition does exist." This should always be accompanied with recommendations. For instance, a retired employee of a metal-plating operation claims that chromic acid waste was consistently disposed of in an obsolete well on the premises. The well contents and possibly some of the associated soil should be evaluated, and confirmation of contamination should be followed with a Phase III assessment to clarify the extent of the contamination in the soil.

The simplest, most direct means to classify a site is through grouping the risks and assigning a qualitative risk. For instance, the property has a water well which is known to be contaminated with pesticides. A farmer formulated the pesticides on-site. The soil is sandy, and a slow moving stream of non-potable groundwater is five feet deep. The risks are: 1) high for the soil contamination; 2) high for groundwater contamination; and 3) high for migration potential. The overall impact may be the contamination of community drinking water.

The bottom line is, "What is the probability for impact? What may be impacted? How many people may it involve?"

RECOMMENDATIONS

Recommendations are generally based on the level of risk. Yet, even a low risk may warrant a recommendation. If the possible risk is minimal, but the potential cost for remediation of that risk is high, some assurances may be sought. For instance, a building which was built in the late 1980s has an acoustical surfacing material on the ceilings, throughout the entire 50,000 square feet of office space. The date of construction dictates an improbable chance that the surfacing material is asbestos. However, if it is asbestos, removal may cost a million dollars. An evaluation of the material is indicated.

On the other hand, a recommendation to further evaluate a high probability for contaminated soils from an adjacent, obsolete gasoline station may meet with resistance. The soils are clay. Chances of migration are minimal, and the possible overall risk is low.

A recommendation may be to seek a Phase II or III assessment, or it may be to extend the scope of work. Further research may disclose sufficient information to change from a "moderate" to a "low" risk and significantly keep the costs down where a Phase II may have involved expensive soil and/or water sampling. For example, a property resident was allegedly paid to haul away hazardous materials from his place of employment 20 years ago. The whereabouts of the containerized waste is unknown. There are signs of what appears to be automotive waste oil on the property, and there is an unexplained five foot high soil mound in the back of the house. An attempt to locate the former lessee may be in order. If he can provide evidence of having hauled the waste to another location, the cost for performing a Phase II may be avoided.

Well thought out recommendations are a must. They will impact the client's decisions to proceed or back out of a project. Be prepared to seek an expert opinion to assist in the projections and recommendations. They are the meat of the report.

COST PROJECTIONS

The purpose of an assessment is to determine potential liabilities and evaluation of the property due to the presence of hazardous materials. Once a potential is identified as moderate or high, the client will want to know how much the recommended actions will cost. They don't require an exact figure but do need to know if the projected cost may run around $1,000 or $500,000. If you don't know how to project costs, seek assistance from someone who does (e.g., an environmental firm that performs core sampling or a biologist that knows how to evaluate endangered species). The cost of recommended actions may chase a prospective buyer away, but the present owner may opt to pursue the recommendations at his own expense.

When discussing the circumstances with the party who may ultimately perform the Phase II or III, apprise them of all pertinent information. For instance, if seeking core sampling whereby a drilling rig is required, let them know how accessible the site is and whether traffic will pose a problem. Where raw land must be evaluated and there are no roads or means for getting to the site without going through a ditch, there are bound to be problems and associated higher costs. Failure to mention such possibilities can throw the figures way off.

ROUTINE AUDITS AND UPDATING THE RECORDS

Those who manage repossessed properties (e.g., RTC and banks) require routine audits and record updates. These are done once every six months in some cases. The purpose is twofold. It is a means to check previous work performance and a process for identifying new developments.

If an owner has had a Phase I assessment performed in previous years and wishes to use the property for collateral on a business loan, the loan officer may require an update. The latest methodology may have changed considerably since prior assessments.

SAMPLE SCENARIOS BY PROPERTY CATEGORY

Some consultants have estimated that about ten percent of their total Phase I site assessments may disclose information which may have a considerable impact on a client's decision making process. Each scenario presented therein is typical. They are those most likely to be investigated by the reader. One of each of the property category types is posed to the reader, and the content is simplified for brevity. Phase I assessments, with substantiating documents, typically are packaged in 30 pages to several volume reports, depending on complexity and property type. The following are abbreviated descriptions for clarification only. They are not to be misconstrued as sample reports.

Undeveloped Land

The land is in a rural area, and there are plans to develop a residential area. The property lies on 200 acres of unleveled land with dense vegetation, and the developer has decided it would be wise to seek a Phase I environmental site assessment.

The nearest small population center is 20 miles away. The property is relatively flat and has a river running through it. The soil is of moderate permeability. The groundwater is approximately 200 feet from the surface, and the closest major aquifer is 20 miles away.

The historic usage search indicates all property owners by surname, development in the surrounding areas only in the previous ten years (as observed on the aerial photographs), no listed telephones at the property address, but Peter's Waste Disposal Company was located adjacent to the property 20 years prior and has since gone out of business. There were no fire insurance maps for this area.

The regulatory agency listing discloses no known hazardous waste cleanup sites within a one mile radius, no known hazardous waste sites within a 0.5 mile radius, one small generator within a 0.5 mile radius (a dry cleaner). There are no records of solid waste disposal sites within a 0.5 mile radius, underground storage tanks on or around the property, leaking underground storage tanks within a one mile radius, and hazardous substance spills on or adjacent to the property.

During the site and area reconnaissance, the investigator notices that there are no fish in the river. The property where Peter's Waste Transport was previously located houses damage, deteriorating, 55-gallon drums, many of which are leaking. An old abandoned well, emanating a strong, pungent odor is found on the property.

Interviewing a neighbor who had resided in this area for almost 22 years, the investigator found out that Peter's Waste Transport had leased the property adjacent to the property being assessed. They hauled unknown materials and dumped them on the property for well over a year.

In brief, the property is located adjacent to what used to be a waste collection business and the operator deposited the containers on the premises and possibly dumped some of the wastes on adjoining properties. The assessed has a "high probability for hazardous substance contamination" both from dumping and migration through the soils from the adjacent property to the assessment property.

The investigator recommends a Phase II, projecting an estimated cost of $17,000 for preliminary soil, surface water, and groundwater sampling. The developer then chooses not to incur any additional expenses investigating the possibilities. There are other, less risky properties from which to choose.

Residential Property

The property has a 100-unit apartment building and 50 acres of land. An investor seeks to invest in an apartment complex, and the lending institution has requested a Phase I environmental site assessment.

The site is located on the periphery of large population center. The land consists of rolling hills and has a small pond. The soil is of low permeability. The groundwater is approximately 400 feet from the surface, and the closest major aquifer is 15 miles away.

The historic usage search indicates all property owners by surname or investment firms and development of the area since 1968. There is, however, evidence of what appears to be a landfill at the property location in 1967, and according to aerial photographs the landfill is no longer apparent in 1974. A review of the street directories indicates a municipal landfill at the property address from 1964 to 1970. The remaining listings were either construction companies or apartment residences. There were no fire insurance maps for this area.

The regulatory agency listing discloses no known hazardous waste cleanup sites within a one mile radius, no known hazardous waste sites within a 0.5 mile radius, several small generators within a 0.5 mile radius (i.e., dry cleaners and service stations), no underground storage tanks on or around the property, no reported leaking underground storage tanks within a one mile radius, and no hazardous substance spills on or adjacent to the property. The property is, however, listed under solid waste disposal sites as a closed, sanitary landfill.

During the site and area reconnaissance, the land is landscaped and the vegetation appears healthy. There are no unusual, noteworthy signs of waste disposal on the property. However, stress fractures are observed on the exterior walls of some of the buildings, indicating extensive setting.

The investigator interviews some of the residents and learns that those on the lower level have noticed an unpleasant odor in their apartment. Although they have attempted to locate the source and/or have used an arsenal of air fresheners, the odor seems to keep coming back. Several first floor residents had the same problems but had yet to associate the problem with the building. The present owner indicates that the complex was built on a landfill, but it was not supposed to cause any problems.

In brief, a closed sanitary landfill has been noted in the solid waste disposal site listing, and there is a trend of odor complaints from occupants. This property has a "moderate probability for migration of gases from an old municipal landfill" underlying the apartment complex, but there was no confirmation at the time of the assessment.

The recommendation involves an abbreviated Phase II site assessment, and the estimated cost is $200 for a basic air monitoring evaluation or $4,000 for soil sampling.

The investor likes the property and requests the basic air monitoring evaluation. Methane gas is detected in many of the lower level apartments. As a result of these findings the investor decides to look elsewhere.

Later, the methane problem escalated. City officials identified the problem and condemned the entire complex. Residents were given one week to move, and the property value has dropped.

Commercial Property

The property has a dry cleaning operation on the corner of a city intersection. The owner of the dry cleaning operation has decided to purchase the property which he has been leasing for the past five years. He has been told that the location used to be used for a gasoline station. A business broker advises him to seek a Phase I environmental site assessment.

The site is located around a university. The property is around the top of a small hill, and there is a river within 100 feet of the building. The river is used for fishing and recreational purposes. The soil is of moderate permeability, and the groundwater is 20 feet below the surface. This is non-potable water which flows in the direction of the river.

The historic usage search indicates all property owners by surname, investment firms, then business name. Buba's Service Station owned it from 1953 to 1966. The fire insurance maps indicate an auto repair shop at this location in 1938, and this is confirmed through a street directory review. Frank's Auto Repair was listed at this address between 1938 to 1953. From 1966 to 1977, there were no phone listings and investment firms owned the property. In 1977, Pat's Dry Cleaning was listed. Then, from 1988 on, the present operator was listed. Aerial photographs confirm a building at this site starting with a 1942 Department of Highways aerial.

The regulatory agency listing discloses no known hazardous waste cleanup sites within a one mile radius, no known hazardous waste sites within a 0.5 mile radius, several small generators within a 0.5 mile radius (dry cleaners and service stations), no solid waste disposal sites within a 0.5 mile radius, no underground storage tanks on or around the property, no reported leaking underground storage tanks within a one mile radius, and no hazardous substance spills on or adjacent to the property.

During the site and area reconnaissance, the investigator observes patches in the concrete around the parking lot. A couple of places in the concrete slab are slightly concave and severely cracked. The back door opens to uncovered soil surface, and the vegetation is sparse in the immediate vicinity of the exit, dense in other areas.

The investigator interviews a long-term employee of the operator. This employee had worked for the previous operator and comments that they used to dump used dry cleaning fluid out the back door, onto the ground.

All indications are that the property was used for auto repair work back when lead was used to fill auto bodies and old batteries were stored in the yards. There is no report of an underground storage tank, but prior ownership and the condition of the concrete slab indicate probable abandonment of the underground storage tanks which may by now be leaking whatever contents may have been left behind. The tanks may have leaked in the past as well. The soil permeability and proximity to a river provide a means for migration of hazardous substance from the property and impacting the surrounding environments. There is a "high probability that the grounds are contaminated."

The investigator recommends a Phase II, projecting a cost of $12,000 for preliminary deep soil sampling. The operator chooses not to proceed with sampling and not to buy the property.

Industrial Property

An investor seeks to purchase, not only property, but a manufacturing operation as well. The business is a sawmill, and it lies on 100 acres of leveled, open terrain. The lending institution requires a Phase I environmental site assessment and records audits for this purchase.

The land is in a rural area, surrounded by farms and ranches. The nearest small population center is 80 miles away. The property is relatively flat and has a stream running alongside of the property. The soil is highly permeable, and the groundwater is approximately 75 feet from the surface. The surrounding property owners use groundwater as their sole source of drinking water.

The historic usage search indicates all property owners by surname up until 1957 when the present owner took title to the property and developed an existing sawmill operation. Aerial photographs and street directory listings confirm this. There are no fire insurance maps for the area.

The regulatory agency listing discloses no known hazardous waste cleanup sites within a one mile radius, no known hazardous waste sites within a 0.5 mile radius, no RCRA agents within a one mile radius, no solid waste disposal sites within a 0.5 mile radius, no underground storage tanks on or around the property, no reported leaking underground storage tanks within a one mile radius, and no hazardous substance spills on or adjacent to the property. The records are clean.

During the site and area reconnaissance, the investigator notices that there is a wood preservative treatment area located within 20 feet of a small stream. The wood is treated and taken directly to an uncovered concrete slab, 35 feet from the stream. There are stains on the ground and no vegetation between the off load treatment area to the storage area. There are no fish downstream of the sawmill, but there are in the water preceding the property.

A records audit discloses the use of pentachlorophenol, a highly toxic substance, in the wood treatment process and some old citations, dated 1979, from the EPA for the uncontrolled release of hazardous substances into the adjoining stream. There are no manifests of outgoing hazardous wastes.

When the manager of the plant is asked what became of the citation, he says to ignore it. The EPA hasn't been back since the original citation, and it really is not a problem.

On departure from the plant, the investigator stops at a neighboring farm to get some automotive radiator water. This becomes a water sample which is later found to contain pentachlorophenol.

In brief, the high soil permeability and proximity of both surface water and groundwater indicate migratory potential for soil contaminants. The sawmill has evidence of hazardous substance contamination of the adjacent stream. Although sampling is not generally included in a Phase I assessment the collection of one sample was sufficient confirmation to state that there is a "high probability of hazardous substance contamination of the property, groundwater, surface water, and surrounding areas."

The investigator recommends a Phase II environmental site assessment, projecting a cost of $25,000 for preliminary soil, surface water, and groundwater sampling. The buyer opts to discontinue negotiations with the present owner and search elsewhere.

The developer decides the risk is too high. He chooses not to seek confirmation or denial of the risk with a Phase II site assessment and proceeds to identify another property for investment purposes.

SUMMARY

All the information gathered up to this point culminates with a projection of source components and potential risks linked to an assessed property. Ultimately, the client wants to know:

- Is there a potential for property contamination?
- Is there a potential for migration either to or from the property?
- What kind of impact could be expected?
- What is recommended?
- How much will it cost to follow the recommendation(s)?

Once again, a Phase I environmental site assessment is not always cut-and-dried; and if there are any questions generated during the survey, don't overlook them because they seem minor. "A minor crack in a dam at the right stress point can result in a major catastrophe."

REFERENCES

1. Goss, Frank D. (ed.): *Environmental Evaluations for Real Estate Transactions: A Technical and Business Guide.* 2nd Printing. Diagnostic Engineering Inc., Government Institutes, Inc., Rockville, Maryland, 1989.
2. Wilson, Albert R.: *Environmental Risk: Identification and Management.* Lewis Publishers, Chelsea, Michigan, 1991.

APPENDICES

Appendix 1

Regulatory Definitions of "Pollutant"

CLEAN AIR ACT

Air Pollutant - Any air pollution agent or combination of such agents, including any physical, chemical, biological, radioactive (including source material, special nuclear material, and by-product material) substance or matter which is emitted into or otherwise enters the ambient air. Initial list in 42 USC 7412 §112. See also amendments. [42 USC 7602 §302]

Hazardous Air Pollutant - See "Air Pollutant."

CLEAN WATER ACT

Pollutant - Dredged spoil, solid waste, incinerator residue, sewage, garbage, sewage sludge, munitions, chemical wastes, biological materials, radioactive materials, heat wrecked or discarded equipment, rock, sand, cellar dirt and industrial, municipal, and agricultural waste discharged into water. [33 USC 1362 §502 (6)]

Toxic Pollutant - Those pollutants, or combinations of pollutants, including disease-causing agents, which after discharge and upon exposure, ingestion, inhalation, or assimilation into any organism, either directly from the environment or indirectly by ingestion through food chains, will, on the basis of information available to the Administrator, cause death, disease, behavioral abnormalities, cancer, genetic mutations, physiological malfunctions (including malfunctions in reproduction) or physical deformations, in such organisms or their offspring. [33 USC 1362 §502 (13)]

CERCLA

Pollutant - Any element, substance, compound, or mixture, including disease-causing agents, which after release into the environment and upon exposure, ingestion, inhalation, or assimilation into any organism, either directly from the environment or indirectly by ingestion through food chains, will or may reasonably be anticipated to cause death, disease, behavioral abnormalities, cancer, genetic mutation, physiological malfunctions (including malfunctions in reproduction) or physical deformations in such organisms or their offspring; except that the term "pollutant or contaminant" shall not include petroleum, including crude oil or any fraction thereof which is not otherwise specifically listed or designated as a hazardous substance under subparagraphs (A) through (F) of paragraph (14) and shall not include natural gas, liquefied natural gas, or synthetic gas of pipeline quality (or mixtures of natural gas and such synthetic gas). [42 USC 9601 § 101 (33)]

Hazardous Substance [paragraph (14)] - The term means (A) any substance designated pursuant to §311(b)(2)(A) of the Federal Water Pollution Control Act, (B) any element, compound, mixture, solution, or substance designated pursuant to §102 of this Act, (C) any hazardous waste having the characteristics identified under or listed pursuant to §3001 of the Solid Waste Disposal Act (but not including any waste the regulation of which under the Solid Waste Disposal Act has been suspended by Act of Congress), (D) any toxic pollutant listed under §307(a) of the Federal Water Pollution Control Act, (E) any hazardous air pollutant listed under §112 of the Clean Air Act, and (F) any imminently hazardous chemical substance or mixture with respect to which the Administrator has taken action pursuant to §7 of the Toxic Substances Control Act. The term does not include petroleum, including crude oil or any fraction thereof which is not otherwise specifically listed or designated as a hazardous substance under subparagraphs (A) through (F) of this paragraph, and the term does not include natural gas, natural gas liquids, liquefied natural gas, or synthetic gas, usable for fuel (or mixtures of natural gas and such synthetic gas). [42 USC 9601 §101 (14)]

OSHA

Air Contaminants - Listed in Tables Z-1, Z-2, and Z-3, Toxic and Hazardous Substances. [29 CFR 1910.1000]

RCRA

Hazardous Waste - A solid waste, or combination of solid wastes, which because of its quantity, concentration, or physical, chemical, or infectious characteristics may: 1) cause or significantly contribute to an increase in mortality or an increase in serious irreversible, or incapacitating reversible, illness, or 2) pose a substantial present or potential hazard to human health or the environment when improperly treated, stored, transported, or disposed of, or otherwise managed. Wastes listed in 40 CFR 302.4. [42 USC 6903 §1004]

SARA TITLE III (Emergency Planning and Community Right-to-Know Act)

Hazardous Chemical - Chemicals which are included in: (A) the list in 29 CFR 1910.1200(c), the Hazard Communication Act, (B) any food, food additive, color additive, drug, or cosmetic regulated by the Food and Drug Administration, (C) any substance present as a solid in any manufactured item to the extent exposure to the substance does not occur under normal conditions of use, (D) any substance to the extent it is used for personal, family, or household purposes, or is present in the same form and concentration as a product packaged for distribution and use by the general public, (E) any substance to the extent it is used in a research laboratory or a hospital or other medical facility under the direct supervision of a technically qualified individual, and (F) any substance to the extent it is used in routine agricultural operations or is a fertilizer held for sale by a retailer to the ultimate customer. [SARA §311 (e)]

Appendix 2

Summary of Important Environmental Regulations

Clean Air Act (CAA); Initial Enactment in 1963 - Regulates air pollution and sets emissions standards.

Title I:	Air Pollution Prevention and Control
Title II:	Emission Standards for Moving Sources
Title III:	General
Title IV:	Acid Deposition Control
Title V:	Permits
Title VI:	Stratospheric Ozone
Title VII:	Acid Precipitation Program and Carbon Dioxide Study

Clean Water Act (CWA); Initial Enactment in 1977 - Regulates the amount of discharge of oil or hazardous substances into or upon the navigable waters and adjoining shorelines of the United States in any harmful quantity as determined by regulations.

Title 1:	Research and Related Programs
Title II:	Grants for Construction of Treatment Works
Title III:	Standards and Enforcement
Title IV:	Permits and Licenses
Title V:	General Provisions
Title VI:	State Water Pollution Control Revolving Funds

Comprehensive Environmental Response, Compensation, and Liability Act (CERCLA or the "Superfund" Act); Initial Enactment in 1980 - Requires notification of any release of "reportable quantities" of hazardous substances. (This does not apply to federally permitted releases or to the application of pesticides.)

Title I:	Hazardous Substances Releases, Liability, Compensation
Title II:	Establishment of Hazardous Substance Response Trust Fund
Title III:	Miscellaneous Provisions
Title IV:	Pollution Insurance

Occupational Safety and Health Act (OSHA); Initial Enactment in 1970 - Regulates occupational exposures to hazardous substances.

Resource Conservation and Recovery Act (RCRA); Initial Enactment in 1976 - Gave EPA the power to regulate hazardous wastes.

Title II: Solid Waste Disposal

Subtitle C - Regulates the ongoing generation, transportation, treatment, storage, and disposal of hazardous wastes.

Subtitle I - Regulates management of underground storage tanks. Each owner must notify the state or local controlling agency as to the existence of such a tank, detailing the age, size, type, location, and uses. Releases must also be reported and corrective actions taken.

Subtitle J - Regulates medical waste.

Safe Drinking Water Act (SDWA); Initial Enactment in 1974 - Establishes and regulates Maximum Contaminant Levels (MCL) of hazardous substances for public drinking water systems. MCLs are used by EPA as the basis for groundwater cleanup criteria under CERCLA.

Superfund Amendments and Reauthorization Act (SARA); Initial Enactment in 1986 - Amplifies CERCLA requirements.

Title III: Emergency Planning and Community Right-to-Know Act of 1986 - Requires certain businesses to prepare inventory reports listing hazardous chemicals in their possession, to assist in the development of local emergency response plans, to prepare annual reports of releases of hazardous substances, and to report immediately certain ultrahazardous releases.

Title IV: Radon Gas and Indoor Air Quality Research

Toxic Substance Control Act (TSCA); Initial Enactment in 1976 - Regulates the manufacturer and distribution of hazardous chemical substances within the United States. Participants must maintain records and submit reports to EPA on a routine basis.

Title I: Control of Toxic Substances
Title II: Asbestos Hazard Emergency Response Act of 1986 (AHERA) - Regulates asbestos management and control procedures in public schools.

Appendix 3

Some Methods Used for Phase I Environmental Site Assessments

American Society for Testing and Materials

This standard will likely serve as the prevailing national standard for scope of work in real estate site assessments. Final draft not available at the time this book was printed. Write to: ASTM, 1916 Race Street, Philadelphia, PA 19103-1187.

Federal Home Loan Bank Board (Office of Thrift Supervision)

- An historical review
- A review of building, zoning, planning, sewer, water, fire, environmental, and other department records
- A review of the Department of Health Services, Solid Waste Management Board, Regional Water Quality Control Board, Air Quality Management District, and other boards or agency records and files
- An investigation of the Environmental Protection Agency's National Priority List or Comprehensive Environmental Response Compensation and Liability Information System (CERCLIS) List and similar state lists
- An inspection of the site
- A verification as to whether present or past owners/tenants have stored, created, or discharged hazardous material or waste and

whether appropriate procedures, safeguards, permits, and notices are in place
- An analysis of old aerial photographs
- Interviews with neighbors
- A review of building records and a visual inspection of the building(s) for asbestos-containing materials
- A review of the potential for radon in the soil

RESOLUTION TRUST CORPORATION (RTC)

- Site history
  - Title search
  - Aerial photographs
  - Maps and data
  - Site questionnaire
  - Fire department
- Site visit and investigation
  - Present use and improvements
  - Wetlands
  - Permits
  - Material safety data sheets
  - Site inspection
  - Chemicals and raw materials
  - Polychlorinated biphenyls
  - Asbestos-containing material
  - Radon
  - Lead
  - Wells
  - Hazardous and solid wastes
  - Landfills
  - Pits and sumps
  - Storage tanks
  - Off-site underground storage tanks
- Interviews
  - Employees
  - Neighboring properties
  - Others
- Regulatory agency review (including, but not limited to, the NPL and CERCLIS)

MAJOR COMMERCIAL LOAN BANKS

- Site overview
- Background/operating history
  - Current ownership
  - Prior ownership
  - Review of aerial photographs
  - Historical city directories
  - History of property use
- Environmental setting
  - Surface water characteristics
  - Subsurface geologic characteristics
  - Groundwater characteristics
- Site inspection
  - Site observations and inquiries
  - On-site regulated substance identification/inventory
  - Area reconnaissance
  - Site plan drawings
  - Asbestos-containing material
- Environmental/regulatory agency inquiries
  - Federal/state regulatory agencies
  - Local governmental agencies
  - List of recorded cites
- References
  - Records of communication
  - Regulatory records and public documents
  - Published references

FEDERAL NATIONAL MORTGAGE ASSOCIATION (Fannie Mae)

- Review of government records
- Interviews with people who are familiar with the site
- An inspection of the site
- Inquiry into the presence of the following:
  - Asbestos
  - Polychlorinated byphenyls
  - Radon
  - Underground storage tanks
  - Waste disposal facilities
  - Lead-based paint

- Urea formaldehyde particle board
- Urea formaldehyde foam insulation
- Lead levels in drinking water

Legislative Definition of "All Appropriate Inquiry" (Originally Introduced by Congressman Weldon in 1989)

- A 50-year chain of title search
- Aerial photographs
- Recorded environmental cleanup liens
- Federal, state, and local government environmental records
- A visual site inspection

SMALL BUSINESS ADMINISTRATION COMMERCIAL LOANS

- Inspection of the site and adjacent properties
- Review of files of regulatory agencies
- Interviews with individuals knowledgeable about site operations

Appendix 4

Sources of Aerial Photographs

U.S. DEPARTMENT OF AGRICULTURE

Agricultural Stabilization and Conservation Service (ASCS)
Salt Lake City, Utah 84125

Largest Scale: 1:20,000
Starting: 1930s (black & white)
Photographed by County on a 7-year cycle

U.S. Forest Service (USFS)
Region 1 (Missoula, Montana)
Region 2 (Lakewood, Colorado)
Region 3 (Albuquerque, New Mexico)
Region 4 (Ogden, Utah)
Region 5 (San Francisco, California)
Region 6 (Portland, Oregon)
Region 8 (Atlanta, Georgia)
Region 9 (Milwaukee, Wisconsin)
Region 10 (Juneau, Alaska)

Largest Scale: 1:20,000
Starting: 1934 (black & white)
Recent: (color and color infrared)
Photographed national forest lands on an as needed basis

Soil Conservation Service (SCS)
Hyattsville, Maryland

Largest Scale: 1:20,000
Starting: 1930s (black & white)
Photographed on an as needed basis

U.S. DEPARTMENT OF COMMERCE

National Ocean Survey, Coastal Mapping Division
Rockville, Maryland

Scale: 1:10,000 - 1:40,000
Starting: 1940s (black & white)
Photographed on an as needed basis, over nations's major airports

Department of Defense (1940s - 1972)
Defense Mapping Agency
Topographic Command
6500 Brooks Lane, NW
Washington, DC 20315

Defense Intelligence Agency (1972 - present)
Attn: DS4A
Arlington Hall Station
Washington, DC 20301

Scale: 1:15,000 to 1:40,000
Starting: 1930s (black & white)
Photographed on an as needed basis

U.S. Army Corps of Engineers
Huntsville Division (Huntsville, Alabama)
Lower Mississippi Valley Division (Vicksburg, Mississippi)
Missouri River Division (Omaha, Nebraska)

Scale: Varies
Starting: 1930s (black & white)
Photographed on an as needed basis, civil projects

U.S. Geological Survey (USGS)
Earth Resources Orbiting Satellite (EROS) Data Center
Sioux Falls, SD 57198

Common Scale: 1:24,000
Starting: 1964
Photographed on an as Needed Basis
The depository and dissemination center for many of the federally acquired
aerial photographs.

U.S. Geological Survey
National Cartographic Information Center
507 National Center
Reston, Virginia 22092

Scale: 1:5,000 & up
Starting: 1920s
Collects, organizes, and distributes information about cartographic products
held by federal, state, local, and private organizations, usually restricted to
the United States.   There are 67 state affiliates.   The Texas Natural
Resources Information System of the Texas Water Commission maintains
one of the largest collections (over 500,000 photographs).

U.S. Environmental Protection Agency
Remote Sensing Branch
P.O. Box 15027
Las Vegas, NV 89114

PRIVATE AERIAL SURVEYS

American Society of Photogrammetry
105 North Virginia Avenue
Falls Church, VA 22046

Provides names of private aerial survey firms.

Appendix 5

Federal Sources of Information

ENVIRONMENTAL HAZARDS

Land Disposal

U.S. EPA
Office of Solid Waste
1) Municipal Solid Waste Programs Division - Information concerning former and current municipal disposal sites.
2) Characterization and Assessment Division - Information concerning land disposal restrictions.
Office of Water Programs Enforcement
RCRA Guide and Evaluation - Technical assistance for site evaluation.

Office of Emergency and Remedial Response (Superfund)
Hazardous Site Evaluation Division - Inclusions of sites on the federal/state Superfund lists.

Hazardous Substance Management, Use, Storage, and Disposal

U.S. EPA
Office of Solid Waste
Characterization and Assessment Division - Assess types of waste.

Chemical Emergency Preparedness and Prevention Office
Chemical reporting as per SARA, Title III.

Office of Emergency and Remedial Response (Superfund)
 Hazardous Site Evaluation Division - Scoring information for
 Superfund evaluations.

Office of Water Regulations and Standards
 Analysis and Evaluation Division - NPDES permit listings for waste
 water.

Office of Waste Program Enforcement
 RCRA Enforcement: Technical Assistance - Compliance history,
 permits, etc.

Aboveground and Underground Storage Tanks

U.S. EPA
Office of Underground Storage Tanks

Asbestos

U.S. EPA
Office of Toxic Substances
 Division of Environmental Assistance - Regulations concerning the
 use and management of asbestos-containing materials whereby
 exposure potential involves the general public.

U.S. Department of Labor
Occupational Safety and Health Division
 Regulations concerning worker exposures to asbestos.

Radiation Hazards

U.S. EPA
Radon Division
 Research concerning radon in buildings.

Office of Radiation Programs
 Criteria and Standards Division - Regulations concerning all forms of
 radiation.

U.S. Public Health Service
Department of Health and Human Services

Pesticides

U.S. EPA
Office of Pesticide Programs
     Registration information.

Department of Agriculture
Forest Pest Management
     Regulations

SPECIAL RESOURCES

Archeological Sites

Department of Interior
National Park Service
     Cultural Resources

Bureau of Land Management
     Land and Renewable Resources

Coastal Dunes/Beaches

National Parks Service
Office of Public Affairs

U.S. Fish and Wildlife
Office of Public Affairs

Threatened and Endangered Species/Critical and Unique Habitat

U.S. Fish and Wildlife
Fish and Wildlife Enhancement

Department of Agriculture
U.S. Forest Service
    Fish and Wildlife Management

Wetlands

U.S. EPA
Office of Wetlands Protection

U.S. Army Corps of Engineers
Office of Public Affairs

U.S. Fish and Wildlife
Office of Public Affairs

Wild and Scenic Rivers

National Park Service
Office of Public Affairs

AGENCY ADDRESSES

Bureau of Land Management
200 Independence Avenue, SW
Washington, DC 20201

Department of Agriculture
14th Independence, SW
Washington, DC 20250

National Park Service
1849 C Street, NW
Washington, DC 20240

U.S. Army Corps of Engineers
20 Massachusetts Avenue, NW
Casimir Pulaski Building
Washington, DC 20314

U.S. Environmental Protection Agency
401 M Street, SW
Washington, DC 20460

U.S. Fish and Wildlife
1849 C Street, NW
Washington, DC 20240

U.S. Public Health Service
1849 C Street, NW
Washington, DC 20240

Appendix 6

HUD Standard Practices for Collecting Paint Samples

The inspector should attempt removal of paint in such a manner as to minimize the amount of substrate which adheres to the paint film. Some materials useful in collecting samples are:

- A heat gun.
- Two putty knives; one wide and one narrow.
- Clean, see-through plastic baggies with a zip-lock mechanism. Two sizes, sandwich and larger may be needed.
- Masking tape or labels.
- A permanent marker, not water-based.
- Sharp, durable, cutting knife with a fine edge or thin scalpel blade.
- A two-handed paint scraper may be necessary to scrape down to the bare substrate when removing for X-ray Fluorescence (XRF), Substitute Equivalent Lead (SEL), corrections.
- Small boxes for mailing.

The samples taken for laboratory analysis should be about 2 square inches; the larger, the better. Samples removed for determining an XRF SEL should be larger than the minimum sensitive area of the SRF being used. Typically, about 3″ × 3″. These samples, although not usually submitted for lab analysis, should be retained by the PHA until all abatement is complete. Samples should contain all layers of paint down to the substrate.

Preparing the sample container:

- On a strip of tape or label, identify the exact location where the sample was taken (e.g., ceiling, room #2, 1st floor, 401 Maple Avenue, Jones City, SS) and the sample number assigned on the inspection form.
- Affix the label to the outside of the baggie.

There are three general methods that are suggested, all of which are fairly messy. A tray or other container should be held under the sampled surface to catch debris which falls. Inspectors should practice these methods to become proficient.

The first method is the cutting or punching method:

1. Apply clear, pressure sensitive adhesive tape over an area slightly larger than the sample to be collected.
2. Cut through the paint layers with a punch or template/sharp knife combination of *known area.*
3. Remove the paint and a thin layer of substrate beneath it using a sharp chisel having the same dimension as a side of the square.
4. Use the brush or mini-vacuum to clean the area and dispose of any residual material in a plastic disposal bag.

Samples collected in this manner are for analysis results to be reported in area concentrations.

The second method is a cutting method:

1. Using a sharp knife or scalpel, score the area of paint in question to an appropriate size, attempt to lift the paint off by sliding the thin blade along the score and underneath the paint, and remove a section down to the wood or plaster, making sure all layers of paint are intact. Care should be taken to avoid including wood, paper, or plaster in the sample if the analysis results are to be reported in weight percent.
2. Use the brush or mini-vacuum to clean the area and dispose of any residual material in a plastic disposal bag.

The third method utilizes the fact that paint and substrate materials heat and cool are different rates. It does not work well on plaster, work moderately well on concrete, works very well on steel and wood. With practice, an inspector can effect the removal of an entire paint film down to, but not including the substrate. Materials needed are a heat gun, two *sharpened* putty knives (one wide, one narrow), and a paint scraper.

1. Direct hot air from the heat gun about 4 to 6 inches from the surface while pressing the edge of the knife into the paint. Heat gently to soften the paint; don't overheat or cause smoking.
2. Heat for a few seconds, and cool for a few seconds while gently pressing the knife edge into the paint.

3. Use the knife to lift off the paint, scrape the surface with the scraper to remove residual paint, if any.
4. Use the brush or mini-vacuum to clean the area and dispose of any residual material in a plastic disposal bag.

After using either method, recheck to ensure that the samples are properly labeled for shipment to the laboratory, or for storage until after abatement is complete. The samples may be needed for testing to determine if they will be considered a hazardous waste, depending upon the abatement method used. Finally, having obtained a sample:

1. Place the sample into the corresponding pre-labeled baggy, and secure with the zip-lock mechanism.
2. Using a separate baggy, collect the next sample following one of the above procedures.

Be certain that the samples are not mixed with dirt or soil. Do not put more than one sample in a single bag. You may put several small bags, each properly labeled, into one large bag labeled as to the location where the samples were collected for storage purposes. If samples are mailed, use boxes, not envelopes, for shipping samples and enclose a cover letter to ensure that the ASTM D 3335-85a preparation procedure is followed. It is best to express mail samples or ship so that the samples are traceable in the event they are lost in the mailing.

This information does not disclose laboratory methodologies and/or sampling strategies which are contained in a manual of guidelines. Copies of the entire report are available by prepaying $45.00 ($35.00 for NIBS members) in check or money order, payable to the National Institute of Building Sciences. This payment should be sent with the title (Lead-based Paint: Interim Guidelines for Hazard Identification and Abatement in Public and Indian Housing) to:

National Institute of Building Sciences
1201 L Street, NW, Suite 400
Washington, DC 20005

Source: Housing and Urban Development: *Lead-Based Paint: Interim Guidelines for Hazard Identification and Abatement in Public and Indian Housing.* U.S. Department of Housing and Urban Development/Office of Assistant Secretary for Public and Indian Housing, Washington, DC, September 1990. pp. A5-24-26.

INDEX

APPENDIX 4   287